HOUSE OF
HORRORS

NIGEL CAWTHORNE

HOUSE OF HORRORS

THE HORRIFIC TRUE STORY OF JOSEF FRITZL, THE FATHER FROM HELL.

JOHN BLAKE

Published by John Blake Publishing Ltd,
3 Bramber Court, 2 Bramber Road,
London W14 9PB, England

www.johnblakepublishing.co.uk

First published in paperback in 2008

ISBN 978 1 84454 696 1

British Library Cataloguing-in-Publication Data:

A catalogue record for this book is available from the British Library.

Design by www.envydesign.co.uk

Printed in the UK by CPI Bookmarque, Croydon, CR0 4TD

5 7 9 10 8 6 4

Papers used by John Blake Publishing are natural, recyclable products made from
wood grown in sustainable forests. The manufacturing processes conform to the
environmental regulations of the country of origin.

Every attempt has been made to contact the relevant copyright-holders, but some were
unobtainable. We would be grateful if the appropriate people could contact us.

CONTENTS

INTRODUCTION

By a curious irony, I am writing this book in a basement... but this is not a House of Horrors. Twenty years ago when I moved in, I was told by my then landlord that the converted cellar in Bloomsbury, not far from the British Museum in central London, had once been the studio of the photographer David Bailey. I never checked that out in case it wasn't true and, as I was familiar with Bailey's work, I would rather live with the idea that the space had once been inhabited by numerous beautiful models, frequently and pleasingly *déshabillé*. My then landlord told me that he had bought the basement studio and converted it into five flats. Mine – I have just measured it – is 43 square metres. The cellar that Elisabeth Fritzl and her subterranean family lived in was, by all accounts, 35 square metres. However, the height of her ceiling was an oppressive 1.7m – 5ft 6in – while mine is 2.4m, a dizzying 8ft.

On the street side, my apartment is below the level of the pavement. But there is a broad walkway in between and light, especially on the sunny summer mornings while I was writing this book, comes pouring in. When the landlord was making the conversion, the council ordered him to dig out the back to allow more light in, so I have a broad patio area and bank planted, after a fashion, with greenery. I overlook this small city garden from the large French windows where I work. These let in so much sunlight that, on sunny days, I have to close the curtains so that I can see the screen of my computer. For Elisabeth Fritzl, this would have been an unimaginable inconvenience. Some days, I put garden furniture out there, open up the umbrella and work outside.

Although the floor space of my flat is comparable to that of Elisabeth's cellar, after years of back-breaking excavation, I only have to share the space with one other person – my son. He is 24, born less than two months after 18-year-old Elisabeth disappeared from the world of light and greenery. Although there are only the two of us, we often get on each other's nerves. This is despite the fact that we have doors on our bedrooms and on the bathroom and lavatory, so we can enjoy some privacy, or lock ourselves away if we are feeling tetchy or antisocial.

While all basements suffer to some extent from damp and mould, it would be hard to imagine a place more light and airy than my apartment. I have a front-door key and can come and go as I please. Friends, relatives and lovers come round. But despite all these advantages, some days, when I have been working hard at home, I feel a twinge of cabin fever. Come evening time, I need to go out to the restaurant next door, to the swimming pool and steam room in the hotel at the end of the road, or to the pub in the square, just for a change of scenery and some company and conversation. More than a couple of days without some contact with the outside world and I would go stir-crazy.

Consequently, I find it hard to put myself in Elisabeth's shoes. Our lives could not be more different. Her tyrannical father stole her life between the ages of 18 and 42 – the years that most people would consider the best of part of their lives. These are the years when most people have adventures, love affairs and indulge in youthful indiscretions that, though they blush about them in middle age, they would not have missed for the world.

That is certainly true in my case. Between 18 and 42, I travelled much of the world. I had written for newspapers and magazines in the UK and USA, had a handful of books to my name, been married, divorced and returned to a life of philandering, appeared in the dock of the Old Bailey for a youthful indiscretion – I was acquitted, I might add – and testified to a US Senate Select Committee.

For Elisabeth Fritzl, these same precious years were stolen from her by the one man who ought to love and protect her, who should have allowed her the follies of youth and been there to rescue her, if and when things went wrong. While her father pretended that he was keeping her safe from the dangers of the modern world, he was merely indulging his own selfish lust. Not only did he rob her of her life and freedom, he subjected her to an unimaginable hell of torture, physical violence, intimidation and sexual humiliation.

He then inflicted this hell on three of the children he sired by her. There are not the words to condemn this man, nor is there any sufficient punishment for what he has done, but this book is not only about the depths of cruelty and vice a man can descend to, it is also a tale of courage. This young woman somehow endured everything her vile tormentor put her through. She suffered years of solitary confinement in the certain knowledge that no one was looking for her or even imagined her fate. With no possibility of escape, the only company she could hope for was her jailer, who would most likely be visiting to rape her once again. Her only contact with the outside world was a man without a scintilla of pity or compassion.

She faced the terrifying prospect of giving birth alone. And, when the children came, she helped extend her own jail, digging out new rooms with her bare hands. She was also forced to relinquish some of those children. But the ones she kept, she did her best to rear and educate, given the appalling circumstances in which they found themselves. She did not go mad – an astonishing achievement in itself. Somehow, she found the strength to remain sane. And when the opportunity came to free herself and her children, she succeeded.

By any standard, Elisabeth Fritzl is a remarkable woman. Her ordeal is over, but let's not forget about her brutal tormentor. He will die in prison or in mental hospital. There is no retribution that he can make or be forced to make, no recompense for what he has done. Instead, let us hope that the world can find some way to give this young woman and her children every pleasure and fulfilment life offers.

Meanwhile, the world must atone. The people of Elisabeth's home town of Amstetten and the Austrian authorities failed to notice that she was physically and sexually abused as a child. And when she disappeared, they did not ask the questions necessary to rescue her and thwart her father's evil plan.

Around the world, there have been some who have

attempted to prove that, after a number of high-profile cases, the imprisonment and abuse of children is a uniquely Austrian phenomenon tied to that country's Nazi past. Of course, history is a factor, but the abuse of children is not a problem exclusive to Austria. In Britain and America – and just about every other country – there are numerous cases of children being abused or neglected, actions that could have been prevented by the vigilance of neighbours and friends. Sadly, too many of us end up looking the other way.

Nigel Cawthorne
Bloomsbury, July 2008

1

A LIVING TOMB

In 1984, two weeks after the end of the Olympic Games in Los Angeles, a young woman in a small town in Austria was drugged, dragged into a cellar and repeatedly raped by her own father. This ordeal would not just go on for one day, or one week, but 8,516 days – just a few months short of 24 years. In all that time, she would not see natural light or breathe fresh air. With the exception of her father – her jailer – no one knew what had happened to her.

And while Elisabeth Fritzl languished in her purpose-built dungeon, the global events of the end of the 20th century inexorably rolled by: the IRA bombing; the Tory conference in Brighton; the assassination of Indira Gandhi; Ronald Reagan's second term; Bhopal; the Sinclair C5; Gorbachev announcing *glasnost* and *perestroika*; the end of the British miners' strike; Live Aid; Boris Becker winning Wimbledon; the race riots on Broadwater Farm Estate; the explosion of the space shuttle *Challenger*; Chernobyl; the election of former UN General-Secretary Kurt Waldheim, president of Austria, and the revelation of his Nazi past; Argentina's 'hand of God' victory in the World Cup; the marriage of Prince Andrew and Sarah Ferguson; the City of London's 'Big Bang'; the AIDS 'Don't Die of Ignorance' campaign; *Mona Lisa*; Irangate; the first-ever episode of *EastEnders*; the Zeebrugge disaster; *Spycatcher*; the Hungerford massacre; England's 'storm of the century'; the Remembrance Day bombing of Enniskillen; the King's Cross fire; the SAS shootings on Gibraltar; the Piper Alpha disaster; the 1988 Seoul Olympics; the election of George Bush Sr; Lockerbie; the Ayatollah Khomeini's *fatwa* on Salman Rushdie; Tiananmen Square; the fall of the Berlin Wall; the US invasion of Panama; Paul Gascoigne's tears; Colin Powell becoming the first black Chairman of the Joint Chiefs of Staff; Nelson Mandela's release; the reunification of Germany; the fall of Mrs Thatcher; the First Gulf War; the break-up of the Soviet Union; Boris Yeltsin being elected President of Russia; the break-up of Yugoslavia; the beating of Rodney King; the election of Bill Clinton; Maastricht; Waco; South Africa adopting majority rule; Nelson Mandela becoming president; Rwanda; the siege of Sarajevo; the 'Supreme Truth' nerve-gas attack in Tokyo; the OJ Simpson trial; the arrest of Fred and Rosemary West in the Gloucester 'House of Horrors' case; 'mad cow' disease, the Spice Girls topping the charts; Robbie Williams' record-breaking world tour; the Taliban taking over in Afghanistan; Tony Blair becoming British Prime Minister; Hong Kong being returned to the Chinese; the death of Princess Diana; the Heaven's Gate cult committing mass suicide; the Oklahoma City bombing; Kosovo; the Good Friday agreement; al-Qaeda bombing the US embassies in Kenya and Tanzania; the introduction of the Euro; Pinochet's arrest in London; Monica Lewinsky; the

A LIVING TOMB

Columbine High School Massacre; East Timor; Y2K; the Sydney Olympics; neo-Nazi Freedom Party joining the Austrian coalition; the conviction of Harold Shipman; the Internet bubble; George W Bush becoming the 43rd US President, thanks to 'hanging chads' in Florida; 9/11; the US and Britain retaliating in Afghanistan; the trial of Slobodan Milosevic; Hugo Chavez coming to power; Chechen rebels taking 763 hostages in a Moscow theatre; the second Gulf War; Burmese opposition leader Aung San Suu Kyi being placed under house arrest; the publication of the *Da Vinci Code*; the space shuttle *Columbia* exploding; Saddam Hussein being caught, tried and executed; the train bombings in Madrid; the Athens Olympics; Chechen terrorists taking 1,200 schoolchildren hostage in Beslan; Abu Ghraib; Guantanamo Bay; a tsunami hitting south-east Asia; the death of Pope John Paul II; London's 11/7 bombings; Israel's evacuation of the Gaza strip; Angela Merkel becoming German Chancellor; Elton John's civil partnership with David Furnish; Danish Islamic cartoons causing riots in the Middle East; Hurricane Katrina; Austria's first girl-in-a-cellar, Natascha Kampusch, being released after six years in captivity; Nicholas Sarkozy election as President of France and marriage to Italian model Carla Bruni; Live 8; Tony Blair standing down; the Spice Girls tour (again); the assassination of Benazir Bhutto; the killings in Kenya; John McCain securing the Republican presidential nomination; Barack Obama securing the Democratic nomination; the Virginia Tech shootings; then, three days later …

On Saturday, 19 April 2008, a young woman arrived by ambulance at the Mostviertel Red Cross hospital in the small town of Amstetten in Lower Austria, 75 miles west of Vienna.

She was in a coma and no one could tell what was wrong with her. An hour later, 73-year-old Josef Fritzl turned up at the hospital. He said the girl was his 19-year-old granddaughter Kerstin. The unconscious teenager, he said, had been left outside his house.

Apparently, this was not an unusual event in the Fritzl household. Fritzl told anyone who would listen that his daughter Elisabeth had run off to a mysterious religious sect in August 1984 when she was just 18. In the 24 years since then, she had not been seen by her family or friends, but she had written to them. Seemingly unable to cope with motherhood, Elisabeth had left three babies outside the family home with notes begging her parents to look after them – at least, that was Josef Fritzl's story. He and his wife Rosemarie, now in her late sixties, had taken them in and, in due course, adopted one and officially fostered the other two.

The patient, Fritzl's granddaughter, was having convulsions and was bleeding from the mouth. She had lost nearly all her teeth, was severely malnourished and deathly pallid. According to the doctor who treated her, 'She hung in a state between life and death.' She would remain that way for weeks.

Despite her shocking state, her grandfather seemed unconcerned. Instead of staying at the hospital – at least long enough to get a diagnosis – or waiting until the girl's condition stabilised, Fritzl rushed away, adding somewhat puzzlingly that the doctors should not call the police. He left a note from her mother, which he said he had found with the unconscious child. It read, 'Wednesday, I gave her aspirin and cough medicine for the condition. Thursday, the cough worsened. Friday, the coughing gets even worse. She has been biting her lip as well as her tongue. Please, please help her! Kerstin is really terrified of other people, she was never in a hospital. If there are any problems please ask my father for help, he is the only person that she knows.'

There was a curious postscript to the note, addressed to the stricken girl, 'Kerstin – please stay strong, until we see each other again! We will come back to you soon!'

This seemed an unlikely sentiment from a woman who, the medical staff had been told, was unable and unwilling to look after her own children; a woman who had simply dumped her children outside her parent's three-storey house at 40 Ybbsstrasse in Amstetten.

Dr Albert Reiter, who was in charge of the case, said, 'I could not believe that a mother who wrote such a note and seemed so concerned would just vanish. I raised the alarm with the police and we launched a TV appeal for her to get in touch.'

Kerstin's condition deteriorated. The fits continued, she lapsed in and out of consciousness, and her immune system did not seem to be working. The doctors needed to know more about the medical history of their mysterious patient, but the appeal for her mother to come forward brought no response. A week went by, during which time Kerstin deteriorated. Eventually, she was placed on a ventilator; her kidneys had stopped working. She was on a dialysis machine and was being kept in a medically induced coma, yet still no mother appeared.

Elisabeth Fritzl, however, had seen the TV appeal and suddenly turned up in Amstetten as if returning from the dead. This was no surprise to the family and those who knew them. Around Christmas 2007, another letter arrived from Elisabeth, telling her parents that she intended to leave the cult and return home. 'If all goes well, I hope to be back within six months,' she wrote. Now, prematurely, she had returned.

She, too, was in an appalling condition – deathly pale and prematurely aged. This was explained by the cult's bizarre ascetic lifestyle, which also seemed to have had a shockingly deleterious effect on Kerstin.

On Saturday, 26 April 2008, Elisabeth Fritzl appeared on the streets of Amstetten for the first time in 24 years. She was seen with her father and was heading towards the hospital, on her way to see her sick daughter. When they reached the grounds of the hospital, the police, tipped off that they were on their way, detained them. Kerstin was in such a bad condition that they wanted to question her mother with a view to bringing charges of child neglect. Father and daughter were taken to the police headquarters where they were questioned separately. At first, Elisabeth stuck to her father's story that she had been in a cult, but, from the start, the police sensed there was something very odd about her. Although she was only 42, she had grey hair, no teeth and a morbidly pallid complexion. She looked like a woman in her sixties, who had been locked up in an institution. It was also quite plain that she was terrified.

Suddenly, she said that she would tell them everything, provided they could guarantee she and her children would never have to see her father again. This was a shock to the detectives. Fritzl was a pillar of the community; a retired electrical engineer and the owner of a number of properties in the town, he had lived there all his life. He had brought up three of Elisabeth's abandoned children and had even taken her critically ill daughter to the hospital after she had, apparently, neglected the child. But Elisabeth then told them a story that beggared belief.

She said she had not run away to join a cult and her father was not the caring family man that he pretended to be. A strict disciplinarian, he had been beating her brutally from the time she was old enough to walk. The sexual assaults had begun when she was 11. She then said that, when she was 18, he had drugged her, dragged her to a concealed cellar in his house, raped her, and had continued to do so for the next 24 years. The rapes had resulted in seven children. For nearly a quarter-of-a-century, she and three of the children had lived in a windowless hell-hole beneath the family home. The children had never seen the outside world or breathed fresh air; they had never known freedom, nor had had any contact with wider society. The only other person they had seen was their jailer, a man who would alternately play with them and terrorise them.

She said that he told them that the doors to the cellar were electrified and, if they tried to escape, they would be gassed. He raped their mother in front of them and yet, with the boxes of groceries and meals he shoved through a hatch, he was their only lifeline. The good family man of Amstetten was, in truth, a brutal monster, and the respectable family home at 40 Ybbsstrasse was, in fact, a House of Hrrors.

All this was hard to believe, but the police could not put aside the evidence of their own eyes. Elisabeth was in such a shocking state that she had clearly gone through some terrible ordeal – possibly the one she had just described.

The police had to put her allegations to Fritzl. Initially, he refused to talk, even producing the letter from his daughter saying that she was intending to return from the religious sect where she had spent the last 24 years in an attempt to deflect her accusations. Later, he even complained that he was disappointed that Elisabeth had seized her opportunity to 'betray' him so rapidly.

The following morning, the police took Josef Fritzl back to his house at 40 Ybbsstrasse. The front was a typical suburban townhouse on an ordinary street, but at the rear was an imposing concrete structure, not unlike a wartime bunker. Although it was set among leafy suburban gardens where those neighbouring the Fritzls' property were all visible, the back of the house was screened off by high hedges. Fritzl's garden was the only one not overlooked by neighbours.

At first, the police could not find the dungeon where Elisabeth said she had been held; it was so well hidden. But, sensing the game was up, Fritzl led them down the cellar stairs and through eight locked doors and a warren of rooms. Concealed behind a shelving unit in his basement workshop was a heavy steel door just 1m high with a remote-control locking device. After some prompting, Fritzl gave the police the code to open it; he was the only one who knew the code. He had told Elisabeth and her children that if they harmed him or overpowered him while he was in the cellar, they would find themselves locked in there for ever. He taunted them that, if he died suddenly from a heart-attack outside, they would starve. Their prison was also rigged with security systems that would electrocute them if they tried to tamper with the door, and led them to believe toxic gas would be pumped in, should they try to escape.

Later, he told Lower Austria's top criminal investigator, Oberst Franz Polzer, that the lock on the heavy steel door that shut the basement dungeon off from the outside world worked on a timer. It would open automatically if he was away for a protracted period, so his daughter and her children would be freed if he died, he said.

8

'But there was no mechanism in place that we have found to release them,' said Chief Investigator Polzer. 'I do not want to think about what would have happened to the mother and her three children if anything had happened to Fritzl.'

Beyond a basement workshop, Fritzl had built a perfectly concealed bunker to imprison his own daughter and her children. Ducking through the first door – just 3 feet 3 inches high – the police found a narrow corridor. At the end was a padded room, sound-proofed with rubber cladding, where he would rape his daughter while the children cowered elsewhere. It was so well insulated that no scream, cry or sob could be heard in any other part of the building. Beyond that was a living area, then down a passage little more than a foot wide that you would have to turn sideways to negotiate were a rudimentary kitchen and bathroom. Further on, there were two small bedrooms, each with two beds in them. There was no natural light and little air.

On the white-tiled walls of a tiny shower cubicle, the captives had painted an octopus, a snail, a butterfly and a flower in an attempt to brighten their prison. The furnishings were sparse. The police found a toy elephant perched on a mirrored medicine cabinet and scraps of paper and glue that the children had used to make toys. The only other distraction was a small TV, which provided flickering images of the outside world, which the children had never experienced and, for Elisabeth, was an increasingly dim memory. There was also a washing machine and a fridge and freezer, where food could be stored when Fritzl took off on the holidays he denied his captives.

The entire space was lit by electric light bulbs – the only source of light – although Elisabeth had begged her father to give her vitamin D supplements and an ultraviolet light to prevent her kids from suffering growth abnormalities. The lights went on and off on a timer to give them some sense of day and night, something else that the children had never experienced.

The police found two children who had survived these appalling conditions – 18-year-old Stefan and 5-year-old Felix. They were in a poor physical state and unused to strangers; they were so lacking in social skills that the police found they were practically feral. Because of the low ceilings in the dungeon – never more than 1.7 metres, or 5 feet 6 inches – Stefan was stooped. In his excitement, young Felix resorted to going on all fours. Having never been required to communicate with anyone beyond their immediate circle, the police found the boys had difficulty talking and, between themselves, resorted to grunts. For the first time in their lives, they were taken out into the daylight.

Confronted with the evidence, Fritzl confessed that he had imprisoned his daughter. 'Yes,' he told the police, 'I locked her up, but only to protect her from drugs. She was a difficult child.'

While admitting to having repeatedly raped her, he rejected his daughter's allegations that he had chained her to the cellar wall and kept her 'like an animal', claiming he had been kind to the 'second family' he kept in the cellar. He admitted that the children were his own, the offspring of incest with his own daughter, and subsequent DNA tests confirmed that he was their father. However, the police did not understand why he had decided that three of the children – Lisa, 16; Monika, 14 and Alexander, 12 – should live upstairs with him and his wife and go to school, while the other three – Kerstin, 19; Stefan, 18 and Felix, 5 – should remain downstairs in their subterranean prison. Asked by police how he had come to that decision, Fritzl told them he had feared the noise of their cries might lead to their discovery. 'They were sickly and cried too much in the cellar for my liking,' he said.

There had been another child, Alexander's twin, who had died at just three days old, back in 1996. The infant's sex has not been determined, but it is now thought to have been a boy and has posthumously been named Michael. Fritzl had taken the child's tiny body and burnt it in the furnace that provides hot water and central heating for the family home that lay just beyond the steel door in the more open part of the cellar.

Fritzl confessed in an almost matter-of-fact manner to the abduction and rape of his daughter, and to the imprisonment and enslavement of Elisabeth and their children, as well to incinerating the body of Michael. Otherwise, he was not particularly forthcoming during his interrogation, officers said. He did not bother to explain himself; he just said he was 'sorry' for his family and announced that he wanted to be left in peace.

Despite the DNA tests confirming that Fritzl fathered the cellar children, in court he may yet plead not guilty to rape, incest and false imprisonment. His lawyer Rudolf Mayer declared, 'The allegations of rape and enslaving people have not been proved. We need to reassess the confessions made so far.' It is also widely believed that he will be angling for a plea of insanity.

'Every case that has got a psychological background is interesting,' said Mayer. 'We defence lawyers believe that there are good souls ...' He added that Fritzl was 'a shattered and ruined man. He is emotionally broken.'

Fritzl showed no emotion when he was remanded in

custody while the police continued their investigation of the whole grizzly story. He faces up to 15 years in prison, if convicted on rape charges, although he could be charged with 'murder through failure to act' in connection with the infant Michael's death. That is punishable by up to 20 years in prison. A second murder charge could await if Kerstin did not recover from her critical state. However, Josef Fritzl is already 73 and unlikely to serve the full term of any sentence the courts might impose. There is no death penalty in Austria and, as he has managed to remain undetected for so long, he will effectively escape without punishment. Even if he could be executed, it would hardly expiate his crime. As it is, he is in a poor state of health and it is thought unlikely that he will live long enough to stand trial.

2

HEART OF
DARKNESS

Josef Fritzl has said little to explain the brutal rape and incarceration of his daughter and the appalling maltreatment of at least three of their children. However, he has claimed to be a victim of his Nazi past, and there may be some truth in this.

He was born on 9 April 1935, in Amstetten, and was nearly three when his home town turned out to raise their arms in a '*Sieg Heil*' salute as Adolf Hitler drove by in an open-topped car on 12 March 1938. The *Führer* was on his way to Vienna, where he was greeted by huge crowds celebrating the *Anschluss* – the German annexation of Austria. In the First World War, Austria had fought alongside Germany and, in defeat, lost its central European empire. Subsequently, the country suffered similar political and economic upheaval to its larger neighbour. The Nazi Party then grew in power in Austria and many Austrians, even those who were not Nazis, favoured a union with Germany. Hitler was, after all, a local boy, an Austrian who only took

German nationality in 1932 at the age of 43, the year before he became German Chancellor.

Born in Braunau am Inn on the Bavarian border just 85 miles from Amstetten, Hitler spent most of his childhood in Linz, less than 30 miles from Fritzl's home town. Linz remained his favourite city and he said that he wanted to be buried there. In his 'Private Testimony' written in the *Führerbunker* in Berlin on 29 April 1945, the day before he died, Hitler wrote, 'The paintings in the collections which I had bought in the course of the years were never collected for private purposes, but solely for the gradual establishment of an art gallery in my home town of Linz. It is my heartfelt wish that this bequest should be duly executed.'

Fritzl was an only child. His mother Rosa was disabled and he grew up for the most part without a father as Franz Fritzl was in the Army. School friends remember a boy so poor that other parents gave his mother food. She lived by herself after divorcing Franz, a scandalous event in the small, traditional Austrian town.

'My father was somebody who was a waster; he never took responsibility and was just a loser who always cheated on my mother,' Fritzl said. 'When I was four, she quite rightly threw him out of the house. After that, my mother and I had no contact with this man, he did not interest us. Suddenly there was only us two.'

It seems that Fritzl's father was killed in the war. The name Franz Fritzl appears on the town's war memorial, which also bears the carved image of a Nazi stormtrooper. Although after the Second World War, most Austrians claimed to have been unwilling victims of the Nazis, many were enthusiastic party members. It is known that Amstetten, particularly, was a hotbed of Nazism. Hitler's visit in 1938 was greeted with wild excitement by the residents, and every house in the town flew the swastika. A local history book says of the visit, 'The crowd was screaming and yelling and waving.'

Amstetten went a step further than other Austrian towns in its enthusiasm for the *Anschluss* and made Hitler an honorary citizen. The *Führer* sent a thank-you letter, saying the town's tribute 'filled him with great pleasure'. According to Fritzl, the Hitlerian past of Amstetten, where he grew up, affected him profoundly. 'I grew up in the Nazi times and that meant the need to control and the respect of authority,' he said. 'I suppose I took some of these old values with me into later life. It was all subconscious, of course.'

After Hitler invaded the Soviet Union in June 1941, Amstetten found itself on a main rail line for troops and material heading for the Eastern Front. The RAF bombed the rail lines there repeatedly and the inhabitants, including the young Fritzl, would have regularly sought shelter in their cellars as the bombs were dropped. Throughout this time, slave labourers were brought in to help reopen the vital rail link that ran from Linz to Vienna.

Just a short walk from the cellar where Fritzl repeatedly raped his daughter and imprisoned their offspring is the site of a Nazi concentration camp, where 500 women were caged during the war. In Amstetten itself, there were two concentration camps – Bahnbau II, which held the women, and Bahnbau I, which held some 3,000 male slave labourers used to rebuild the railway lines. These two camps were branches of the infamous Mauthausen-Gusen concentration camp 25 miles away. Although the camp had been initially designed for 'extermination through labour', in December

1941 it opened a gas chamber where inmates were murdered 120 at a time and Nazi doctors performed cruel experiments on their captives. Up to 320,000 people died there. While the camp officers indulged themselves with Austrian beer and women in Amstetten, hundreds of thousands of prisoners were being starved, tortured, raped and murdered close by.

Again, the Austrians enthusiastically embraced this most evil aspect of the Third Reich. Some 40 per cent of the staff and three-quarters of the commandants of concentration camps were of Austrian origin, and it was largely Austrians who organised the deportation of the Jews. Some 80 per cent of the staff of Adolf Eichmann, the logistics planner of the Holocaust, were from Austria. It is unlikely that, even as a child, Fritzl would have been unaware of the death camps near his home.

Even the clinic where Elisabeth and the Fritzl family were cared for by doctors and psychologists after their release has a Nazi past. Hundreds of patients were put to death at Amstetten's Mauer clinic under the Third Reich's euthanasia laws. At least another 800 were transported to other institutions to be killed.

A book called *Amstetten 1938–1945*, commissioned by civic leaders in Fritzl's home town, includes a chapter on the Mauer clinic's wartime atrocities. 'The first step to eliminating inherited and mental diseases was sterilisation,' it says, citing 346 cases in Mauer. 'The last was euthanasia.'

The euthanasia programme officially began in 1941. It started with psychiatric patients, but moved on to those in nursing homes and homes for the elderly. In 1944, a notorious doctor named Emil Gelny visited the Mauer clinic to dispose of what he deemed to be 'unnecessary mouths'. He killed at least 39 people with drugs such as barbitone, luminal and morphine, the book says.

It is not known how much young 'Sepp' – the Austrian diminutive of Josef – Fritzl was aware of, but he may well have been a member of the Hitler Youth. Enrolment was, by then, compulsory after the age of ten. However, local officials say the records were burned at the end of the war so, like those of many other Austrians and Germans from that era, his Nazi past was conveniently buried. That is not to say that having been a member of the Hitler Youth necessarily turns you into a monster. The current pope, Benedict XVI, had been enrolled in the Hitler Youth in 1939, despite being a bitter enemy of Nazism, believing it to conflict with his Catholic faith. But this was not a concern for Fritzl who, like most Austrians, was a Catholic. The conflict between Nazism and Catholicism did not bother Hitler either – he never renounced his Catholic faith.

By his own admission, Fritzl was affected by the politics of the era. He called his secret cellar his '*Reich*' and he openly admitted that he got the iron discipline needed to live a double life from growing up under the Nazis.

'I have always placed a great deal of value on discipline and good behaviour,' he said. 'I admit that. My behaviour comes from my generation; I am from the old school. I was brought up during the time of the Nazis that meant discipline and self-control – I admit that took over me to a certain extent.'

Although his character may have been shaped by being brought up under Hitler and the Nazi regime, it is no excuse – any more than it was for those who committed atrocities in Hitler's name at the time.

Four days after Fritzl's tenth birthday, Vienna was

liberated by the Red Army following several days of vicious hand-to-hand fighting. The following month, Soviet tanks rolled into Amstetten. Fresh from seeing the Nazis lay waste to their country, Russian troops embarked on an orgy of rape and pillage. Reports in the Austrian media say that, as a child, Fritzl 'suffered badly' during this post-war occupation, a period marked by the high incidence of sexual assaults perpetrated by Russian soldiers on German and Austrian women – so much so that Vienna's memorial to the 'unknown soldier' was sardonically referred to as the memorial to the 'unknown father'. The Red Army stayed in Austria until 1955.

Although Austria was spared the rigorous de-Nazification programme inflicted on Germany, Fritzl would have been acutely aware of the shame of his nation's defeat in the post-war era. A 1951 school photograph shows a surly 16-year-old youth glowering at the camera. Nonetheless, he was said to have been a very bright and resourceful boy. He did well at school and was always well behaved. This has been credited to his mother.

'My mother was a strong woman; she taught me discipline and control and the values of hard work,' Fritzl said. 'She sent me to a good school so I could learn a good trade and she worked really hard, and took a very difficult job to keep our heads above water.'

Rosa Fritzl was strict, but they were living through hard times. There was little food in post-war Austria and it was years before the country's economy was back on its feet. His mother reflected the period. 'When I say she was hard on me, she was only as hard as was necessary,' he said. 'She was the best woman in the world. I suppose you could describe me as her man, sort of. She was the boss at home and I was the only man in the house.'

There has been some speculation that there may have been something unhealthy about their relationship. 'It's complete rubbish to say my mother sexually abused me,' said Fritzl. 'My mother was respectable, extremely respectable. I loved her across all boundaries. I was completely and totally in awe of her. That did not mean there was anything else between us, though. There never was, and there never would have been.'

However, when asked if he had ever fantasised about a relationship with his mother, he answered, 'Yes, probably ... But I was a very strong man, probably as strong as my mother and, as a result, I was capable to keep my desires under control.'

His sister-in-law told another story in an interview with an Austrian newspaper. 'Josef grew up without a father and his mother raised him with her fists,' said the women identified only as Christine R. 'She used to beat him black and blue almost every day. Something must have been broken in him because of that. He was unable to feel any kind of sympathy for other people; he humiliated my sister for most of her life.'

Others got a better impression. A friend at high school said, 'He was a very positive influence on his younger colleagues, but he was also a bit of a loner. We all thought he'd do quite well for himself and he always came to class reunions with his wife. We were shocked to learn what he had done. That wasn't the man we knew.'

But some had already noticed a darker side. An old classmate of Fritzl painted a picture of a fiend obsessed with power and torture. Gertrude Haydn, now 73, said, 'His family was very poor. People said he tortured his pets and killed cats and dogs inside his house. I was too afraid to ever go in there.'

Leaving school at 16, Fritzl went on to study electrical engineering at a nearby polytechnic and took up an engineering apprenticeship where he excelled. Then he took a job with a local steel company, Voest. Working there, he managed to get out from under the thumb of his mother and began to take an interest in other women.

'I became older and I managed to meet other women,' he said.

By all accounts, he was also something of a moustached charmer, although hardly in the David Niven mould. He was insufferably arrogant and self-absorbed. Known for his lecherous innuendoes, it was clear he was unnaturally obsessed with sex. 'I had affairs with a few girls,' he boasted, 'and then a short while later I met Rosemarie.'

It was 1956. He was 21 and Rosemarie was 17 when they married and started a family of seven. Of course, it was difficult for Rosemarie to live up to the standard of his mother, but for what Fritzl had in mind, his new wife fitted the bill perfectly.

'Rosemarie was also a wonderful woman ... *is* a wonderful woman,' he said. 'I chose her because I had a strong desire then to have lots of children.'

And the reason Fritzl wanted lots of children lay in his own childhood. 'I wanted children that did not grow up like me as single children,' he said. 'I wanted children that always had someone else at their side to play with and to support. The dream of a big family was with me from when I was very small, and Rosemarie seemed the perfect mother to realise that dream.'

The other advantage was that she had little in common with his mother, the redoubtable Rosa. 'She is just a lot more shy and weaker than my mother,' he claimed. He could dominate her and she would not question him, although this was of particular concern to her family who distrusted him from the outset.

From 1969–71, Fritzl worked for Zehetner, a construction materials firm in Amstetten, where he was described as 'an intelligent worker and a good technician'. Yet even in those early years, he was demonstrating a tendency towards sexual deviancy. His first brush with the police came when he was 24 after a complaint that he had exposed himself. The police say he went on to rape at least two women in Linz, where he was working in the 1960s. Only one of the victims brought charges. In 1967, Fritzl was convicted of rape and sentenced to 18 months in jail.

He still struggles to explain why he betrayed his wife and his, by then, four children, by breaking into a ground-floor flat and raping a young nurse. 'I do not know what drove me to do that,' he said. 'It's really true I do not know why I did it. I always wanted to be a good husband and a good father.'

Despite his conviction for rape, his wife, the long-suffering Rosemarie, took him back. He later claimed he was grateful. 'I always loved her and I will always love her,' said Fritzl, even after confessing to the rape of their daughter. This can have been of little comfort to Rosemarie.

Details of the 1967 rape case have now been expunged from the records. Under Austrian law, as part of the process of rehabilitation, details of previous convictions are destroyed after ten years. 'When such a crime has been atoned for, it's been atoned for,' a senior police officer explained.

However, another victim, who claimed that she had been too frightened to press charges at the time, came forward after Elisabeth had emerged from her dungeon, saying that she was

'100 per cent sure' it was Fritzl who had raped her in September 1967, when she was 20 years old. She recognised him as her attacker when she saw his photograph in the newspapers.

'I was raped by Fritzl,' the woman, who refused to disclose her identity, told the local Linz newspaper, *Upper Austrian News*, on 30 April 2008. 'When I saw his picture yesterday, I knew, yes, that is him.' There was no doubt in her mind. 'I recognised him immediately,' she said. 'I will never forget those eyes.'

At the time of the rape, she was a recently married young mother. While her husband, an Austrian railway worker, was away on a night shift, Fritzl slipped through her ground-floor bedroom window. 'I felt the bedclothes being pulled back,' she told the newspaper. 'At first I thought it was my husband coming home but then I felt this knife being pushed against my throat. He told me, "If you make a noise, I'll kill you." Then he raped me in my own bed.'

At the time, she was too ashamed to report the rape, and neither did she want to risk alienating her husband. She kept the memory of her terrifying attack to herself for over 40 years. The woman admitted that she had had her suspicions about Fritzl from the start and feared she might not be the only victim of his sexual deviancy. She said she had seen Fritzl on a number of occasions in Linz before she was assaulted by him. He had attracted attention because he behaved like a peeping Tom. 'He was a voyeur. He used to ride around on his bicycle and watch everyone,' she said.

Once Fritzl had been exposed as the dungeon rapist in the Austrian press and on television, it was then that the memory came flooding back and she realised that he was the same man who raped her more than 40 years before.

A third woman from Linz also went to the police in April 2008 to complain of an attempted rape by Fritzl. She had been 24 at the time and a work colleague of his. On 2 May, officials said a rape file had been found and was being studied. However, the Austrian justice authorities say the offence is irrelevant because it happened more than 15 years ago and was beyond the statute of limitations.

However, Fritzl was convicted and went to prison at the time. As a result, he lost his job. But he was such a good engineer, and such was his ability for inventing new devices that, in 1969, when he was released, he immediately found work, despite his record.

'My father often said he was an absolute genius,' said a daughter of his late boss, Karl Zehetner. 'He was amazed at what he could do.'

Fritzl's ingenuity would later be put to sinister use when constructing the elaborate dungeon where he imprisoned the hapless Elisabeth and their children, complete with its electronically-controlled sliding steel door.

When the sister-in-law of the company's manager was told that Fritzl had been taken on, she spoke up. 'I don't want that,' she protested. In her mind, Fritzl was a danger and she repeatedly warned her children to stay away from him.

A spokeswoman for a company where Josef Fritzl was employed as an engineer and procurement manager during the 1970s also had misgivings. 'He did an excellent job,' she said, 'but there was always something uneasy about him as it was widely known that he had served time in prison for a sexual offence.'

Neighbours in Amstetten also knew of his record. 'I was ten at the time,' a 50-year-old resident now recalls, 'but I remember how we children were afraid to play near Fritzl's house because of the rumours that he had raped a woman and spent some time in jail for it.'

Later, Fritzl became a travelling salesman for a German company and then worked as an electrical engineer at a company that made industrial drills. In 1973, he and his wife bought a summer guesthouse and camping ground at an idyllic tourist spot in the mountains on the shores of Lake Mondsee in the Vöcklabruck district of the Salzkammergut near Salzburg, which they ran until 1996. Then, in the 1980s, he decided to move into real estate, buying several buildings around Amstetten. He already owned the large grey town house at 40 Ybbsstrasse in Amstetten, which he extended into the back garden to provide accommodation for up to eight tenants at a time. The family lived on the floors above; below was the cellar.

Over the years, Fritzl bought a further five properties and started an underwear company. But his attempts at property development came to nothing and his businesses failed. It is now known that he had run up debts of more than €2m (£1.56m) as a result of his various endeavours, but in the eyes of the townsfolk, he became 'a man of stature', as the local police chief put it. He was a respected, well-connected figure in Amstetten, often seen at the wheel of a Mercedes. He dressed in fine clothes, with gold rings on his fingers and a gold chain round his neck. Even when running errands, locals said, he wore a natty jacket, crisp shirt and tie.

Generally, Fritzl was known in Amstetten as a polite man who loved fishing, drinking beer and sharing a bawdy joke with his neighbours. But he was a private individual; he was not active in community or church groups. Even fellow members of his fishing club say he was something of a question mark. Fritzl made little attempt to socialise, but always paid his dues. 'There was never a problem with him,' said club treasurer Reinhard Kern. 'Whether he actually went fishing or not, how am I to know? Maybe it was an alibi.'

However, most neighbours or townsfolk remember only an affable, if unremarkable, fellow who liked to keep himself to himself. In fact, he was part of a well-heeled coterie of businessmen who were not short of friends in all the right places.

With all record of the rape conviction eradicated after ten years under Austria's statute of limitations, Fritzl was at liberty to present himself as the strong, wholesome family man. In a devoutly Catholic country like Austria, it is necessary for a 'paterfamilias' to sire a large brood and Fritzl fathered five girls and two boys. Ulrike was born in 1958; Rosemarie followed in 1961; Harald in 1964; Elisabeth in 1966; the twins Josef Jnr and Gabriele in 1971; and Doris in 1973.

Outwardly, all was well. Josef Fritzl was the smartly dressed engineer who drove a nice car and had such well behaved children. True, he was an autocratic task-master behind closed doors, but that was not an unknown characteristic among provincial Austrian men of his generation.

Fritzl said that his favourite daughter was Elisabeth, the fourth of his seven children with Rosemarie, but that did not mean that she was given an easy time. Because she was pretty, it appears that he was harder on her than the others and beat her mercilessly. Fritzl had no time for spoiling children. At home, in this traditional Austrian family, father ruled the roost – though, even in the eyes of others who shared his background, he was inordinately strict.

'For me, I always had the impression that Sepp was an intelligent and successful man,' said Leopold Stütz, deputy mayor of Lasberg, a town 30 miles from Amstetten. Stütz was a close friend of the Fritzls and even went on joint holidays with the family. 'He often talked about his perfect family. He was very strict with his children, a strict but fair father, I would say. It was enough for him to snap his fingers and the youngsters would be in bed. He always stressed that, for him, education and career were the most important things.'

Others were not so sanguine. Fritzl's sister-in-law Christine told the Austrian newspaper *Österreich* that her brother-in-law was a 'disgusting despot', who cleverly covered up his excesses. 'Every person that looked in his eyes was fooled by him,' she said.

The family lived in fear of his outbursts. 'He tolerated no dissent,' said Christine. 'When he said it was black, it was black, even when it was ten times white.' She loathed the way he was so harsh on the kids. 'I always hated him,' she said. 'He was like an army drill instructor with his children. They had to stop whatever they were doing and stand still when he entered the room. Silence fell over everyone immediately – even when they were in the middle of playing a game. You could sense their constant fear of being punished.'

The children were required to remain silent while their father was in a room. If they failed to comply, or if they forgot to say 'please' or 'thank you', he would hit them until they toed the line. They were very rarely allowed to have friends round. If they did, the children's friends had to leave the house immediately when he came home from work.

Christine believed that Fritzl's tyrannical behaviour towards the seven children he had with her elder sister Rosemarie was the main reason why most of them had married young. 'The only chance for the children to escape this atmosphere was to marry,' she said. 'And that's what they all did as soon as they were old enough.'

When Elisabeth finally escaped the House of Horrors and the police eventually took an interest, they confirmed what Christine was saying. 'We have spoken at length to Elisabeth's brothers and sisters,' said the detective in charge of the case, Chief Investigator Polzer. 'All of them said their father wasn't just very strict, aggressive, dominant and power-mad, he was a "real tyrant". They weren't ever allowed to address him or ask him anything. That was why every child except one son left the house as soon as they could.'

However, none of them moved very far. Their eldest daughter Rosemarie married at 21 and now lives with her husband, Horst Herlbauer, in an apartment in the Linz suburb of Traun, 30 miles from the family home. With his wife, Harald moved into an orange-painted cottage in the village of Mitterkirchen im Machland, eight miles from Amstetten. Doris left home when she married a man named Henikl and set up home with her husband in a villa in the Alpine province of Styria, not far to the south. However, she and her family would join her parents at family reunions and sometimes go on holiday with her mother.

Ulrike married a man named Pramesberger and became a teacher. She moved to Bad Goisern in the foothills of the Alps, some 65 miles from Amstetten, to an impressive chalet-style property set in extensive grounds. Gabriele lives with her partner and child near Amstetten in a small chalet. Only Josef

Jnr, Gabriele's twin brother, continued to live in the family home, although he is now in his late thirties. Very much under his father's thrall, he remained a virtual slave.

'One son wasn't allowed to leave,' said Polzer, 'just like Elisabeth. He is very slow and has a few problems and difficulties. Josef kept him, using this son as his slave and house-boy. I believe it was Josef's youngest son. He had to wait on his father hand and foot, and skivvy for him.'

Christine described how Fritzl expected his wife to play a subservient role from the start of their married life. 'When Rosemarie married Sepp she was 17, and had no professional qualifications, so she was always dependent on him – and for 51 years he exploited that,' she said.

Rosemarie was poorly educated and had trained as a kitchen help. Fritzl's pride in his own intelligence and resourcefulness prevented him from taking his wife seriously, Christine said. He was completely in control in their marriage.

'Listen, if I myself was scared of him at a family party, and I did not feel confident to say anything in any form that could possibly offend him,' she said, 'then you can imagine how it must have been for a woman that spent so many years with him. He was a tyrant. What he said was good and the others had to shut up. He was a despot and I hated him.'

Asked what would have happened had Rosemarie challenged Fritzl, Christine said, 'We don't know what he would have done to her. Maybe he would have slapped her.'

It never happened. Fritzl had intimidated her far too much for it to come to that. He frequently mocked his wife, put her down and took a sadistic delight in humiliating her in public. 'He was relaxed and sociable with everyone in the family apart from Rosi,' said Christine. 'He used to tell her off in front of the others. The worst things were his crude, dirty jokes, which he used to laugh loudly about. This was embarrassing for everyone, because we all knew they hadn't had sex with each other for years.'

Rosemarie secretly confided this to friends, but Fritzl was quite open about it. 'He would always say, "My wife is much too fat for me,"' said Christine. It was a comment he made regularly to others, often within Rosemarie's earshot.

She also said the narcissistic Fritzl spent a fortune on a hair transplant after she said he was bald. 'Josef would be spiteful about my weight, but I would say, "Better to be chubby than bald,"' Christine said. 'He is so vain he went to Vienna for a hair transplant.'

The most difficult time for the family came in 1967, when Fritzl was convicted of rape and went to prison for 18 months. Christine is 12 years younger than her sister, and was young and impressionable at the time. 'I was 16 when he was locked up for rape and I found that crime truly disgusting – all the more so seeing as he already had four children with my sister,' she said. 'I have always hated him. He was born a criminal and will die a criminal.' She could not understand how her sister could take him back.

Despite his protestations of love for Rosemarie, Christine said that Fritzl showed no gratitude for his wife's tolerance and understanding. Prison had not chastened him and his conviction taught him no humility. Instead, he began to batter and brutalise his family. Rosemarie and their seven children were subjected to regular vicious beatings as he unleashed a relentless reign of terror against his cowering victims. According to a friend, Rosemarie was so desperate that she plotted to flee the monster with her two boys and five girls at least 20 times, but she told her friend that she feared, 'Josef will hunt us down and drag us back'.

Details of the harrowing home life of Rosemarie and the children were provided by Elfriede Hoera, now 69, who became close to Rosemarie after she and her husband Paul met the Fritzls on a camping trip in 1973. Elfriede said Rosemarie lived in total fear of her husband, whose 'father was a Nazi stormtrooper who died fighting for Adolf Hitler'. Elfriede said her best friend had told her, 'We must escape – he has hit me many times and beats the children. He slaps me hard in the face if I don't do what he wants and he makes the children cry. I can't stand it any longer – I want to run away from him.'

Fritzl was still working at the time so there was some respite. 'I am always happy when he is out of the house,' Rosemarie confided, but she dreaded his return. 'That swine beats me up – and the children,' she said. 'All the time he treats us like rubbish. I really hate the bastard. My marriage is made up of quarrels and arguments. We haven't had sex for a very long time – though I'm very happy when he doesn't touch me.'

It seemed to Elfriede that Rosemary had resigned herself to her fate. 'I must stay for the sake of my children,' she said. 'Josef will find us if we all run away.'

Elfriede knew Rosemarie for many years and was in a position to assess how she and the children suffered. 'Fritzl was a tyrant who terrorised his family,' she said. 'He bossed them around and brutalised them like an army officer. I saw him beating his children and Rosemarie told me how he beat her many, many times – too many times for me to remember.'

Elfriede said she also had regular talks with Fritzl's

daughter Elisabeth when, as a teenager, she spent three years working as a kitchen helper at a guesthouse they owned. Although Fritzl said Elisabeth was his favourite, this appeared to be belied by his brutal treatment of her. Elfriede recalled, 'Josef did not like Elisabeth at all and she was a very shy, sad child – not happy at all. I never saw her laugh once and she seemed somehow disturbed.'

But Elfriede failed to find out what the root of the problem was. 'I tried to get close to her but she never confided in me what was happening to her,' she said. 'I once asked her why she was so sad and she just said, "Papa is so dominant and strict."'

It appeared to Elfriede that Fritzl only liked three of his children – his daughters Gabriele and Ulrike, and his son Josef. The other four – Rosemarie Jr, Doris, Harald and Elisabeth – routinely suffered the full fury of his hate-fuelled rages. 'Josef was very cruel to them,' Elfriede said. 'Rosemarie told me it was common for him to attack them.'

Elfriede witnessed this for herself. 'When I saw Josef hit his children with his open hand across the face they always burst out in tears,' she said. 'I felt so sorry for Rosemarie and her family.'

One day she saw Fritzl drag his daughter Rosemarie from a caravan by the hair before slapping the weeping youngster across the face for disobeying him. There was nothing discreet about his abuse. Elfriede told how she had witnessed Fritzl openly lash out at his children in public outside their home.

'Josef was driving down the road one night and saw the kids running around,' she recalled. 'He stopped the car and got out in the middle of the street and started beating them. It was awful – I heard the screams.' Elisabeth was also subject to these assaults and had bruises all over her body.

Elfriede, who now lives in Munich, across the border in Germany, said she often asked Rosemarie why Fritzl doted on some of his children while appearing to loathe the others. 'Rosemarie said she did not know,' Elfriede recalled. 'But she once told me, "Ulrike is Josef's favourite – she is the only one to answer him back." He seemed to respect that.'

Elfriede even begged Rosemarie to take the kids and run away from the brute who had turned their home into a living hell.

'I tried to convince her to go but she was helpless,' she said. 'She told me she wanted to leave Fritzl – but she knew she could not escape with all seven of her children. She knew Fritzl would hunt them down and drag them back. She stayed in the marriage because of the kids. Many times she told me how she was afraid to stand up to him for fear of being beaten up. And she feared for the safety of the youngsters because he beat them so brutally.'

Mother-of-two Elfriede lost touch with Rosemarie when her own marriage broke up. She and her husband Paul divorced in 1984, some months before Elisabeth's dungeon ordeal began.

Elfriede later speculated that Rosemarie might have had some inkling that something was going on in the cellar. 'Rosemarie once told me, "Josef is busy at home at the moment – he has lots of building work to do,"' Elfriede said. 'she did not know what he was doing.'

Elfriede is sure that Rosemarie did not know what her husband was up to, because she was too cowed by his brutality even to ask questions.

However, in 1973, Rosemarie plucked up the courage to leave her husband, although she was not allowed to take the children with her. It seems she simply made the excuse that she had to stay at a guesthouse at Mondsee to take care of business there. It was two hours from the family home. Fritzl insisted their seven children stay with him at Ybbsstrasse, although she was allowed to see them occasionally.

Rosemarie's former colleague Anton Klammer said, 'Josef beat her and she was petrified of him. She loved her kids but the guest house they owned was a good excuse to leave him. She thought that if she didn't leave, he may kill her. Rosemarie was happy and normal but when he was around she used to shrink away. You could tell she was terrified of him. The children stayed with Josef because they had to go to school but sometimes he would come up and drop the children off with Rosemarie for a few nights. She was a loving mother.'

Rosemarie had to move back into 40 Ybbsstrasse nine years later when the guesthouse was burnt down. Soon after Fritzl was arrested for arson. A local newspaper published a picture of Fritzl taken at a court hearing in 1982. However, he was released due to lack of evidence.

Beate Schmidinger, the owner of a nearby café, said, 'Everyone thought he set fire to the place because we knew he had money trouble.'

Despite the appearance of prosperity, it is clear that Fritzl was already badly in debt, but the real motivation for the fire might have been to force Rosemarie to return to Ybbsstrasse, where he could control her.

Paul Ruhdorfer, who took over the guesthouse after it had been restored, said, 'There were two Rosemaries. One was the owner and competent businesswoman who was happy and carefree. The other was a timid victim, controlled by her overbearing husband.'

While Fritzl was a tyrant, that did not mean he could not enjoy life as well. A friend, who went on holiday with him to Thailand, filmed him having a massage on a beach and cheerfully tucking into a knuckle of roast ham. A home video from this Thailand trip, shown widely on Austrian television, showed Fritzl and a friend from Munich riding on an elephant. The off-camera commentary says, 'Hey, Sepp, you had better show this to your wife to convince her that we're on safari, not hunting for humans.' The police do not believe this was significant. It may simply have been a reference to his predilection for seeking out young Thai prostitutes. However, the remark now appears chilling.

It is clear that Fritzl had, indeed, once hunted humans – his rape victims. Even before his daughter disappeared into the cellar, he could have feasibly perpetrated a series of ghoulish crimes. Despite the removal of his 1967 rape conviction from the record, the Linz police now believe he was a suspect in two other sex attacks, in 1974 and 1982. He was also investigated for arson and insurance fraud on more than one occasion and there are indications that he had at least one other conviction. However, once again, the records have been expunged and the authorities said they were unable to give further details of the crime.

'I don't know what happened then,' said District Governor Hans-Heinz Lenze. 'It happened too long ago. It's beyond the statute of limitations and it's therefore no longer of relevance to the authorities.'

Along with Austria's laws governing the lapsing of criminal records for the purpose of rehabilitating criminals, Fritzl has also been the beneficiary of an informal 'Masonic' network that has brought 'good chaps' with murky pasts back into main-stream respectability. Without a de-Nazification programme, a large number of former Nazis – some of whom were involved in the concentration camps or implicated in the Holocaust or other atrocities – managed to find their way back into society. As a result, it was usually best not to ask too many personal questions. Austrian diplomat Kurt Waldheim, for example, had served two terms as Secretary General of the United Nations and was standing for election for the Austrian presidency when it was revealed that he had not been studying law at the University of Vienna during the war as he claimed. Instead, he had been with a German unit in the Balkans that took brutal reprisals against Yugoslav partisans and shot civilians, and was responsible for the deportation of the Jews from Salonika in Greece to the death camps in 1943. Nevertheless, he won the election and served for six years as President.

In Fritzl's case, the Austrian unwillingness to ask questions may have covered up some more recent crimes. On 22 November 1986, 17-year-old Martina Posch was found dead on the southern shore of Mondsee Lake, opposite the Fritzls' guesthouse and camping ground near Salzburg. Two divers found Martina's naked body, bound and wrapped in two green plastic sheets, ten days after she had gone missing from her home. She was thought to have been raped and murdered before her body was dumped in the lake.

No one was arrested. Fritzl's best friend, Paul Hoera, who first met him at Mondsee on a camping holiday with his wife, Rosemarie's friend Elfriede, in 1973, said he made regular trips to the lake and could have been in the area when Martina went missing. Since Fritzl hit the headlines, the police made the connection between the two cases and

Martina Posch's 22-year-old murder file has been re-opened. A pretty 17-year-old, Martina bore a striking resemblance to Elisabeth who, by then, had already been in captivity for over two years.

'We have found no sign of a concrete link up to now,' said Alois Lissl, Chief of Police of Upper Austria province, but he said Fritzl would be questioned about the murder as he could have been in the area when Martina was killed.

Although Fritzl was no longer co-operating with the police, he had claimed earlier that he had an alibi for the day Martina Posch was killed and dumped in the lake. This has yet to be tested in court, but his close friend Andrea Schmitt said that her husband was staying at Lake Mondsee at the time – and she believes Fritzl was there, too.

The police were also hoping to find a DNA match, and they searched Fritzl's house for the murdered girl's missing possessions, which include a blue jacket, a grey purse and a pair of black ankle boots.

'The perpetrator could have kept these items as a kind of trophy,' said Police Chief Lissl, adding, 'What really stands out is that, without her permanent wave, Martina looks similar to Fritzl's daughter Elisabeth. When we put the portrait photographs next to each other, it was unbelievable.'

The artist's drawing of Elisabeth published so far bears little similarity to the only photographs of Martina released to date. Observers say Elisabeth now looks more like the sister of her mother, Rosemarie, who is 69. However, a black-and-white snap of Elisabeth as a smiling teenager and a colour picture of her as a 14-year-old secondary school pupil are said to bear an uncanny resemblance.

Austrian police are also investigating the possibility that

Fritzl was involved in another unsolved sexually-motivated murder of a teenager in the 1960s. In 1966, prior to Fritzl's first conviction for rape, the body of 17-year-old Anna Neumauer was found in a cornfield near her home in Pfaffstaett bei Mattinghofen in Lower Austria, 65 miles from Amstetten. She had been killed with a captive bolt pistol, the type used for slaughtering livestock.

The police are reviewing the case of 16-year-old Julia Kuehrer, who disappeared from Pulkau, 60 miles from Amstetten, in June 2006, and they are also looking for any possible connection between Fritzl and the murder of Gabriele Supekova, a 42-year-old prostitute, whose body was found in August 2007 near the Austrian border, where Fritzl is said to have spent time on holiday.

It may be that the police are just trying to write off their unsolved cases. On the other hand, Fritzl might have been conducting a parallel career as a serial killer. It is not unknown for criminals to progress from minor crimes such as flashing or theft, via rape to murder – and, in this case, possibly, to incest, imprisonment and enslavery.

After his arrest, Fritzl condemned the media coverage of his case, saying that he could have killed the family he kept in the cellar, but he didn't. For those who have not killed before, surely this is a daunting prospect – particularly if the victim is your own flesh and blood. Perhaps he knew that he really could kill his dungeon captives because he had already killed elsewhere. He was plainly a man who placed little value on the lives of others – whether they were strangers or his own flesh and blood.

3

THE APPLE OF
HIS EYE

Elisabeth was the prettiest of Fritzl's daughters when she fell prey to her monstrous father. With her picture-book Austrian good looks – high cheekbones, wide eyes and a rosebud smile – she was always the apple of his eye. Despite Rosemarie saying that Ulrike, the oldest girl, was Fritzl's favourite, he himself insisted it was Elisabeth. Ulrike answered him back, Rosemarie said, and Fritzl respected that, but it was no good for his purpose: he needed someone he could intimidate.

During a crucial part of Ulrike's development, Fritzl had been away in jail. Perhaps that's what had made her so single-minded. But Elisabeth was still an infant when her father was in prison. By 1977, Ulrike was 19 and getting ready to slip from his grasp by leaving home, but Elisabeth was only 11 and had not begun the 'youthful rebellion' he complained of later. She still took care to hide the evidence of the beatings she suffered from her teachers and school friends. What began as a vicious over-indulgence in discipline and punishment

39

developed into a sadistic fixation and Fritzl began to sexually assault his helpless daughter. This may have begun while her brother and sisters were enjoying a holiday with their mother. Having lost interest sexually in his wife, Fritzl began to go on vacation on his own. One holiday snap released to the press shows him on a trip to the Mediterranean in the late 1970s – at a time when it is thought he was already sexually abusing the ill-fated Elisabeth.

Elisabeth said that the abuse started when she was 11. Fritzl denies it, saying that it began much later, but there is circumstantial evidence to substantiate Elisabeth's allegation. In 1977, Rosemarie took Ulrike, Rosi (then 16) and their brother Harald (13) to Italy. Family pictures show the sisters enjoying their two-week vacation. But Fritzl refused to let Elisabeth go and so she spent the fortnight at home with her depraved father. His perverted lust was the driving force behind his later crimes and, being at home alone for two weeks with the child he had already cowed, he had manufactured the perfect opportunity to inflict himself on her.

Family friend Paul Hoera joined the Fritzl family with his own children for the break. 'I can't bear to see them any more,' he said, after discovering the secret of Fritzl's House of Horrors. 'While we enjoyed ourselves, he could have been putting Elisabeth through goodness knows what.'

Paul, now 69, added, 'Elisabeth as a child was withdrawn and shy. I got the impression Josef didn't like her much. He didn't treat her as well as his other kids. He used to beat her a lot more. She used to get a slap for small things. I feel sick every time I think of her under the house when we were sitting in the garden laughing and joking.'

Denied the simple pleasures of a family holiday, Elisabeth

was trapped at home with her tyrannical and sexually predatory father. That year, Fritzl had begun raping her, the police report says – although, even now, she can barely bring herself to speak of it and the details are yet to come out.

As a young girl, she could not understand her predicament. Although her father was a domineering man, as a child she had offered him total obedience, but somehow he was now treating her differently from her brothers and sisters. 'I don't know why it was so,' she said, 'but my father simply chose me for himself.'

She later told the police that Fritzl would rape her without warning, in his car and on walks through the forest – even in the cellar. He denied this, saying that he only began to have sexual contact with his daughter some time after he locked her in the dungeon. Elisabeth was terrified of the days when he came to her, when he would mercilessly abuse her because, in his eyes, she belonged to him. She was nothing beyond being his possession to do with as he pleased.

'I am not a man who would molest children,' he said. 'I only had sex with her later, much later.'

However, it seems plain now that something was going on – the signs were all too obvious. Elisabeth, already an outsider at school, became more withdrawn. Her best friend at Amstetten High School, Christa Woldrich, said that she always had to be home half an hour after school finished.

'I was never allowed to visit her,' said Christa. 'The only explanation she ever gave was that her father was very strict. I did not see him, but he was always there between us because of his influence over her, like an invisible presence you could always feel.'

Another school friend recalled how Elisabeth was 'terrified

of not being home on time'. 'When we went to her home, we had to leave as soon as her father appeared,' she said.

Christa Woldrich said the teenage Elisabeth was noticeably reserved when speaking of life outside the classroom. 'I did get the impression that she felt more comfortable at school than at home,' said Christa. 'And sometimes she went quiet when it was time to go home again. It was the same for both of us – it was like a silence descending.'

It was clear that Elisabeth was being physically abused by her father. Other school friends said that she had sometimes avoided gym classes for fear that the teacher would ask about the bruises all over her body. Classmate Christa Gotzinger, who also had a violent father, said, 'We learnt to take the beatings ... We learnt how to pull ourselves together when the pain was unbearable.'

Another friend, who refused to be identified, said that Fritzl punched his children. 'He didn't slap or spank them,' she said. 'He hit them with his fists. Her brother once told me, "The pig will beat us to death one day".'

As Elisabeth grew older and began to show the first signs of becoming a woman, Fritzl grew frighteningly possessive over his daughter. He flew into a tempestuous rage if she attempted to dress fashionably, wore make-up or mentioned boys. Christa Woldrich noted the effect these furious outbursts had on her. 'Elisabeth became very sullen and withdrawn,' she said. 'She wasn't allowed out in the evenings or to invite friends to the house. I think she was comfortable only at school, though she wasn't very good at anything.'

It was clear that she was not developing along the lines of other girls. There was no chance that she could get close to a boy, or even develop a crush. 'She was so pretty she could have had boyfriends, but she never did,' said Christa. 'She just sat quietly and no one noticed her. When I think about it, I wonder why the teachers never realised something was wrong.'

Though it was widely known at school that Fritzl was violent towards his daughter, not even Elisabeth's best friend Christa knew about the sexual abuse at the time. 'The abuse at 11?' said Christa, after it eventually came out. 'I have thought about it a lot recently, whether I noticed anything when we were back at school. Now it is easier to understand why she didn't talk about boys or about sex. Now, with hindsight, I understand why she didn't talk about certain things or why she was distant and quiet, but we didn't realise it back then. You just think, oh, you're having a bad day.'

In 1978, when Elisabeth was just 12, Josef Fritzl applied for planning permission to turn his basement into a nuclear shelter. This was not unusual during the Cold War years. Austria was on the front line in the confrontation between the Soviet Bloc and the West. At the end of the Second World War, much of the country was in Russian hands and the Red Army stayed on as an occupying force in the Soviet zone for ten years. When they withdrew in 1955, eastern Austria was left surrounded on three sides by the Iron Curtain with Communist Czechoslovakia to the north, Hungary to the east and Yugoslavia to the south. Amstetten was barely 30 miles from the heavily guarded border that divided East from West. Both sides of the frontier bristled with nuclear weapons. The situation remained that way until the fall of the Berlin Wall in 1989.

Fritzl worked single-handedly on building the shelter over the next five years. However, in due course, he would need help to install the steel-and-concrete door which weighed nearly a third of a ton.

He was anything but discreet about the building work. On one occasion, he fixed an industrial winch to the roof of the house. The heavy-duty lifting device was installed directly above the entrance to the cellar. Fritzl brought it in to raise massive concrete blocks as he turned the bunker into an unbreachable fortress. It may have also been used to help shift the dungeon's heavy concrete-filled steel door that could only be opened by an electric motor operated by a remote control.

In 1983, local officials came to inspect his handiwork and gave their approval. Building inspectors checked out the underground bunker and fire safety officers checked the incinerator that was later used to burn his child's body, metres away from the hidden dungeon. The inspection team pronounced the ventilation shaft safe, gave Fritzl the appropriate stamp and left. They even advanced him State funds towards the construction shelter and later gave him permission to extend the basement and put in running water. In the eyes of the authorities, he was simply a good family man, trying to protect his wife and children in the event of a nuclear attack. This now looks like paranoia, but fear was running high at the time. Given the chilly political climate, nobody gave it a second thought. It is now apparent that Fritzl was actually building a prison where he had planned all along to incarcerate Elisabeth.

Elisabeth left school at 15 and, while her older siblings escaped by marrying, she remained under her father's constant gaze and was put to work full time at his lakeside guesthouse and campsite.

At the age of 16, Elisabeth ran away. She found work as a

waitress at a motorway truck stop and lived in a hostel, but Fritzl caught up with her and brought her back. Elisabeth's attempts to escape her father were common knowledge, according to Alfred Dubanovsky, who knew her when she was at school. 'After she vanished, we all talked about it,' he said. 'We knew she had run away before and thought she had done it again because she had told someone in our group that she had had enough, couldn't stand it any more at home and that her father had beat her, and had hurt her. She said she was scared of him.'

Even before her captivity, Elisabeth had spent most of her time indoors, he said, as her father did not let her out. However, as she got older, she began to come out of herself, even though her father tried to prevent it. 'She was a great girl, but very shy and pretty nervous,' said Dubanovsky. 'You needed to know her before she would trust you, but we got on really well. We used to spend a lot of time together, we were in the same class and we were friends. We had even danced together a couple of times. We all used to go the Belami disco at the bottom of her road, but she was rarely allowed out to see us.'

Joseph Leitner, now a waiter who lives in Neustadt near Amstetten, had also heard about the abuse. He attended the Amstetten Institute of Technology with a friend of Elisabeth's who knew her by the nickname 'Sissi'. Later, he became a lodger who rented a room from Fritzl, even though he had been warned by a friend about his behaviour before he moved in.

'I knew Sissi was being raped by her father before she disappeared,' he said. 'I had a good friend from school who was really close to Elisabeth. I would say they were best friends; they spent a lot of time together. She confided in me, and she told me what a monster Josef was – and what he had done to Sissi.'

Elisabeth made another attempt to escape, this time with their mutual friend. 'They came up with a plan to run away together,' said Leitner. 'It was in 1983. Elisabeth packed her bags and left the house. She and my friend were 17, and the two went to Linz but also spent some time in Vienna. Josef was furious and eventually found Elisabeth and dragged her home. Sissi was banned from having anything to do with my friend again. Her mother also made sure of that. She banned Elisabeth from seeing her – and watched her carefully to make sure they were kept apart.'

Leitner also knew of Elisabeth's earlier attempt to flee when she was 16. 'She could not take it living at home any more and tried to escape,' he said.

There were also indications around this time that Elisabeth was suicidal. However, the authorities unaccountably took no notice of her plight and aided Fritzl in getting her back. 'She had taken sleeping pills and went to Vienna,' said Leitner. 'But the police found her and they, or her father, brought her back home.'

Again, Leitner and his friend were not surprised when Sissi disappeared for a third time, nor was Leitner surprised that her friend kept quiet about what she knew. 'When Elisabeth vanished again just a year later, my friend thought she had run off again,' he said. 'She never said anything because she was scared. It wasn't only Elisabeth that was terrified of Fritzl, my friends were, too. They never went to the police because they were too scared of what Fritzl would do. That was why my friend kept quiet for so long.'

46

Leitner himself was also frightened of Fritzl, but now regrets taking no action. 'I feared he would take revenge,' he admitted. 'I have been tormented by nightmares ever since.'

Others knew of Elisabeth's distress and her plans to flee the family home. Classmate Susanne Parb, now into her forties, said, 'Elisabeth used to say, "It would be great if only I could escape. I can't wait for the day when I'll be free of him." When she was 16, she ran away to Vienna but he tracked her down. I wish he had never found her because all this may never have happened. She then got a job in a motorway restaurant and was saving money. Her plan was to leave when she was 18 because then he couldn't force her to come back home. She had her bag packed and was bracing herself to say goodbye to her mother when she vanished. It made sense that she had run off to a cult because everyone knew she lived in fear of her father.'

The reason she wanted to leave was clear enough. 'Before she vanished, Elisabeth told me she was beaten very badly at home,' said Susanne. 'Her father was clever, though, to make sure he didn't hit her where anyone could see the bruises and that's why the teachers didn't know. But Elisabeth never spoke about the rape. I think she must have been very ashamed.'

There was no love lost between Fritzl and Elisabeth's friend Susanne. 'I went to her house a few times to play but never when the father was there,' she said. 'He didn't like me because I asked questions about why Elisabeth could not leave and come to mine for dinner. Soon, he banned me from meeting her. Elisabeth didn't seem sad at school but was just very quiet. She had a good relationship with her brother Harald and her younger sister Doris.'

Susanne also knew that Elisabeth was not the only one in

the family who suffered abuse. 'After Elisabeth disappeared, I spoke to Harald a few times and when he had been drinking he told me how his father beat him,' she recalled. 'He used to say, "I'm very afraid that one day he will kill me."'

In 1982, Elisabeth spent three weeks in hiding in Brigittenau, Vienna's 20th district. The police picked her up and returned her to her parents. By making repeated attempts to escape and failing, Elisabeth unwittingly helped to provide her father with the cover story he would later use when he took her down to his basement and kept her imprisoned there. When he said that she had run off again, people naturally believed him; she had a track record. After all, she was a proven runaway, a rascal, a troublesome child. She was just the sort of delinquent who would end up in the hands of some strange sect. In the eyes of the good people of Amstetten, she had finally gone completely off the rails, leaving her parents distraught. She was an ungrateful child. Consequently, no one really cared where she had gone or what had happened to her.

It seems only natural that a teenager who was suffering extreme physical and sexual abuse at home would want to run away, but Fritzl still claims Elisabeth was in the throes of 'teenage rebellion' that had to be curbed at all costs. 'Ever since she entered puberty, Elisabeth stopped doing what she was told; she just did not follow any of my rules any more,' he said. 'She would go out all night in local bars, and come back stinking of alcohol and smoke. I tried to rescue her from the swamp and I organised her a trainee job as a waitress.'

He also accused her of 'promiscuity'. 'I have always had high regard for decency and uprightness,' he said. 'I was growing up in Nazi times, when hard discipline was a very important thing. I belong to an old school of thinking that just does not exist today.'

After Elisabeth was returned from Vienna, her father didn't touch her during the first few weeks, but then, she says, it started all over again. She decided to stick it out until she was 19. At that age, the Austrian police would have no further jurisdiction over her; youngsters of 19 upwards could leave home and go where they pleased, and the police would have no authority to pursue them. In the meantime, she had entered a training programme as a waitress at the Rosenberger highway rest stop near Strengberg on the A1 autobahn that ran from Linz to Vienna. She and other girls in the programme slept in a dormitory below the kitchen. After the years of abuse, it must have felt liberating to get away. For the first time, she felt safe from her father. However, Strengberg was little more than ten miles from Amstetten, so he could still keep an eye on her.

Later, she was sent to a catering college, where she lodged. The sexes were strictly segregated there, but she managed to meet an apprentice chef named Andreas Kruzik. The 18-year-old trainee was struck by Elisabeth, whom he described as a 'pretty, but serious and withdrawn girl'. Twenty-four years later, the 42-year-old divorced father-of-one recalled, 'My heart jumped into my mouth when we first met and I saw how beautiful she was. I struck up a conversation with her, talking about school and exams and trying to make her laugh. I knew then that I had fallen in love with her.'

It seems that his feelings were reciprocated. 'I noticed that she was slowly opening up and started to show interest in me,' he said. 'It was not so simple to be intimate because such things were not allowed in the school and there were only few

49

opportunities to make out. The girls' dormitory was a strict taboo and any boy caught there would have been expelled from the school.'

During their busy two months at catering college, they used to go for long walks in the woods and spend time together. 'We became inseparable,' said Andreas.

It is plain that Elisabeth had found a soul-mate, someone she could unburden herself to – up to a point, at least. 'She really confided in me,' said Andreas. 'I knew that she was under pressure from her parents and that she ran away from home when she was 14 or 15 and that she was closer to some of her other siblings. There was a trusted sister whom she stayed with often.'

Although they were physically intimate, the couple never had full sex because Elisabeth 'would suddenly pull back', Andreas said. 'She told me that she couldn't have sex with me. At the time, I thought it was because she didn't feel ready, but I know now that she must have been traumatised by what her father had done to her.'

By then, she had already been sexually abused by Fritzl for over seven years, according to what she told police, but she was reticent about her home life. 'She spoke of her parents and her home only once, and said that she had a very strict father,' Andreas said. 'She said he got her a waitress apprenticeship at a tank station, but that she would have preferred to become a cosmetician.' They even talked of running away together and getting married, although Andreas now fears that Fritzl may have learnt of their plans.

The couple finally decided to sleep together at his house but, before they had the chance, Fritzl turned up at the college gates, forced Elisabeth into his car and took her home. 'That night, she said she wanted to sleep with me and planned to stay at mine, but her father arrived to take her home,' Andreas said. While Fritzl waited outside, they snatched a passionate farewell. 'I kissed her goodbye and said I would be down at Amstetten to visit her, but she was worried about her dad. He was waiting in the car and she feared that if he found out about me she would be punished. She was very depressed and worried. She had failed part of the exam – the theory part – but I was cracking jokes and trying to cheer her up. I said, "Don't worry, you can repeat the exams." But it seemed like there was something else bothering her.'

Before she left, Elisabeth made Andreas promise to keep their love secret. Under the circumstances, it seemed a reasonable precaution. He knew that her father was a strict disciplinarian, but it would have been impossible for Andreas or anyone else to appreciate the lengths this tyrannical, self-centred beast would go to in order to dominate his own child. 'She told me her dad was strict but I had no idea he would do anything like this. Who would? We were madly in love and said we would write,' he said.

Andreas was not allowed to say goodbye to Elisabeth as she climbed into her father's grey Mercedes because she was banned from talking to boys. He remembers their hurried, secret farewell. 'As we kissed goodbye, we promised each other to write as often as possible,' he said. But when he received no reply, he thought she had lost interest in him. 'Now I realise she was no longer able to answer my letters.'

Elisabeth plainly did not get his letters, as she would have replied. Before she disappeared underground, she was already in correspondence with another male friend who lived Wiener Neustadt, a small town south of Vienna, 70 miles from

Amstetten. During her last month of freedom, she wrote three letters to him. The first was dated '9 May 1984' and the recipient was named only as 'E'. Her letter was clearly a reply to another from him as she said that she was very happy to receive a 'nice long' message from him. 'Basically, I'm doing pretty fine,' she wrote. 'Sometimes, I still feel some pain and feel sick. I'm still in contact with …' When the letter was released to the press, the name had been blanked out, but this was plainly Andreas. 'He went into the next hospitality class for cooks and waiters. I've been dating him since the course. Sometimes there are problems because he is from Enzesfeld-Lindabrunn [just a few miles north of Wiener Neustadt]. This is very far from my place and this is why I'm very sad.'

She confided her plans to leave home. 'After the exams … I'm moving in with my sister and her boyfriend,' she wrote. 'As soon as I've moved, I will send you my new address. You could come and visit me with your friends if you want to.'

She also talked about applying for a job in a nearby town and told E, 'Keep your fingers crossed for me.'

Her letter was also full of delightful, girlish trivia. 'I had my hair cut – layered on the sides and on the fringe,' she wrote. 'At the back, I want to let it grow long.' Then she asked, 'Do you have parties when your parents are at home, too? You are a crazy guy.'

E was plainly living a family life completely alien to Elisabeth. He seemed to be a normal, everyday teenager, whose parents tolerated a certain amount of youthful high spirits and disorder – out of love for their children. The idea that such a life was possible must have been a comfort. In E, Elisabeth had clearly found someone she could depend on for friendship and support, someone she did not want to lose contact with.

'I have a sensitive question I want to ask,' she wrote. 'I'd like to know if we're going to stay friends when you have a girlfriend? Most of the time friendships break up because of that. And it is very important to me. If you can believe it, I deal with boys much better than girls.'

She then explained why it was much easier to unburden herself to him than to her girlfriends at school. 'Girls are not as trustworthy as boys,' she wrote. 'Probably that's because I was around my brother from when I was a little child. I'm very proud of my brother who is now 21 years old. I know his problems and he knows mine, and I wouldn't say anything bad about him.' And she signed off the letter by saying, 'I hope we see each other soon. Best regards.'

Elisabeth sent the letter with Polaroid snap of herself attached. It shows her wearing a checked blouse, sitting on the steps of her parent's roof-terrace swimming pool on a balmy summer's evening in 1984. The sun has caught her bobbed red hair and a smile is starting to emerge on her lips. She wrote at the bottom of the letter, 'PS: the picture is a little bit dark but I will send you better ones soon, OK?' And on the back of the picture, she scrawled, 'Think of me!!! Sissy.'

This is the last known photograph of Elisabeth Fritzl before she disappeared into her long captivity underground. She appears momentarily happy: she has a boyfriend and has found another friend she can rely on, and she now faces the tantalising prospect that she may soon be able to escape the family home and her father's abusive tyranny.

Her second letter to E, dated 29 May 1984, was written on notepaper decorated with a cartoon girl dancing in a yellow dress. It read, 'Hello E. It is now already half-past ten and I'm lying in bed. Of course, I went out on Saturday. Can you imagine how hammered I was? At first we went to a couple of clubs. At about 5.00am we all went to my place to get a coffee because we'd had so much fun, and they all slept at my place. That was a mess. It took me half a day to clean up the flat.'

Her father could hardly have been pleased. She went on to talk about her waitressing job, saying, 'Most of the time, I'm off two days a week. That's when I go swimming, play tennis or even football. I like listening to music and daydreaming. But if life consists just of dreams – well, I don't really know about that.'

But, in a dungeon, all you can do is dream.

She called the friends with whom she went clubbing her 'crew' and said, 'They are really cool.' She urged her friend to 'keep your promise that you'll visit me as soon as you get your driving licence,' adding, 'I have six siblings, four of them are girls and two brothers. My brother H is 21 years young. He is the one I like most.'

She signed off as 'S' and told her friend, 'Stay safe, keep being a good boy. Don't drink too much.'

In the third letter, posted from Amstetten on 3 August, less than a month before she disappeared below ground, Elisabeth revealed her plans to move in with one of her sisters. She told E she was 'living fully in stress' due to an upcoming exam, but she had been to a fair with work pals, saying, 'It was something.' And she talked again of leaving home. 'As soon as I've moved, I will send you my new address,' she said. 'You could come and visit me with your friends if you want to.' She added, chillingly, 'Cross your fingers for me – when you get this letter, it will all be over.'

But her impending ordeal was just about to begin.

In all other respects, her tone was blithe and even

54

apologetic for not writing a longer note. 'Now I'm very tired because it's very late and also the evening movie (*Duel*) is so exciting. I can't write while watching this.' She concluded, 'Bye, see you soon, S. Write back soon and don't get drunk for no reason!'

In the letters, Elisabeth Fritzl seems a completely normal, happy girl – totally unaware of the terrible fate that hung over her.

Her boyfriend Andreas Kruzik had been writing, too. 'I wrote two letters to Elisabeth, telling her how much I loved her,' he said, 'and I was heartbroken when she did not write back.'

Unaware of the evil machinations of her depraved father, Andreas naturally jumped to the conclusion that he had been dumped. 'I thought she had gone off me, despite the fact that we had talked about the future and getting married,' he said. 'She had spoken of running away with me and getting married, but he must have known of her plans.'

But he never saw or heard from her again and was horrified to learn of her fate through the media, more than two decades later. He now fears it was his secret love letters that led to her incarceration. 'Now I fear he must have flown into a rage,' said Andreas. 'It's horrific he would act like that.'

When Elisabeth completed her training programme in the late summer of 1984, she figured that she would soon be free. Her bags were packed, she had money saved and a job prospect in Linz. It seemed she was on the verge of getting away from her abusive father. The long nightmare of her home life finally seemed to be over and freedom, love and happiness beckoned, but that life was to be snatched away and she would enter a longer and darker nightmare.

4

INTO THE ABYSS

On 28 August 1984, Elisabeth's underground nightmare began. Her father woke her that night and whispered to her to come down to the cellar that he normally stopped anyone else from entering. He asked her to help him fit the steel door, the final section of the prison he had built beneath the family home in Amstetten. This must have seemed a strange request, but he often worked downstairs in the cellar at night and absolute obedience had been drilled into her.

After the two of them had grappled the heavy door into place, Elisabeth said that her father grabbed her from behind and knocked her out with ether. When she came to, she found she was handcuffed to a metal pole, where she remained for the next two days. Then she said he put her on a five-foot dog leash which allowed her to reach the makeshift lavatory in the corner but otherwise restricted her movement. Already the bunker had been transformed into a prison: the heavy steel door was electronically controlled and the small room insulated and soundproofed. For the first few weeks, the terrified teenager was held there in total darkness.

Elisabeth tried to fight back. She banged on the walls and screamed until she could no longer speak, but nobody responded and eventually she gave up. When she stopped battling her father, the beatings lessened, although he kept demanding sex and she was kept on the leash for the next nine months. Her father only visited her to rape her, or give her food to keep her alive. This presented her with a vicious dilemma.

'I faced the choice of being left to starve or being raped,' she said. It was a stark choice – but, in the end, it was no choice at all.

She said she could not remember how many times her father raped her while she was on the leash, or how many times he had raped her before, or how many times he raped her in all the years she was in the dungeon. In the end, her only alternatives were to endure the unendurable, or struggle and add to her suffering with another beating. There was no way out.

Fritzl denied handcuffing his daughter or keeping her on a dog leash, as she had told police. 'That would not have been necessary,' he said callously. 'My daughter had no chance of escape.'

Nevertheless, at first the frantic Elisabeth spent hours screaming and banging her bruised body against the walls of her prison in the slim hope that she might attract help, but the dungeon was so deep below the main house and so well soundproofed that no one came. For four years, Fritzl kept her in complete isolation. Her only human contact was with her vile jailer, her only pastime counting the hours until he would return to brutally beat and rape her again.

Fritzl justified the captivity of his daughter, saying, 'Why should I be sorry? I took good care of her. I saved her falling into the drug scene.'

There are no indications that she was on drugs. Her boyfriend certainly knew nothing of it. 'What her father has said was not true at all,' said Andreas Kruzik. 'In no way whatsoever, that she went off the rails, that she took drugs … It is not true at all.'

Even today, there is only a minimal drug scene in Vienna, centred on the Karlsplatz. Elisabeth ran away to Vienna, she stayed in Brigittenau, which is over 3km away. The drugs of choice for Austrian teenagers seem to be alcohol and cigarettes, a fact confirmed by Elisabeth's own letters.

Her father complained that, even though he had found her a job, there were days when she would not go to work. But then, she was a teenager. 'She even ran away twice and hung around with persons of questionable moral standards, who were not a good influence on her,' he said. It is hard to imagine that any she met had more 'questionable moral standards' than Josef Fritzl himself.

'I had to bring her home,' he said, 'but she always ran away again. That is why I had to arrange a place where I gave her the chance – by force – to keep away from the bad influences of the outside world.'

But the bad influences were much closer to home.

While Elisabeth was safely restrained in her subterranean dungeon, there were loose ends to be tied up. It was two years since she had started as a trainee at the Rosenberger restaurant in Strenberg. Then, her boss Franz Perner said, Elisabeth 'suddenly vanished'. Fritzl told him that she had run away from home and would not be coming back to work.

The day after Elisabeth disappeared, Rosemarie Fritzl promptly – and properly – reported her daughter as 'missing'. A short time later, Fritzl handed over a letter to the police, the first that Elisabeth was forced to write in captivity. It was dated 21 September 1984 and carried the postmark of the nearby town of Braunau am Inn, Hitler's birthplace. According to the letter, Elisabeth had had enough of living at home and was staying with a friend. She warned her parents not to look for her, otherwise she would leave the country.

According to the German news magazine *Der Spiegel*, 'The letter was practically made-to-order for a quick decision by the relevant bureaucracies. Nowadays, perhaps, even officials at Austrian youth agencies would ask themselves why a girl who was considered well-adjusted and shy would run away from home twice. But, at the time, the letter conformed perfectly to the standard prejudice that runaways are little more than ungrateful brats who ought to be thinking about what they are doing to their poor, suffering parents.'

As days turned into weeks, Fritzl ordered Elisabeth to write other letters to her mother. In them, she was to pretend that she had run away to join a religious sect and asked the police not to look for her. These letters must have been agonising to write. With each, she was robbing herself of any chance that someone would come looking for her; she was adding a new lock to her dungeon door, digging herself deeper into her grave. She must have been tempted to litter them with clues that would alert the reader to her terrible plight. But they were dictated and read by her father. However callous he may have been, he was not stupid. Nothing would get past him – no hint, no clue, not the slightest indication that anything was wrong. Besides, her browbeaten mother and the compliant authorities seemed to believe anything they were told. Any hope she might have had in these communications with the outside world must have soon been extinguished. No one, it seemed, was interested.

The letters duped the police searching for her into winding down the hunt. Meanwhile the local authorities simply did what was expected of them. They forwarded the missing-child report to the Austrian Interior Ministry, the State financial authority and all State educational authorities in case the name of Elisabeth Fritzl appeared in their records, but that was where their interest in the case ended.

'Josef Fritzl had merely helped provide the authorities with an excuse for dropping the case when he told police that his daughter must have run off to join a sect,' said *Der Spiegel*. It seemed plausible enough at first glance. No one even bothered to check with Dr Manfred Wohlfahrt, the officer concerned with sects at the St Pölten diocese; he would have seen through it in a moment. Sects that isolate members from their family and friends are practically unknown outside Japan and the English-speaking world, where their strange antics often generate massive publicity.

It was only a matter of weeks before investigators apparently gave up on Elisabeth Fritzl. And after she turned 19, her disappearance was no longer of police concern. 'This is something the police see time and time again. As we all know, every child leaves the family home at some point,' said Chief Investigator Franz Polzer. 'Then her 19th birthday arrived. The Austrian police aren't allowed to search for missing persons over the age of 19 because, from this age onwards, an Austria citizen can go anywhere in the world they want to.'

In planning Elisabeth's imprisonment, Fritzl was clearly meticulous. He was widely known to be highly organised, a quality appreciated by those he did business with. He had dealings with Anton Graf, a neighbour of the summer guesthouse the Fritzl family ran in the mountains, who rented land to Fritzl. 'We had a business relationship,' said Graf. 'He was correct. If he gave you his word, you could count on it. If he borrowed a tool and said he would return it two days later, then two days later it was back. What he said, he did. You could always count on it.'

However, sometimes Graf found Fritzl difficult to get along with. 'He was inflexible and had no sensitivity,' said Graf. 'You were sick, something happened, he didn't care ... there was a rule – and that was it.'

Anton Graf saw the Fritzls every summer and knew Elisabeth throughout her childhood. So when she 'disappeared', Fritzl was sure to let him know all about it. 'One day he came to see us in a right old state,' said Graf. 'And he told us, "Lizzy won't be coming home. She is involved in a sect and has disappeared."'

The letters Elisabeth had written from captivity were used to reinforce the idea that she had fallen into the hands of some crazy cult and to deflect any further questions. 'A bit later on, he told us a letter had arrived,' said Graf. 'The letter said that it was pointless to search for her. She was deeply involved in a sect and she was so happy there that she was not coming home.' He added that Fritzl delivered the story with such aplomb that no one was suspicious.

Other acquaintances, such as Fritzl's friend, the deputy mayor of Lasberg, Leopold Stütz, also assumed the tale that his daughter Elisabeth – or Liesel, as he called her – had run away to join a religious sect was true. 'Whenever we asked him about Liesel, he used to say that Interpol was looking for her,' Stütz said. 'He said that he was so worried that he even went to a fortune teller to try and learn what had happened to her.'

None of them questioned him, or checked any further. Even some of her school friends were duped by Fritzl's cover story. 'I remember how afraid Elisabeth was of her father and how she panicked about being home on time,' said one former school friend. 'When I heard she'd run away to a cult, it seemed like the logical consequence of trying to free herself from home and her domineering father.'

Nobody asked any questions.

Elisabeth's boyfriend, Andreas Kruzik, did not believe her father's story, however. 'That she joined a sect? It is not true at all,' he said. 'She wasn't the type to be influenced by a sect. She knew exactly what she did and what she wanted to do.'

The lie was transparent. But, sadly, Kruzik was only wise after the event. He did not hear Fritzl's fabrication at the time. He thought he had simply been unceremoniously dumped and was heartbroken. 'We were a couple. We wrote to each other, we saw each other,' Andreas said. 'But all of a sudden, all contact ended. When I called, I was palmed off. It was over and I didn't hear from her again.'

What lovesick youth would enquire further, especially when he was sworn to kept his love a secret from his beloved's tyrant of a father?

While Fritzl went to great lengths to keep the imprisonment of his daughter a secret, he claimed that he longed to confide in a sympathetic soul – perhaps similarly to master criminals who risk being discovered purely so that others can see how clever they have been. 'With every week that I kept my daughter prisoner, my situation became more crazy,' he said. 'I often thought about telling a friend, but I was scared of being arrested.'

Full of self-pity, Fritzl considered that it was he who was ensnared, rather than his daughter. 'I got myself into a vicious circle from which there was no escape,' he said. 'I just kept putting off a decision ... Really, it is true, I often thought if I should set her free or not, but I just was not capable of making a decision, even though, and probably because, I knew that every day was making my crime that much worse. I was scared of being arrested, and that my family and everybody that knew me would know about my crime. That was why I kept putting off the day I would make a decision, putting it off again and again. Eventually – after a time – it was just too late to bring Elisabeth back into the world.'

As the weeks below ground stretched into months, Fritzl kept up a sickening pretence of normality with his daughter. He would tell her how work on the garden above her was progressing, and would also chat about films he had seen on TV, describe trips he had made and even kept her updated on the progress of her brothers and sisters. Unable to see any of these things for herself, this must have been an additional torture for her.

Then there was the sex. Elisabeth insisted that her father had been sexually assaulting her since she was 11, contrary to Fritzl's claim that the rapes had not begun until he had incarcerated his daughter – as if that made it any better. Initially, he controlled himself, he said, but 'my desire to have sex with Elisabeth also got much stronger as time went by'. Eventually, his lust for forced incest overwhelmed him.

'We first had sex in spring 1985 – nine months after I imprisoned her,' he claimed. 'I could not control myself any more. I wanted to have children with her. It was my dream to have another normal family, in the cellar, with her as a good wife and several children ... At some stage, somewhere in the night, I went into the cellar. I knew that Elisabeth did not want it, what I did with her. The pressure to do the forbidden thing was just too big to withstand.'

Elisabeth did not fight him, he said, but she cried quietly afterwards, making small whimpering noises. Then, every two or three days when he went into the cellar to bring her food and a change of clothes, he had sex with her. 'It was an obsession with me,' he said.

For Elisabeth, the choice was always brutally simple – 'It was either starve or be raped.' And it was not her recollection that her father held off his sexual attacks for nine months. They began straight away, while she was in chains. Her father's lust for her was not a consequence of her incarceration, but the cause of it.

While Fritzl might be planning to enter an insanity plea, he had already admitted that when he was raping his daughter in the cellar he knew right from wrong. 'I knew what I was doing was wrong and that it was hurting her,' he said. 'But I was driven and, in the end, that desire was just too great for me.'

For most people, any inkling of such feelings would have been a good reason to release her, but Fritzl had no such qualms about turning the full force of his libido on his unfortunate daughter. Friends said that, by this time, Rosemarie's 27-year marriage was a sham. In 1984, with his new sex slave installed in the basement, Fritzl stopped even sleeping with his wife. He told his wife brutally, 'You're too fat for sex.' And he told family and friends in her hearing, 'Fat women are below my standard.'

According to Roswita Zmug, who later took over a restaurant and guesthouse from the Fritzls in the nearby village of Aschbach, 'The marriage was over.'

Although Rosemarie put on a brave face, Roswita sensed her stoicism was illusory. 'There was a coldness between them and they didn't even talk to each other,' she said. 'Fritzl would just sit in the bar all day, ogling the women customers and grinning as if he had no care in the world, while she ran around doing all the hard work.'

Fritzl's friend Paul Hoera also thought there was something amiss with the marriage, though he thought it was partly his wife's fault. 'I thought she was a cold person,' he said. 'I don't know what their relationship was like – but I know that she was not his type. He told me he liked thin women and that he had a girlfriend. I never guessed it was his daughter.'

Fritzl admitted he did not even bother to use contraception while raping Elisabeth. 'In reality, I wanted to have children with her,' he said. 'I was looking forward to the offspring. It was a beautiful idea for me, to have a proper family also down in the cellar.'

There seemed no depth to which his depravity would not stoop. He already had his daughter confined to one small room as his sex slave, to be beaten for his sadistic pleasure or penetrated on a whim. For the first four years of her incarceration, he kept her utterly alone. According to her own account, the only visitor she had was her captor, who raped her every few days. During those years, she must have sunk into utter despair. He could not have failed to inform her that everyone had swallowed his tissue of lies. The letters she had written had worked; no one had come to find her and no one was going to come – not her mother, not her brothers and sisters, not her friends, not the social services, not the police. An arrogant man, he would have crowed about it. How clever he was; they were not even looking. As far as they were concerned, she was having a wonderful time in some hippie commune. And if they had been looking for her, the last place they would have searched was in 40 Ybbsstrasse, her home, just metres below their feet. She had been buried alive.

Then, just when it seemed things could not get any worse, the luckless Elisabeth fell pregnant.

'If we want to discuss when things deteriorated for Elisabeth, then certainly there was the moment that she realised she was pregnant for the first time, and then the worry throughout the pregnancy whether the child would be healthy,' said Professor Max Friedrich, head of the Child and Adolescent Psychiatry Clinic, Medical University, Vienna. 'And the births themselves would have taken their toll, especially given there was no help on hand, like a midwife or a doctor.'

Her situation was hopeless. He was in total control. She was helpless – just a captive to be beaten for pleasure, raped at will and now carrying her own father's child.

Parallels have been drawn with the case of Natascha Kampusch. Kidnapped from a Viennese street while she was on her way to school at the age of 10, she was held for eight years in a cellar before escaping in 2006. Professor Friedrich was the psychiatrist in the Kampusch case. He said that, like Natascha, Elisabeth Fritzl would have had to reach some sort of compromise with her captor simply to survive.

'Since she was taken prisoner at the age of 18, and kept imprisoned, she must have been extremely scared,' said

Professor Friedrich 'The question is, how did she cope with this fear and at what point was her will broken – because that's a thing we would expect to happen. And then you see something called Stockholm Syndrome, which is when the victim becomes resigned to their abuse.'

Stockholm Syndrome is a psychological response often seen in people taken hostage, where the victim shows signs of loyalty to the hostage-taker, regardless of what they have suffered or the danger the hostage has faced. There are reports that hostages have even fallen in love with their captors. The syndrome was first identified after the robbery of the Kreditbanken at Norrmalmstorg, Stockholm, Sweden, in 1973. The robbers held the bank employees hostage from 23 August to 28 August. In this case, the victims became strongly emotionally attached to their captors and even defended them after they were freed from their six-day ordeal.

The term Stockholm Syndrome was coined by the criminologist and psychiatrist Nils Bejerot, who assisted the police during the robbery. Famous cases include that of Patty Hearst, the heiress to the US newspaper empire of William Randolph Hearst, who was kidnapped by left-wing radicals calling themselves the Symbionese Liberation Army in 1974. After two months in captivity, she was filmed taking part in a robbery with her captors and issued statements condemning the capitalist 'crimes' of her parents, using the name 'Tania' – the *nom de guerre* of Tamara Bunka, the comrade-in-arms and lover of Argentine revolutionary Che Guevara. The rest of the SLA were killed in a shoot-out in May 1974, but Patty Hearst remained at large until September 1975, when she was captured by the FBI. She was charged with bank robbery and firearms offences.

In her defence, she claimed that she suffered from Stockholm Syndrome and had been coerced into aiding the SLA. She was convicted and imprisoned for her actions in the robbery, though her sentence was commuted in February 1979 by President Jimmy Carter, and she later received a Presidential pardon from Bill Clinton.

Another case that more closely mirrors that of Elisabeth Fritzl was Colleen Stan. She was held captive under the name Carol Smith from 1977 until 1984, by Cameron and Janice Hooker in northern California. Colleen was kept in locked wooden containers, sleeping in a coffin-like box under the bed Hooker shared with his wife. Throughout her captivity, she was consistently tortured and sexually assaulted to the point of complete physical and mental subservience. However, when given the opportunity to escape, she stayed – even signing a 'slavery agreement' and writing letters saying she was falling in love with Hooker.

Eventually, Janice Hooker grew tired of the attention her husband lavished on Colleen and arranged for her to leave. Even then, Colleen did not go to the authorities; neither did she tell her family the whole story and repeatedly telephoned Hooker, although she refused to return to him. Eventually, Janice Hooker left her husband. She began to reveal what had gone on and Cameron Hooker was arrested and charged with kidnap, rape and other sexual offences. His defence was that Colleen had become his slave voluntarily and that the sex was consensual, citing her letters and phone calls. But the jury did not believe him. He was convicted of ten felony counts and sentenced to 104 years' imprisonment.

Plainly, Elisabeth Fritzl was not broken to this extent. In her 24 years in the cellar, she was never presented with any opportunity to escape. When one came – and she was assured that it really was a cast-iron bid for freedom – she took it.

But the most interesting parallels occur between the Kampusch and Fritzl cases, of course – firstly, because they both took place in Austria. Natascha Kampusch had been much younger than Elisabeth at the time of her kidnap, and was been abducted by a stranger, although the allegation has now been made that her mother was involved in the kidnapping or the cover-up. However, her captor Wolfgang Priklopil was, like Fritzl, a technician, having worked for some time at the German engineering giant Siemens. She was held in a small nuclear bunker under Priklopil's garage. The entrance was hidden behind a cupboard and had a steel door. The cellar had no windows and was soundproofed. It had a floor space of just 5 square metres – approximately 54 square feet – smaller than the padded cell where Elisabeth Fritzl was first held. Natascha also attempted to make a noise to attract attention by throwing bottles of water against the walls.

However, she was only confined to the dungeon for the first six months. After that, she spent increasing amounts of time upstairs in the rest of the house, but each night was sent back to the chamber to sleep and was also locked up there while Priklopil was at work. Natascha said that she and Priklopil would get up early each morning to have breakfast together. Priklopil gave her newspapers and books, so she could educate herself. Stacks of school books were found in her cell. He also encouraged her to listen to classical music and educational programmes on the radio, and she taught herself to knit. So, in some ways, she had an easier time than Elisabeth Fritzl. But there was no escape. Priklopil had warned her that the doors and windows of the house were booby-trapped with high explosives. He also claimed to be carrying a gun, and warned that he would kill her and anyone she spoke to if she attempted to escape. Natascha said she fantasised about chopping his head off with an axe, although she dismissed the idea.

In later years, she was seen outside in the garden alone, and one of Priklopil's business partners also said that he met Natascha at his home nearby when her kidnapper came to borrow a trailer. Natascha, he said, looked 'cheerful'. After she turned 18, she was allowed to go on shopping trips with Priklopil. He threatened to kill her if she made a noise, although she did make vain attempts to attract attention. He even took her on a skiing trip to an Alpine resort near Vienna. She initially denied that they had made the trip, but eventually admitted that it was true, although she said she had had no chance to escape during the excursion.

On 23 August 2006, the 18-year-old was cleaning and vacuuming Priklopil's BMW in the garden when, at 12.53pm, someone called him on his mobile phone. Priklopil walked away from the car because of the noise of the vacuuming. Seeing her chance to escape, Natascha left the vacuum cleaner running and ran away, unseen by Priklopil, who completed the call without noticing she had gone. Natascha ran for some 200m through gardens and a street, jumping fences, and asking passers-by to call the police, but they took no notice. After about five minutes, she knocked on the window of a 71-year-old neighbour and said, 'I am Natascha Kampusch.' The neighbour called the police.

Unlike Elisabeth Fritzl, when Natascha escaped she was found to be in good physical health, although she looked pale and shaken and weighed only 48kg – approximately 7st – almost the same weight she had been eight years earlier when she disappeared. She had grown only 15cm – about 6in – and was identified by a scar on her body, DNA samples and her passport, which was found in the room where she had been held. Sabine Freudenberger, the first police officer to speak to her after her ordeal, said that she was astonished by Natascha's 'intelligence and her vocabulary'.

Unable to recapture Natascha, Priklopil realised that the police would soon be after him and he killed himself by jumping in front of a suburban train near the Wien Nord station in Vienna. It seems he had planned to commit suicide rather than be arrested, having previously told Natascha that 'they would not catch him alive'. She said she had not cried when she learned of his suicide, but she admitted that, in some way, his death had affected her. 'He was part of my life,' she said. 'That is why, in a certain way, I did mourn him.'

They had had a close relationship. In interviews, she referred to him only by his first name, Wolfgang, rather than Priklopil. She said he rarely worked and they would talk while she did the cooking and housework for him. 'He was not my master … I was equally strong,' she said.

Natascha now owns Priklopil's house, which was given to her as compensation. She has no plans to have it demolished like the homes of American cannibal Jeffrey Dahmer or Fred and Rosemary West. And, since her release, she has visited the cell where she was held captive.

Some sentiments expressed in the official statement Natascha issued after her escape eerily echo the justifications of Josef Fritzl. She said that her captivity spared her many things. 'I did not start smoking or drinking,' she said, 'and I did not hang out in bad company.'

Like Elisabeth Fritzl, Natascha Kampusch is a remarkably

strong and resilient young woman. She said that, in general, she did not feel she had missed out on anything during her imprisonment and somehow gained strength from the hopelessness of her situation. 'I always had the thought, "Surely I didn't come into the world so I could be locked up and have my life completely ruined,"' she said. 'I gave up in despair about this unfairness. I always felt like a poor chicken in a hen house. You saw my dungeon on television and in the media, thus you know how small it was. It was a place for despair.'

Natascha Kampusch seems to have made a full recovery. She has managed to exploit the media interest in her, gaining some recompense for her suffering by charging for interviews. She also published a book giving an account of her imprisonment and has begun a well-deserved career as a TV chat-show host.

However, it seems that she prefers to put on a brave face and tends to minimise the abuse she suffered. According to her media adviser, Priklopil 'would beat her so badly she could hardly walk. When she was beaten black and blue, he tried to smarten her up. Then he would take his camera and photograph her.'

She has also refused to give any details of how her captor might have sexually abused her over the years. 'Everyone always wants to ask intimate questions that are nobody's business,' she said. 'Maybe I will tell my counsellor some day, or someone else when I feel the need to, or maybe never. The intimacy is mine alone.'

Professor Friedrich, her psychologist, said that the language she uses is clear and powerfully expresses the complex relationship she developed with her captor.

In the case of Elisabeth Fritzl, there can be no doubt about the sexual abuse she suffered. Her father admits it and the DNA evidence is there. Indeed, unlike Natascha's experience, Elisabeth's life in her underground bunker included no visits to neighbours, no shopping trips, no visits to ski resorts, no glimpse of the outside world and no cause for hope. And now with her pregnancy, she could simply have given up.

Perhaps for some brief moment she might have thought that her father would have had to take her to hospital for the birth. She must have been terrified, too, that a child produced by incest would suffer from some genetic impairment. Fritzl, of course, feigned concern. 'Elisabeth was, of course, very worried about the future,' he said. 'But I bought her medical books for the cellar, so that she would know when the day came what she had to do. I also arranged towels and disinfectants and nappies.'

When Elisabeth was about to give birth, Fritzl drove hundreds of miles to stock up on baby food, clothes and disposable nappies at shops where no one would recognise him. When he returned, it must have been plain to her that he was not going to allow her out of the cellar for the birth. With the medical books to hand, it was clear that he was not going to provide her with any medical assistance. What doctor or nurse could possibly have visited her in her tiny cellar to help her give birth and then left without asking questions? The poor girl was clearly going to have to suffer the ordeal unaided.

In 1989 – the year the Berlin Wall came down – Elisabeth gave birth to her first daughter, Kerstin, whose life-threatening condition caused by a lifetime starved of light and fresh air eventually led to their release. Her terrified 22-year-old mother gave birth to her firstborn entirely alone. The only possible midwife could have been her abusive father and he had no incentive to be around.

'We think he went off sex with Elisabeth when she was heavily pregnant and left her alone to have her babies underground,' said a police spokesman. 'All he cared about was satisfying his lust and keeping the terrible secret of his hidden family. The more we learn about him, the more his actions defy belief. He is morally sub-human.'

However, with the help of the medical books Fritzl had brought, Elisabeth and her baby survived the ordeal. They were lucky; aside from having no professional assistance, the risk to her newborn child was also substantially increased by the lack of proper facilities, said Patrick O'Brien, a spokesman for the Royal College of Obstetricians and Gynaecologists. Elisabeth herself was also at massive risk during the birth.

'Most babies will be delivered absolutely fine, even without medical assistance,' he said, 'but there is a huge rise in the chance of serious complications for both mother and baby when there is a lack of care during pregnancy, and particularly around the time of birth.'

Kerstin was sickly from the moment she was born. She suffered from cramps, now diagnosed as a form of epilepsy that is linked to incest. However, there was an up-side. To have a child – despite its paternity – would have given Elisabeth something to live for. Now she would have someone to love and she would not have to live alone in the cellar. On the other hand, her poor child would have to suffer the same life of captivity that her mother endured.

Indeed, after Kerstin's birth, Elisabeth's life did improve. 'There was a change,' said Chief Investigator Franz Polzer. 'She said herself that even before she was incarcerated, she had been abused by her father. And after being taken prisoner, she had endured brutal physical violence in some shape or form. And then she told us this had lessened.'

The beatings may have become less brutal, but the rapes did not stop. In Fritzl's warped mind, his daughter was now his mistress and he bought her skimpy outfits and lingerie which no one, bar him and their children, would ever see her wear. He also dressed smartly for his nocturnal visits to the cellar and, the following year, she gave birth to a son, Stefan, now 18. Margaret Thatcher had just resigned and Elisabeth Fritzl had already been entombed for five years.

5

WHO KNEW?

Although the police and Elisabeth's mother Rosemarie had long since given up looking for the girl, not everyone believed Fritzl's story that she had run off to join some secret religious sect. At school reunions, when the talk turned to how Elisabeth had left to become part of a cult, her close friend Christa Woldrich would always say, 'Don't be crazy … she would never do such a thing.'

It was all the more unbelievable as, while such secretive sects are well known in the United States and Britain – more recently in Japan – they were few and far between in Austria, a traditional Catholic country. But Christa Woldrich was in no position to pursue the matter. She had never been allowed to visit the Fritzl house and she knew that Elisabeth's father was an ogre who discouraged her friends. There was no reason to believe her mother would be any more forthcoming. She too, apparently, believed the story of Elisabeth running off to join a sect. If she didn't, why wasn't she doing anything about it? Whatever had happened to Elisabeth was clearly, first and foremost, a matter for the family.

There were other people close to hand who might have been expected to know where Elisabeth was. Fritzl rented out rooms in 40 Ybbsstrasse. During Elisabeth's incarceration, more than 100 tenants had lived in the ugly three-storey concrete bunker in the centre of Amstetten – directly above her prison, but none of them suspected anything.

The signs were there though. Joseph Leitner moved into the house on Ybbsstrasse in 1994, despite knowing that Fritzl had raped his own daughter before she disappeared. Though Fritzl banned pets, Leitner kept a dog, a husky-Labrador-sheepdog mix named Sam. 'The dog always used to bark when we walked past the cellar,' he said. 'I thought he was just excited about going outside.'

Fritzl warned all his tenants that the cellar was strictly off-limits – and anyone going near it would be thrown out.

Sam would often wake with a start in the middle of the night and was 'hugely terrified'. He also used to bark suddenly in the small hours – but always slept peacefully once they had moved out. Leitner now believes his pet could hear noises from the cellar below, but even though he already had his suspicions concerning Fritzl and his daughter, he kept quiet.

'I decided I did not want to get involved,' he said. 'I did not want to get kicked out of the flat – I did not want to lose it. I kept myself to myself.'

There was another oddity about the bedsit Leitner rented from Fritzl that should have alerted him. He was baffled about the exorbitantly high electricity bill that Fritzl asked him to pay. A waiter who worked long hours, Leitner was barely ever there and never used the washing machine – yet his monthly electricity bill was more than €400 (£312). Leitner even asked a friend from a cable TV company to check the electricity in the house, but even when all the gadgets in his room were unplugged, the meter continued to click around at high speed.

It was only much later that Leitner discovered the answer to the riddle. It lay just a metre or so beneath his feet. His bedsit was directly above the cellar where Fritzl had imprisoned his daughter Elisabeth and their growing family, and his landlord was siphoning off electricity from his tenants to power the lights and appliances in the dungeon below.

Sam, the mongrel, may also have had his suspicions. Usually a friendly dog, he would growl menacingly whenever he saw the landlord. The antagonism was mutual and eventually, Sam was the reason Leitner had to leave.

'Every time I walked up the stairs, the dog tried to run to the cellar door and barked,' he said. 'When Fritzl noticed, he kicked me out by changing the locks on my flat. He was furious.'

Leitner's summary eviction came 14 years before Elisabeth's imprisonment was discovered. He now feels guilty that he did not pursue his suspicions or follow up on what his dog had been telling him. 'If I had put more effort into finding out what was behind all that, maybe the dungeon would have been discovered much earlier,' he said. 'I'm now angry at myself that I failed to do that.'

Another tenant who had his suspicions was Alfred Dubanovsky, who had known Elisabeth at school. He had also been aware of her harrowing home life and her sudden disappearance – though he assumed, reasonably enough, that she had simply run away again. However, when he got a job at a petrol station near Ybbsstrasse, he moved into number 40. 'I lived there for 12 years and all the time that poor family was suffering so much down below. It is too awful to think about,' he said when the cellar dungeon was discovered.

The floor he lived on was split into a number of flats, let to as many as eight different tenants at a time. His 42-square-metre flat was just a few feet above the cellar where Elisabeth and her family were incarcerated.

Like his fellow tenant Joseph Leitner, Alfred Dubanovsky found there were a great many puzzling aspects to life at 40 Ybbsstrasse. 'There were many things I found strange but I never would have guessed what they represented,' he said. 'Herr Fritzl banned any of the tenants of the eight flats from going anywhere near the cellar or back yard. He told us the cellar was protected with a sophisticated electronic alarm, and whoever went there would have their contract cancelled without notice.'

Plainly, he had something to hide, and there were other odd goings-on concerning the cellar in the household of Herr Fritzl. 'He used to take food and shopping down there in a wheelbarrow – always at night,' said Dubanovsky. There were a great many mouths to feed. Though Fritzl was careful enough to go to outlying supermarkets to do the shopping for his captives, all the food for both Fritzl's second family in the basement and the remaining family upstairs had to be delivered to his home. There, the quantity could not be concealed. According to Dubanovsky, 'The amount was far too much for Josef, his wife and the three kids still at home.'

According to Elisabeth's testimony, her mother knew nothing of her captivity, neither was she involved. It was only her father, Elisabeth said, who supplied her with food and clothing. Even before they questioned Rosemarie, the police had ruled out her involvement. 'What woman would stay silent if she knew that her husband had seven children with his daughter and was holding her prisoner in the cellar?' asked the Chief Investigator.

Rosemarie's younger sister Christine is convinced that, 'She would never have believed him capable of it'.

Her former colleague Anton Klammer said, 'People ask how she could not have known, but she was living away from him for a long time' – at least while Fritzl was developing his plans. 'She was a loving mother – I'm sure she had no idea of what was going on. She was terrified of him.'

Joseph Leitner did not mention Rosemarie's involvement, but he recalled how Fritzl would 'unload plastic bags full of shopping from his silver-grey Mercedes and bring them into the garden between 10.00 and 11.00 at night'.

If that was not puzzling enough, there were other things that could have alerted the tenants. 'At other times, I remember I could sometimes hear a knocking from the cellar that I couldn't explain,' said Alfred Dubanovsky. 'Right below my room, I heard banging, bashing, knocking noises. One time, I asked Fritzl what it was and he said it was coming from the gas heating below.'

Dubanovsky believed his landlord's assurances when Fritzl told him that the cellar below was empty. He also noted, though, that Fritzl had established a routine. When he worked, he visited the cellar in the evening, but once he retired, he disappeared into the cellar at 9.00am each morning, ostensibly to work on electrical engineering plans. He remained there 'at work' long after his wife had gone to bed. She was told never to disturb him.

Given his tyrannical demeanour, the family must have been grateful that Fritzl withdrew for hours on end into his cellar where he had his workshop and office, as well as the well hidden entrance to the dungeon. The entrance to the cellar itself was the back garden, which was obscured by a tall hedge. The back garden was Fritzl's kingdom, one neighbour said, and intruders were not welcome.

'Every day at nine every morning Sepp would go to the cellar, supposedly to produce blueprints for machines he had been commissioned to build,' said his sister-in-law Christine. Often, he even stayed there overnight, she continued, telling his wife under no circumstances was he to be disturbed. 'Rosi was not even allowed to bring him a cup of coffee,' she said. 'His word was law.'

No one queried his behaviour – for good reason. 'Questions about why he was down there so long were banned,' said Christine.

Fritzl had acquired a reputation locally for being somewhat reclusive, so an obsession about some secret project in his basement did not seem out of character to his tenants. 'Herr Fritzl spent every day in his cellar but I thought his behaviour was pretty normal,' said Alfred Dubanovsky.

Dubanovsky also said that Fritzl was enormously house-proud of the unattractive concrete building with its sheer featureless walls and small, cell-like windows on Ybbsstrasse. 'Fritzl was strange,' said Dubanovsky. 'He told me, "One day, my house will go down in history." Now I know what he meant by that. Only he was allowed to go into the cellar; he went there almost every day.'

It was clear, at the very least, that whatever was going on in the cellar was of dubious legality. The seemingly respectable

Fritzl was paranoid about the police. 'He would fly into a panic at the merest mention of the police or the law,' said Dubanovsky. 'When I moved out, there was a dispute over who should pay for repairs to a door. I threatened to sue. He went pale and caved in immediately.'

But who could have imagined what was really going on under the house? 'I never in my wildest dreams thought he was behind anything like this,' said Dubanovsky. Nevertheless, he admits, 'there were so many clues – the noises at night, the amount of food that he used to load into a wheelbarrow and push to the cellar ... I wish to God that I could turn back the clock. The signs were all there but it was impossible for me to recognise them. Who would ever believe something so terrible was going on right under my feet? It is a regret I will have to live with for the rest of my life.'

Another tenant, 32-year-old Anita Lachinger, a neighbour who briefly rented the flat above Dubanovsky's, had no suspicions at all. 'The Fritzl family made a very nice impression,' she said after her brief stay. 'I felt good in the house. They were a perfectly normal family to me. The only thing that was odd was that the grandparents were fostering their grandchildren. When I heard the news about Herr Fritzl, I was genuinely shocked. It is incomprehensible to me. He seemed, whenever you saw him, like such a harmless old man. No one would have guessed the truth. It's incredible.' However, she, too, was warned to steer clear of the cellar. It was out of bounds.

There were other telltale signs that something untoward was going on. Joseph Leitner said food often went missing from his kitchen and that of fellow tenants. Sausage, fresh milk and cheese, for example, would disappear overnight from the fridges. It was as if the little people from *The Borrowers* were foraging for titbits. The real reason things were going missing was that Herr Fritzl would use his master key to slip into the tenants' flats to pilfer provisions for Elisabeth and their children on the days when he did not have time for a shopping expedition.

'I took care of them all,' Fritzl told police during his first interrogation. 'I meant well.'

With Elisabeth and two growing children in the tiny cellar, things were becoming terribly cramped. Only a small, 20-square-metre room had been approved by planning officials as a nuclear-attack shelter. All three lived in one room until the sickly Kerstin was five and Stefan was three, and were present when Fritzl continued raping their mother. To be seen by her growing children being sexually humiliated in this fashion by her father can only have increased Elisabeth's distress.

As the children grew, the overcrowding grew worse and, when Lisa was born in 1992 – the year Prince Charles and Diana separated – there was no room for her. She cried a lot, possibly because of a heart defect that may derive from the genetic composition of her parentage. Fearful that someone might hear the child, Fritzl decided that she should be brought up above ground by his obedient wife. That way, the child could receive proper medical attention. The infant was ill so often that it was not difficult to persuade Elisabeth to go along with his plan.

'Elisabeth and I planned everything together, because we both knew that Lisa, because of her poor health condition and the circumstances in the cellar, had no chance to live had she remained there,' Fritzl said. Elisabeth was easily coerced into writing a letter saying she had abandoned the baby because she could not cope. She may not have wanted to give up the child, but if she loved it and wanted it to survive, again, she had no choice.

On 19 May 1993, a cardboard box containing baby Lisa was found on the doorstep of the Fritzls. She was nine months old, and weighed only 12lb (5.5kg) and measured 24in (61cm).

It was the luckiest day in little Lisa's life because it was the first time she had ever seen the light of day. The only light she had experienced since birth was the harsh glare of an underworld, the never-changing, cold, artificial light of a basement. It was the only light that her mother, Elisabeth, had seen in the six years leading up to Lisa's birth and it was also the only light Lisa's brother, Michael, would ever see as he died in the basement only a few days after his birth.

There is no doubt that her move to the world above ground saved Lisa's life. She would live a life of relative normality for 15 years, but then the secrets of the House of Horrors would be revealed and that world would come crashing down.

Along with the baby in the box was a letter; there was no envelope and no return address. The only thing that identified it was the signature 'Elisabeth', the Fritzls' daughter, who had apparently disappeared nine years before.

'Dear parents,' she wrote in a clear, feminine hand, 'You will probably be shocked to hear from me after all these years, and with a real-life surprise, no less ... I am leaving you my little daughter Lisa. Take good care of my little girl.'

It went on to maintain the fiction that she was still with the sect and had no time for children. This, in itself, was suspicious as secretive sects are usually keen to nurture and indoctrinate the next generation. As she could not bring the child up in those circumstances, she begged her parents to raise Lisa for her. Nevertheless, the note was full of tender detail: 'I breast-fed her for about 6½ months, and now she drinks her milk from the bottle,' it said. 'She is a good girl, and she eats everything else from the spoon.'

The letter was also filled with an air of normality: 'I hope that you are all healthy,' it read. 'I will contact you again later, and I beg you not to look for me, because I am doing well.'

In the supposed circumstances, it seemed only natural that Elisabeth would politely ask her parents not even to attempt to find her. It was as if she was asking them to respect and tolerate her alternative lifestyle – even though it necessitated her thrusting an unwarranted child on them.

Rosemarie seems to have been sceptical, but then she received a phone call purportedly from her daughter, in which she was begged, once again, to look after the child. It is unclear who made this call. According to some sources, it was Fritzl faking his daughter's voice on the telephone. But even Rosemarie would surely have seen through her husband putting on a high-pitched woman's voice. A mother would have known her daughter's voice even after a separation of nine years and it is rare to find a man who can sound convincingly like a woman. Subsequently, Fritzl resorted to using the taped messages that he had coerced Elisabeth into making.

The phone call – however it was contrived – stilled her qualms and Rosemarie then took in the child without further investigation. Friends were told the same story. Mondsee neighbour Anton Graf said Fritzl told him how he had 'discovered' one of Elisabeth's children on his doorstep and Graf said he never doubted the tale. 'He was so convincing of the sorrow he felt and the suffering of his family,' he recalled. 'Nobody had any clue.'

However, some had their doubts. One such was Roswita Zmug, who knew Rosemarie from the guesthouse. 'Once, after a child had mysteriously appeared on their doorstep, I asked how it could possibly have happened,' she said. 'Rosemarie told me all about her daughter going off to join the cult. It seemed incredible to me, but not to her. Still, I'm convinced she didn't then know anything about her husband's life below stairs.'

To Roswita Zmug, Fritzl's story that her wayward daughter had simply dumped the children on the doorstep before scuttling back to her non-existent sect was ludicrous. Elisabeth may have had a reputation for being a little unruly as a teenager – a reputation hardly borne out by the fact – but what mother would do that? It could only have been someone on drugs or who otherwise seriously needed help. It was odd, too, that when Rosemarie expressed the slightest misgivings, she received a mysterious phone call that, apparently, convinced her. Something here needed further investigation.

Not only was the credulous Rosemarie taken in, but so too were the authorities, once again. The social services did not even ask themselves why Elisabeth would entrust her daughter to parents from whom she herself had run away. Instead, five days after Lisa's appearance on the Fritzls' doorstep, Amstetten's youth welfare office wrote, 'Herr and Frau Fritzl have recovered from the initial shock. The Fritzl family is taking loving care of Lisa and wishes to continue caring for her.'

To ward off even the slightest hint of suspicion, Fritzl showed the letter that had come with Lisa to the police along with a few of his daughter Elisabeth's old school notebooks that he happened to have. He said that he wanted the notebooks and the letter given to a handwriting expert so that he and his wife, as the grandparents, could be completely certain that the child they planned to adopt was indeed their flesh and blood. It worked. Despite everything, Josef and Rosemarie were allowed to keep Lisa and, within a year, they were permitted to adopt her.

Asked why social services allowed Herr Fritzl to adopt the child despite his alleged criminal record, the District Governor, Hans-Heinz Lenze, said that in 1994 when the first child, Lisa, was adopted, neither Fritzl nor his wife apparently had any conviction – at least there were none on the record. 'In such cases, giving the child to members of the family is always preferred to committing it to a foster home,' said Lenze, insisting that the social services had not broken with the standard procedures.

But why had records of such serious offences, including sexual assault and arson, not been kept, he was asked. 'I am only a civil servant and not a law-maker,' was his reply.

However, after Fritzl was arrested, it took journalists only a short time to find reports of his rape conviction among the cuttings. Knowing that such an offence would be expunged from the official records under Austria's statute of limitations, it would not have been difficult for someone from the social services to have checked in newspaper archives.

In bringing Lisa above ground, Fritzl had taken unnecessary risks. And it didn't suit his overall plan, either. What he wanted was a second family underground – one that he could dominate completely. And as he was not about to stop having unprotected sex with his abused daughter, there were bound to be more children, so something would have to be done.

In 1993, Fritzl began extending the dungeon with extra rooms to give his growing subterranean family proper living quarters. By then, Elisabeth had been entombed in that single padded cell for nine torturous years.

As her presence in the basement was a secret, there was only one person he could call on to help dig out the dungeon – Elisabeth herself. Together, they dug out an estimated 116 cubic metres of earth – some 200 tons of it – by hand. Over the years, Fritzl managed to smuggle the equivalent of 17 lorry-loads of earth and rubble out of the cellar without his tenants, the neighbours or his family noticing. At the same time, he managed to smuggle tiles, bricks, wooden wall panels, a washing machine, a kitchen sink, beds and pipework into the underground cellar without anybody being any the wiser. He excavated a dungeon seven times the size of the nuclear bunker he had permission to construct. On top of everything else, he was violating all manner of building codes, but the authorities knew nothing of it. In any other circumstances, undertaking such a Herculean task successfully would have been an astonishing – and admirable – achievement. 'Fritzl did it all,' said a police source. 'It's phenomenal by anyone's standards.'

Although Fritzl was a talented engineer and electrician, it seems that plumbing was beyond him. Upstairs tenant Alfred Dubanovsky said he saw another man going down into the cellar. Fritzl introduced him as a plumber who had come to help him install a toilet. 'He didn't get many visitors,' said Dubanovsky, 'but only he alone was allowed in the cellar, which I thought was a bit strange.'

The police do not think this man was an accomplice; they believe Fritzl acted alone. Somehow, this man had entered the cellar, installed the lavatory and gone away again without noticing Fritzl's imprisoned daughter and the children. As there was no door between the room in the dungeon, Elisabeth, Kerstin and Stefan must have been hidden away out of sight, probably bound and gagged, when the plumber visited.

Another major risk Fritzl took in securing expert assistance was the fact that a professional plumber would surely have noticed that the now-extended underground bunker violated the building code. Yet he did not report it to the authorities, and neither has he come forward since. Who he was and how he was involved in the imprisonment of Elisabeth and her children remains one of the unanswered questions of the investigation.

Although the cellar was getting bigger, there was no chance of improving the ventilation system. This would have necessitated breaching the walls or ceiling of the dungeon, allowing sound – possibly a cry – out. While Fritzl later gave his cellar family vitamin D tablets and installed a UV light in an attempt to stop them developing health problems due to lack of sunlight, these provisions were no match for daylight and fresh air.

Household waste from the dungeon family was put into the underground furnace so as not to attract attention. The bathroom, kitchen and toilet were plumbed into the main house's waste disposal system. To further allay suspicion, Fritzl kept a room full of building materials, which could then be brought out when repairs needed to be made to the house or other buildings he owned. No one would note that more went in than ever came out. As his workshop was also down there, it was only natural that he would be seen taking material in. This subterfuge worked. Fritzl's son-in-law, Juergen Helm, now in his late thirties, said, 'I have lived in the house for three years and have been in the cellar at least once. It was scattered with junk and I had no idea this family was living a few metres away. It's incredible.'

Neighbour Erika Manharter spotted nothing amiss either, though he had known Fritzl from childhood. 'I grew up with Josef and he always appeared friendly, though he never seemed to want close contact with anyone,' Manharter said. 'It certainly seemed as if they were a perfect family unit, but it just goes to show you cannot really see what is happening behind closed doors. I am truly shocked.'

Another distinctly un-nosy neighbour was Gabrielle Heiner. 'Everyone used to chat about what might have happened to Elisabeth,' said Heiner. 'My brother was with her in secondary school, then she suddenly vanished. I must admit I always thought the grandfather was a perfect head of the family – someone who cared about his children.'

He cared so much about his children – escaping – that he sprayed the steel door of their dungeon with concrete until it weighed 660lb. There was no chance that Elisabeth and the children could shift it. Without the electric motor running, it eventually took four firemen to push it open.

Despite the extensive evacuations, the labyrinthine complex was no more than 1.7 metres – 5 feet 6 inches – high. In some places, it was a good deal lower. Elisabeth and the children – as they grew – had to stoop. Living with such low ceilings was, by its very nature, oppressive. Added to the sense of confinement were the narrow passageways leading from the original padded cell into the living area and on to the bedrooms beyond.

6

A FAMILY TORN
APART

Rosemarie seems to have taken to the role of foster mother to her granddaughter, now that her own children had flown the coop – or so she thought. Photographs taken on a day trip show a frumpy-looking *frau* in a crimson dress, tending to her 'vanished' daughter's third child, Lisa, then aged two.

When the long-suffering Elisabeth gave birth to Monika on 26 February 1994 – the day Fred West was first charged with killing his daughter Heather – the extension of the dungeon was far from complete and there was still no room for her. It has been reported that, like Lisa, Monika suffered from a heart condition from an early age, again possibly caused by her incestuous heritage, which required surgery. Fritzl took the child upstairs again. He went through the same charade as before, pretending to his wife that he had found the infant on the doorstep.

Nine-month-old Monika supposedly arrived in Ybbsstrasse shortly after midnight on 16 December 1994 – the day Myra

Hindley was to hear that she would never be let out of prison. This time, the new baby was not left at the door in a cardboard box; she was found in Lisa's stroller parked in the vestibule of the Fritzl house. The telephone rang a few minutes later and, when Rosemarie Fritzl answered, she was convinced, once again, that it was her daughter Elisabeth on the other line.

'I just left her at your door,' the caller said. Again, she asked Rosemarie to look after the child.

Rosemarie was in shock, and not simply because her daughter seemed to have contacted her once more after her long absence. The Fritzls had just been given an unlisted number, so how could Elisabeth have found that out? Rosemarie even told the authorities in Amstetten about this. Her comment – that it was 'completely inexplicable' – was noted in the record. Of course there was a simple explanation – Josef Fritzl knew the number. This time, apparently, he used a recording of Elisabeth's voice to make the call, but even this did not ring the alarm bells with Rosemarie. After all, she could hardly have engaged a recording in the sort of conversation she might have expected with her daughter – or, indeed, any conversation at all.

The letter that came with the second child read, 'I am really sorry that I have to turn to you again. I hope Lisa is doing well. She must have grown a bit by now. Monika is now 9½ months old. She was breast-fed for 7½ months. She now eats almost anything. But she still likes the bottle best. The hole in the teat has to be a little bigger for her.'

Once again, the long-suffering Rosemarie accepted that her daughter was either unable or unwilling to rear the child – and that it was her job to do it for her. This time, the Fritzls did not adopt the child. Rather, they fostered Monika because, that way, they would receive a higher state benefit amounting to €400 a month.

The new arrival did not go unnoticed; it even made the local papers. Journalist Mark Perry reported the story at length just after Christmas: 'What sort of a mother must she be?' he wrote. 'That is the second time she put the baby in front of the door of the grandparents. How bad must she be?'

He even got an interview with the secretive Herr Fritzl, whom he quoted as saying, 'Since 1984, we think she is in the hands of some religious group.'

No one who knew the Fritzls expressed the slightest suspicion. At this point, not even Rosemarie's sister Christine, who hated Fritzl, voiced her doubts. 'We spoke about it often when we met,' she said. 'And I would say, "Rosemarie, where can Elisabeth be?" I even told her myself, she is definitely in a cult where you can only have a certain amount of children, or they don't want sick children.'

Once again, social services bought Fritzl's story. And, again, District Governor Hans-Heinz Lenze saw no cause for suspicion. 'If, as people assumed, and her father kept claiming, Elisabeth was living with a sect,' he said, 'it would not have been difficult at all for a member of the sect to give Elisabeth a lift at night and for Elisabeth to leave the baby on the doorstep at a time when she would not have been seen.'

The neighbours also believed him. 'People said that it was irresponsible: "What a bad mother Elisabeth was just to leave the children on the doorstep,"' said Regina Penz, who lived three doors away. 'Frau Fritzl had already had seven children. Now she had to bring up grandchildren as well. It was terrible.'

Two years later, Elisabeth was pregnant again, this time with twins. Again, Fritzl left her to give birth alone. With no scan, Elisabeth may well have been unaware that she was having twins. This would have been all the more frightening for her as the birth pangs continued after she had already delivered one child. Patrick O'Brien of the Royal College of Obstetricians and Gynaecologists said that the risk to Elisabeth's life would also have been greatly increased during a delivery of twins.

One of the children was sickly and, when Fritzl returned to the cellar three days later, it had died. The infant had not been named, but has now been called Michael. Fritzl took the tiny body and burnt it in the basement furnace along with the other household waste.

According to Fritzl's own lawyer Rudolf Mayer, 'He has admitted Elisabeth had the twins on her own in the cellar and that he did not see her until three days after the birth. He told me that when he found one of the babies was dead, he put its body into his furnace. Elisabeth says her baby developed breathing difficulties and Fritzl failed to get medical attention that could have saved its life. Police now say he is guilty of first-degree murder because he did not allow the child to be treated and it died as a direct result.'

Fritzl stopped talking to police after they accused him of murdering the child by neglect – which would bring a charge of murder in the first degree under Austrian law. It is not known whether the life of her seventh child, a twin baby who died shortly after birth, could have been saved if medical care had been at hand.

The surviving twin, Alexander, was taken upstairs and passed off as a foundling as before. Rosemarie was now used to her daughter's 'abandoned' children turning up on her doorstep and no further questions were asked.

'Why this man took these middle children upstairs, we will probably never get a final, clear answer,' said Chief Investigator Franz Polzer. 'You can imagine that it was getting a bit crowded. And you must not forget, the more prisoners in the cellar, the more complicated it became to look after them.'

At the time, the police saw no reason to dig deeper and social services raised no objections. So Fritzl and his wife were named foster parents, entitling them to more state benefits. While officials were happy to hand the children over to the Fritzls, they still took an interest. Following standard procedures, they regularly checked up on them.

Over the years, social workers made at least 21 visits to the Fritzls' house and reported nothing unusual about the family. The Fritzls took pains to 'encourage the children in many ways', the local social welfare agency said in its regular report. They were exposed to 'children's gymnastics, and books and cassettes from the city library,' one social worker wrote, concluding that 'Herr and Frau Fritzl are really loving and warm with their children'.

Fritzl was undoubtedly strict with the children, but this was judged not to be a problem, perhaps because it was his wife Rosemarie who did the day-to-day caring. Almost every day, she would drive her grandchildren to their music lessons, where Lisa learned to play the flute and Monika and Alexander mastered the trumpet.

'Everyone was amazed at how strong she was,' said one of the children's music teachers. Only in one conversation did her voice break and tears come to her eyes, the teacher continued. She was telling him about Elisabeth, about how she had run away to join a sect and how much she missed her daughter.

Austria's justice minister, Maria Berger, now acknowledges that officials made mistakes. 'Looking at everything that we know now, I can see a certain gullibility, especially when it comes to that tale that she had joined a sect,' she said. 'Today, we would surely go about it differently and conduct a detailed investigation.'

One person who does not seem to have been taken in was Elisabeth's school friend, Susanne Parb. 'When the babies started arriving, I knew it wasn't right,' she said. 'Elisabeth hated her father – she would never have left her own children with him.'

This was not a factor that seems to have occurred to the social services.

Fritzl's sister-in-law Christine also grew suspicious. 'When Elisabeth's third child was laid at the door, we asked Sepp if maybe he shouldn't try to find out about this sect,' she said. 'His answer was, "No point." His word was the law.'

His curt answer echoed the letters that he had forced his daughter to write in the cellar. One began, 'Do not search for me, it would be pointless and would only increase my and my children's suffering.' It went on to explain the strictures of the sect's commune. 'Too many children and an education are not wanted there,' it said.

This convenient piece of fiction mirrored her all-too-real plight. Even without the benefits of hindsight, it is odd that Elisabeth's mother and her grown-up sisters or brother never once seem to have mounted any effort to find the author of this distressing note. Their father had drummed into them the importance of education and Elisabeth, as a mother, would not have abandoned that.

Neighbours described Lisa, Monika and Alexander as happy, polite and well-adjusted, and praised their musical ability. They recalled that often they would hear the kids laughing as they played in the swimming pool. Rosemarie was devoted to the three new children she had taken on, they said. Maria, a neighbour of the Fritzls, said that she was a 'wonderful woman' who saved her pennies to buy musical instruments for the children.

Another neighbour stated, 'My children went to the same school together with the Fritzl kids ... there was never anything odd about them.'

At school, the children were regarded as responsible and well-behaved, and appeared happy and popular among their peers. However, some classmates later recalled something odd about them. 'The Fritzl girls and the boy always kept a bit apart in school,' a school friend later revealed. 'They kept away from the others and seemed to lead separate lives.'

A friend of the family said, 'Rosemarie was desperate to give the children a normal start in life, with a proper mum and dad. She was deeply hurt and embarrassed about Elisabeth supposedly running off.'

Brought up by their strict, but seemingly benevolent grandfather and the motherly Rosemarie, the children led a well-ordered life of sports days, karate training, music lessons and school discos. Lisa called the Fritzls 'Mama' and 'Papa' when she started school, but teachers told Rosemarie that she ought to come clean or the children would have problems when they discovered the truth years later. So in the summer of 2000, Rosemarie explained the strange circumstances of their adoption.

The family friend said, 'She hired a counsellor to sit them down and talk about it. Then she threw a party to make them feel positive about the new family set-up. From then on, she and Fritzl were "Omi" and "Opi" – "Grandma" and "Grandad".'

However, others reported that the children continued to call the Fritzls 'Mama' and 'Papa' – unaware that Fritzl really *was* their father.

Rosemarie's sensitive handling of the situation and the family party provided little comfort for the children, though. Unaware of the real circumstances of his birth, Alexander became petrified that his mother would return from her madcap 'sect' to kidnap him. He had visions of her creeping into the house in the middle of the night and snatching him from his bed. 'He was so frightened he almost stopped speaking,' said a family friend.

Despite the social workers' assessment that Josef and Rosemarie were 'really loving and warm with their children', Fritzl continued his tyrannical ways.

'Alexander and Lisa were constantly tense due to Fritzl's bullying,' the friend said. 'Their eyes had a look of sheer terror even when he wasn't there. Rosemarie said he was incredibly domineering.'

Lisa became so desperate to escape life under Fritzl's roof that she begged him to let her go to a boarding school nearby – and he relented. She spent five happy years as a pupil at the private Kloster's girls school in Amstetten, which was run by Catholic nuns. A family photo shows a smiling Lisa starting the school in 2002 at 11 – the same age that her mother had started to endure Fritzl's sexual abuse. She left when she was 16, which was Elisabeth's age when she first found it necessary to run away from home.

Short of money to prop up his ailing businesses, Fritzl seems to have attempted another insurance scam. In 2003, a small fire broke out in the house and he made a claim for £800. Two officers visited the house, but did not follow up their enquiries with a full search and no action was taken, even though Fritzl was charged with arson in 1982 after a blaze destroyed the guesthouse he owned at Lake Mondsee. That case also seems to have been dropped.

Despite the police inaction, there were suspicious circumstances surrounding the 2003 fire. 'It was started in two places – a classic sign of arson,' a police source said. 'But despite all that, the officers only carried out a brief inspection. Senior police officials will be asking why. If a proper investigation had been carried out, the secret family Fritzl kept in his cellar would have been found.'

Neither did police act over two more fires the following year. In 2004, Fritzl claimed another £800 after a power meter somehow burst into flames and £2,300 when he claimed a TV had gone up in smoke. Police carried out no more than a cursory investigation of either incident. Again, they missed their chance to find Elisabeth and family in the dungeon; perhaps they were taken in by Fritzl's outward display of respectability and wealth. Such a man would surely have no reason to attempt to swindle the insurance company out of such paltry sums? But Fritzl was a qualified electrical engineer who did most of the maintenance work around the house. Surely, his electrical wiring should have been sound?

As if Elisabeth and her downstairs children had not suffered enough hell, imagine what might have happened, had any of those fires had got out of hand. It would have been impossible for them to escape; they would have been burnt to death as the building collapsed on them, or – more likely and more mercifully – suffocated beforehand as the fire sucked the air out of the basement. Fritzl would hardly have come running to their aid; he would not have risked his life in the flames to go down into the cellar to let them out, only to expose his own crimes. Better to allow the flames to consume the evidence. Fire investigators may have looked through the embers for the cause of the conflagration, but they would not have been searching for bodies. Even if charred corpses had been found, it would have been impossible to identify them. The children had never been to the dentist and Elisabeth's teeth had fallen out, so they could hardly be identified from dental records.

Neither would they have matched any missing person's report. When Elisabeth disappeared 20 years before, she had had no children. Besides, her file was now inactive. There were no records at all of Kerstin and Stefan; no one would have reported them missing. Besides Fritzl, no one in the outside world knew they existed.

Fritzl was put under more financial stress in 2004 when Monika followed her older sister into the Kloster's school and he had to stump up still more school fees. Again, Monika was happy in school and the other children were too tactful to bring up their mysterious provenance.

'We knew Lisa and Monika were foundling children and had both been abandoned at the front door of the Fritzl home when they were born, almost like a Bible story,' said a classmate. 'But we never spoke to them about it. Lisa told us her story at the start of school but we never mentioned it again out of respect and politeness. The Fritzls were always "Mama" and "Papa" and Rosemarie was a devoted parent.

Josef never came to parent evenings, and was never mentioned by her. It was always Rosemarie who encouraged her to play her flute in the school orchestra or go to sports events.'

Lisa did modestly well academically, learning English, maths and science in a class of 30 before leaving in June 2007. The end-of-school photograph showed her relaxed, apparently without a care in the world.

'Lisa also travelled with the rest of her class on any trips or excursions,' said her school friend. 'She was just a normal, happy kid, not especially clever but very funny. Lisa would always make us laugh in class and was very popular.'

When her year finished school in 2007, they had a big party. 'It was really good fun, and Lisa looked very pretty in her dress,' said her friend. 'But then we went off and I did not know her plans for the future.' No one could have predicted the terrible truth about the circumstances of her birth, which everyone had been too polite to mention, would come out just nine months later.

Monika also showed promise as a musician and 20-year-old Karl Dating, a local volunteer fire-fighter, recalled that she received a perfect score on a fire-safety test he gave at their school. Alexander played the trumpet as well and townspeople remember him as a kind boy, always running errands for the woman he called 'Mami'.

Downstairs in the dungeon, Fritzl showed Elisabeth pictures of Lisa, Monika and Alexander as they grew up and told her how well her children were doing at school. Cruelly, he also would tell his captive daughter about the trees outside and the garden in bloom while she remained confined to her small, dank cell.

As Kerstin and Stefan grew to maturity, Fritzl faced three

adults imprisoned in the dungeon who could, conceivably, have overpowered him. But Elisabeth later explained that, because of the conditions they had been kept in, they were too weak to challenge Fritzl. Even 18-year-old Stefan was too feeble to subdue their ageing tormentor.

'They never trusted themselves to have the strength to attack me,' said Fritzl. But his mastery of the situation did not just come from the appalling conditions in which he had kept his children. Naturally, he had a more self-serving explanation. The secret was the power of his personality. 'It wasn't that difficult to prevent their escape,' he said. 'I was the leader and that was how it was going to be.'

He was, in his own words, their *Führer* – leader – and, like the original *Führer* he had grown up under, he was to lead them to disaster on the pretext that he was saving those he purported to love from a worse fate. However, he added, 'They also needed a code to release the door and none of them had it. They were unable to get out.'

They were also warned that poisonous gas would be pumped into the dungeon if they tried to overpower him or attempted to escape. The door was connected to a high-voltage electricity supply so that anyone who touched it would be electrocuted. And he continually tormented them with the hopelessness of their captivity. 'In any case, only I knew the number code of the remote control that would open the door to the cellar and to close it,' he said. 'I did tell them that they would never get past the door because they would be electrocuted and they would die.'

However, Fritzl was a humane man – in his own eyes at least. He claimed that every time he left the cellar, he activated a delayed reaction mechanism that would release the door in case he died or had an accident that prevented his return to feed his second family. No evidence of this device has been found. Fritzl had also installed a generator in the cellar so his secret family would have electricity, even if the supply to the main house failed, but the oxygen supply was so limited down there in the dungeon that, even if the exhaust was vented, it is very difficult to see how the occupants would not have suffocated, had they attempted to use it.

And still the sexual abuse did not stop. Even though Kerstin and Stefan were teenagers, Fritzl continued raping their mother in front of them. For Elisabeth, this can only have made the degradation harder to bear. In 2003, she gave birth to her seventh child – Felix – by her then 68-year-old father.

There are hints that, for once, Fritzl helped his daughter give birth this time, but it was the one time when she would not have needed him. Before, she had always been alone when she gave birth, or had a young child in tow who could hardly have been expected to help. In fact, they were more likely to have been a hindrance as they would have been frightened by the ordeal their mother was going through. But when Elisabeth gave birth to Felix, she had two sympathetic helpers on hand in the shape of her 14-year-old daughter Kerstin and 10-year-old son Stefan, who would have witnessed their mother giving birth before and would have known what was going on.

By the time Felix was born, Rosemarie was 63 and too old to be expected to bring up another child. Besides, she had her hands full with the three youngsters her husband had already brought upstairs. 'Rosemarie couldn't have handled another child,' Fritzl told authorities during his interrogation. So Felix was doomed to be confined in the dungeon with his older brother and sister and would never know the sunlight and relative freedom of the three siblings his father had taken above ground.

But fortune eventually smiled on Felix. Although he suffered with his subterranean family, he was not to have his entire childhood stolen from him in his father's dungeon. He would see the light in good time to learn to adjust to it.

While the three 'foundlings' were enjoying a normal education, Elisabeth did her best to teach her imprisoned family the basics of reading and writing. They had proper lessons for two or three hours a day and Elisabeth taught them grammar, language and mathematics. However, there were few books in the dungeon, only those Elisabeth had begged Fritzl to bring her. This left their vocabulary severely limited – they would stumble and search for words. Their main source of education, over the years, was the television. This provided flickering images of the outside world they were denied access to by their heartless captor.

Under seemingly impossible circumstances, Elisabeth tried to rear her children with a degree of normality. She strove to give them some sort of structure in the lives and as good a life as possible in the dungeon. By all accounts, the children have been raised very well and have turned out to be very polite and well behaved. And she claims never to have told them that they were actually imprisoned by their own father. Elisabeth was, Fritzl said, 'just as good a housewife and mother' as Rosemarie. There was no higher compliment in his eyes.

In an effort to brighten their drab environment, Elisabeth made rudimentary decorations and hand-crafted toys. She would entertain the kids by making up fairy tales about pirates and princesses, and sang them lullabies. They liked to watch adventures on television together. This was Elisabeth's only reminder of the world outside. For the children, it presented a two-dimensional image of a fantasy world as alien as life on another planet. Elisabeth would also try to pass the terrible hours of boredom by making models with the children out of cardboard and glue. However, the stifling atmosphere in the cellar imbued them with inertia. They spent most of their time sitting nor lying down. There was not the space nor the air for much activity.

Fritzl did provide a fridge and a deep freeze to store food – so he could skip off on holiday to Thailand and elsewhere. Again, he believed he was being generous. 'I even gave Elisabeth a washing machine in 2002, so that she wouldn't have to wash all the clothes by hand,' he said.

He was also 'generous' with his time and his affections. 'It just became a matter of course that I lived my second life in the cellar,' he said. 'I was delighted about the children. It was great for me to have a second proper family in the cellar, with a wife and a few children.'

On top of the necessities of life, he brought treats and presents. 'I tried really as hard as possible to look after my family in the cellar,' he said. 'When I went there, I bought my daughter flowers and the children books and cuddly toys. We celebrated birthdays and Christmas down there. I even smuggled a Christmas tree secretly into the cellar with cakes and presents.'

The birthday and Christmas parties he staged for the three youngsters he had imprisoned from birth mirrored those he held for his family above ground. In a twisted attempt to be even-handed, the decorations in the windows of the children's bedrooms upstairs were replicated in the dungeon bathroom below.

Fritzl took some care with the clothes he bought Elisabeth. She was sometimes allowed to choose them out of a catalogue and they would then have had to be delivered. The question remains whether Rosemarie ever signed for them. On other occasions, Fritzl would choose them himself. Friends he holidayed with in Thailand saw him picking out a glittering evening dress and lingerie at a market – they were clearly much too small for his ageing, rotund wife. When he realised that he had been spotted, he joked about 'having a bit on the side'. Not for one minute did they suspect this could be his own daughter.

But it is clear that he wanted his Liesel to dress up and parade around for him in the squalid, miserable cell he forced her to call home. Then, after raping her, he would settle down at the table while she prepared a meal and they would discuss the children's upbringing.

He bought a video player and would spend hours in the cellar watching videos with the children while Elisabeth cooked his dinner. In a painful parody of normal domestic life, they would have meals together as family, although this would hardly be a cordon bleu affair. Elisabeth did her best, but she was starved of fresh ingredients. His cellar family ate only ready-cooked meals with long sell-by dates so he did not arouse suspicions by making frequent trips to the supermarket to buy fresh fruit or vegetables. The tiny electric rings and the utensils Fritzl provided were barely adequate to cook for a growing family. Elisabeth had no recipe books, no spare food to experiment with and the air in the dank cellar was stale. It would have been impossible to escape from the smell of cooking. These were hardly the best conditions under which to appreciate their meagre diet. The subterranean children

A FAMILY TORN APART

would never even get to enjoy an oven-cooked pizza, like those the other Fritzl children enjoyed on lunchtime treats at the nearby Casa Verona.

After dinner, they would sit down as a family to watch the TV. Fritzl was a fan of Formula 1. He watched motor racing on television with his children and, in a bizarre attempt at playing the normal father, would buy toys for the children and play with them. However, he insisted the children should say 'please' and 'thank you' for every small thing he did for them. 'Elisabeth, Kerstin, Stefan and Felix accepted me as the head of the family completely,' he boasted.

Despite his pretence of normalcy and even-handedness, the world above ground and below could not have been more different. While the children upstairs were restrained only by his strictures, below ground they were confined by walls. And because of the stifling conditions, Elisabeth and the children had to spend long spells moving as little as possible, or simply succumbing to exhaustion caused by the lack of oxygen.

'We know today from the doctors that those who were imprisoned do things at a totally different pace,' said Chief Investigator Polzer, who visited the children after their release. 'The way they talk, the way they now choose to spend their time in freedom – it is simply impossible to imagine what it must have been like to establish a daily routine in this prison and to live with the constant reminder of the world outside, watching the television, seeing pictures and hearing stories from their father telling them what it was like out there.'

While the 'foundlings' were oblivious of their siblings in the bunker, those beneath the ground knew all too well that they had brothers and sisters living above them. Fritzl even brought videos of the 'released' children down to the dungeon so the imprisoned youngsters could see for themselves the way of life they could have lived, had he chosen to set them free. It must have been reassuring for Elisabeth to see that her children above ground were flourishing, although it would also have been a torture to know what she and her subterranean family were being deprived of. The cellar children could be more sanguine; they had never known any life outside their dungeon, so the videos were just more flickering images like others they saw on the TV.

Despite the great play Fritzl made of his 'generosity' towards his second family – particularly buying that washing machine – he admitted that decades underground without daylight, or medical and dental care severely affected his prisoners. They suffered a series of infections and heart and circulation problems, but 'Elisabeth stayed strong,' he said. 'She caused me almost no problems. She never complained, even when her teeth slowly went rotten and fell out of her mouth, one by one, and she suffered day and night with unbearable pain and could not sleep. She stayed strong for the children, but the children – I saw they were constantly getting weaker.'

The children suffered from a range of ordinary illnesses, but in those conditions even a common cold or the 'flu could be life-threatening. Any respiratory condition would have been exacerbated by the damp and fetid air. Fritzl provided nothing but rudimentary store-bought medicines – cough mixture and the like – and there was little Elisabeth could do without proper medical assistance. As far as the children's health was concerned, she was fighting a losing battle.

On top of the normal coughs and colds, Kerstin and Felix suffered from coughing fits and strange, uncontrollable convulsions. Rather than seek medical help, Fritzl dosed them with aspirin. However, the two children appeared to have inherited an allergy to the drug from their grandmother. Felix would shake uncontrollably for hours while Kerstin screamed hysterically. Despite their pitiful condition, it was the only medicine he would allow them. These children had never seen a doctor; they had none of the normal inoculations routinely given to infants. It is a miracle they survived at all.

7

HOLIDAYS
FROM HELL

While Elisabeth and the children were languishing in the dark cellar, Fritzl treated himself to sun-and-sex holidays in Thailand. He made a number of these trips, usually with a group of friends. One of them was his friend Paul Hoera, who twice travelled to the beach resort of Pattaya with him. 'I have known him since 1973,' Hoera said. 'We met on a camping holiday in Salzburg and we spent a lot of time together after that.'

This was when his then wife Elfriede met Rosemarie, although the friendship between the two women came to an end when Paul and Elfriede split up, with their marriage ending in divorce in 1984. However, Paul and Josef remained friends.

'Our friendship was so good we even went on holidays to Thailand,' said Paul. 'One was for almost a month, between 6 January and 3 February in 1998; the other was about three weeks. I went with my girlfriend and stepfather. He travelled alone, without his wife. He told me she had to look after the children.'

Although they had travelled to Thailand together, Paul saw little of his friend Fritzl. 'We planned to spend time together but Josef was always off on his own,' said Hoera. 'He wasn't staying in his room and it was obvious what he was doing. We knew he liked having threesomes but didn't give it any thought at the time.'

Paul and his girlfriend were not into that, but in the Far East, Fritzl began to let his guard down. 'The first time he really admitted to me he was not the perfect family father was in Thailand,' said Hoera. 'He obviously liked women – and good-looking women at that. But I know his wife was not his type.'

Hoera did not consider this unusual. After all, they had been married for 40 years and, after giving birth to seven children, the slim 17-year-old Fritzl had married had turned into a shapeless *hausfrau*. Many men in late middle-age go searching for a younger model, especially when presented with the temptations of Thailand.

However, Fritzl was a little cagey in front of his friends. 'When girls in Thailand approached him to offer sex, he blocked them,' Hoera said. Nevertheless, 'he once had a very long massage from a young Thai girl at the beach – he really loved that, but normally he was more discreet. He always went off on his own at night.'

This was symptomatic of his secretive nature. 'He pulled the wool over all of our eyes,' Hoera said. 'Of course, looking back, there were things you can guess at – but he was really clever at hiding them.'

His friend also noted how Fritzl was happy to blow a bundle on lavish presents for himself on his trips abroad while handing out the most meagre of allowances to Rosemarie. 'He was two-faced,' Hoera said. 'He'd pay for hair transplants and buy crocodile shoes, but not give his wife enough money.'

Rainer Wieczorak, now 62, also accompanied Fritzl on trips to Thailand that sometimes lasted up to six weeks. 'I went to Thailand because the climate was good for my health but Fritzl had other interests,' he said. 'While we would all sit around the hotel bar, he was off on his own. We did not speak about where he went, but it was pretty obvious he had another agenda. We almost never saw him; he was usually sleeping things off during the day, having a massage on the beach and a late breakfast.'

Pattaya is a well known destination for sex tourists, including paedophiles. Brothels and clubs offering erotic entertainments line many streets, while up to 50,000 bar girls, massage girls and prostitutes cater for foreign visitors. However, it seems that Fritzl's tastes were not so conventional as his travelling companions supposed; he also appears to have spent time trawling the notorious gay haunt Boyztown at night.

British holidaymaker Stephen Crickson of Huyton, Liverpool, said that once Fritzl was out on his own, he was flamboyant in his sexual tastes. 'He was a disgusting pervert and all the ex-pats and regular holidaymakers knew what he was up to,' he recalled. 'Rent-boys, ladyboys … he would go with anything. At one point, he was spotted by one bar regular with a 16-year-old.'

He was seen hand-in-hand with the young lad and was known to pay for sex with teenage rent-boys and transvestite hookers. British holidaymakers thought he was a German, rather than Austrian, because of his habit of reserving a sun lounger with his beach towel.

'Fritzl would lord it around us at the beach and treated staff with contempt,' said Crickson, who was holidaying in Pattaya with his girlfriend. 'He was universally unpopular.'

Pictures of Fritzl's 1998 Thailand trip appear in a German newspaper, which deemed the excursion 'a gentlemen's holiday'. They show him smiling and tanned as he lazed bare-chested on the beach, paddled in the surf in tight-fitting Speedos, enjoyed the attentions of a Thai massage girl, dined in open-air restaurants and shopped in local markets at Pattaya, seemingly without a care in the world.

Asked if the police were investigating his trips abroad, Chief Investigator Polzer said, 'His holidays are none of our concern.'

However, his absence on holiday for several weeks at a time raised questions about whether he had an accomplice to look after his underground family. But police believe he was so well organised that it would not have been necessary. 'Based on evidence, we know that this prison had a very restricted living area which was equipped with everything necessary to keep alive – for example, large quantities of food in freezers and fridges,' said Chief Inspector Polzer. 'There was the facility to do laundry – there was a washing machine as well and an electric cooking ring for preparing meals.'

Even so, it is clear that a huge amount of organisation would need to be done before he went away. There would have been extra trips to outlying supermarkets and more late-night work with the wheelbarrow to get the provisions downstairs.

For his captives, his absences must have been a mixed blessing. Elisabeth would not have had to put up with his hideous and rapacious sexual demands and the children would be freed from his admonishments. On the other hand, he was their only lifeline. After several weeks, as the stocks in the fridge and freezers dwindled, they must have worried whether he was ever coming back. The only outcome then would have been facing slow starvation. They must have been both overjoyed and devastated when he returned home.

Despite their different holiday interests, Paul Hoera and Fritzl remained friends and even stayed at each other's homes. 'I was at his home in Amstetten at least three times ... the last time in 2005,' he said. 'I always thought it was a wonderful family.'

When he visited Fritzl at home, the two of them would relax on the roof terrace or watch cartoons on the TV and laugh uproariously – while Hoera, at least, was completely unaware of the sobbing sex slave cowering in the cellar just feet away. 'I did know the cellar was out of bounds but never gave it a second thought,' he said. 'When I think about what was there, I feel ill.'

However, Paul Hoera's girlfriend Andrea Schmitt was a little more circumspect. 'In Thailand, I never noticed anything unusual about him, although he seemed to be spending a lot of time buying things for the children,' she said. 'He had several carrier bags filled with things and I remember thinking what a lot of presents for just three children.'

It was Hoera who caught Fritzl buying clothes for Elisabeth. 'We were at a market and he did not know I was behind him when he bought an evening dress and underwear for a thin woman,' Hoera said. 'It would not have fitted his wife. He was really annoyed when he saw I had been watching him. He then admitted he had a woman on the side and asked me to keep it secret.'

Hoera was shocked when he eventually found out the identity of the recipient. He remembered Fritzl's daughter

Elisabeth as a child; she was introverted and distant. He said Fritzl used to beat her more than his other children. Otherwise, he said there was never a hint of Fritzl's sinister side – in fact, he had quite the opposite impression. 'When we first met Josef, he was a really kind, outgoing and open-minded person who laughed a lot,' he said. 'Josef, Rosemarie, Andrea and I always had so much fun – we laughed all the time.'

Given Fritzl's penchant for humiliating his wife, he must have made off-colour remarks about his activities in Thailand. This would alost certainly have produced embarrassed smiles from Paul and Andrea, but Rosemarie, no doubt, did not share the joke.

While Fritzl was 'a good laugh' when they were out, Hoera described him as 'the master and a bit of a dictator' at home. But it seemed to produce results. 'The children were well mannered and well behaved,' Hoera said, though he admitted that Fritzl probably carried his iron discipline with the children a bit far. 'They were all scared stiff in the presence of their dad. They were never allowed downstairs into the cellar, but we never thought anything of it.'

Like others, he believed what Fritzl told him. There was no point in questioning him. Fritzl had a temper and did not like to be contradicted or crossed. 'He could get really furious and would become another person,' Hoera said. 'His wife always listened to him but always did what he said. Whenever we started to talk about Elisabeth, I noticed Rosemarie would leave the table but I never saw her cry. I thought she was a bit of a cold woman.'

Andrea Schmitt stayed with Paul Hoera at Fritzl's house and brought her own kids. 'My three children always played with his children,' she said.

She first visited the Fritzls' house before Elisabeth disappeared, and she, too, found the child withdrawn and solitary, but this did not seem significant at the time. 'I never thought anything was wrong because we always had such a good time together,' she said. 'Josef loved cartoons and used to laugh his head off. It was such a shock when we found out about him on the news. We got goose-bumps. I've been in total shock since and haven't slept for days.'

Paul Hoera was equally horrified; he had known Fritzl for 35 years and never suspected a thing. 'When I saw his picture on TV, I thought there must be a mistake, a mix-up,' he said. 'I last visited his house in 2005 – we sat out on the terrace and had a really nice evening. Now I think of the dungeon down there and I feel sick. I am ashamed to be linked to him.'

When Fritzl returned from his sex holidays in the Far East with bags full of goodies for his captives, any attempt to ameliorate their plight with colourful clothing would have been painfully belied by the contrast between his sun-browned skin and their deathly pallor. To Elisabeth, this would have been particularly apparent when he raped her.

While Rosemarie tolerated her husband's high-jinks in the Far East, she also enjoyed holidays without him. 'She went on day trips with other older women and she used to go on holiday to Greece without him,' said the lodger Alfred Dubanovsky. 'Rosemarie was pretty quiet when he was around, true, but she knew how to enjoy herself when she was on her own.'

She also took an annual holiday in Italy, while Fritzl stayed at home in Austria. This created suspicion in Dubanovsky's mind. During the 12 years that Dubanovsky lived in the house, they were never both away at the same time. 'In all that time, they never once went on holiday together,' he said.

Again, though, the police believe that Fritzl was such a meticulous man that he was perfectly capable of providing for his cellar family while he was away and see no reason to suspect Rosemarie of being an accomplice. Chief Investigator Polzer was adamant that it 'defies logic' that she had anything to do with it.

Besides Fritzl's sex holidays in Thailand, it seems that he also enjoyed the company of prostitutes closer to home. Sex workers at the Villa Ostende, a brothel in Linz, just 30 miles from Fritzl's home, confirmed he was a regular customer there for years. They said that he paid prostitutes to have sex with him in the brothel's dungeon. One of the girls said he tied her up on a makeshift cross in an underground room not dissimilar from the windowless cellar where he imprisoned his secret family. The 36-year-old blonde said that he ordered her to call him 'teacher' and punched her while having sex with her. He frightened her by losing his temper and staring at her with ice-cold eyes. Like the other girls, she came to dread catching his leering gaze as he entered the downstairs bar.

'I had to call him "teacher" and was not allowed to engage in conversation with him,' the girl said. 'I once asked him about his family and he told me, "I have none." He would pay to have sex inside the brothel dungeon, which I hated. But it was dark and sinister – his favourite place. I was hired by him many times and he was sick beyond imagination,' she said. 'He chose me because he said he liked young, plump girls who were happy to submit to him.'

It is hard not to imagine that Fritzl meted out similar brutal treatment – or worse – to Elisabeth who was completely in his power.

The Villa Ostende's owner, 60-year-old Peter Stolz, said,

'He was a strange character. He liked trips to the dungeon with young girls he had selected personally.'

When the identity of the girl's client came out in the newspapers, she told a reporter, 'To think he was keeping his daughter and her children in a similar place a few kilometres away and abusing them sickens me now ... He belongs in the very depths of hell.'

According to the local press, the Villa Ostende is an old establishment and boasts Adolf Hitler among its former clients. Prostitution is legal in Austria, and the Villa Ostende charges customers €150 (£120) an hour. Most of the prostitutes come from Eastern Europe and the majority are aged between 18 and 25. Fritzl is said to have started going there in 1970, eight years before he began abusing daughter Elisabeth. He continued his visits even after locking her in his own, purpose-built dungeon and making her his personal sex slave.

Some of the brothel's other prostitutes were shocked by Fritzl's sadistic demands and refused to have sex with him again. '95 per cent of the clients are entirely normal; 3 per cent are slightly "derailed",' said the brothel's former barman 38-year-old Christoph Flugel. 'But Fritzl belonged to the last 2 per cent of extreme perverts who are surely mentally deranged ... None of the girls wanted to spend time in a room with him. Two of them even strictly refused to and did without the earnings. He was violent and into domination.'

Fritzl was much the same, apparently, when he was outside the dungeon. 'He acted despotically at the bar,' said Flugel. 'As soon as he liked a particular girl, he would order a glass of champagne for her. But after a short while he would start behaving like a headmaster with pupils and he'd shout things like "Don't slouch", "Sit up straight" or "Don't talk such shit". Such behaviour is unusual in sex clubs – you go there to have a good time.'

There were other allegations. 'Upstairs, in the bedrooms, he got completely off the track,' said Flugel 'He was perverted. He wanted extreme sex and pain and told the girls to pretend to be corpses. No girls wanted to go to a room with him. They were disgusted. I heard about that when talking to the girls. Two of the girls said, "Never again with that guy." Such a thing is very rare in this business. It has to do with excrement, or with pain, or with a game where a girl is asked to play a corpse.'

Apart from his depraved demands, Fritzl was also known for being tight-fisted. 'I worked there for six years and Fritzl was a regular,' said Flugel. 'He was well known for being stingy. If he had a bill for €97 and paid with a €100 note, he'd always want the change and never think of tipping you. Mind you, he wasn't our oldest client. We had one who was 88.'

The barman's tale was printed in the *Österreich* newspaper, but according to the *Sunday Times*, 'It turned out that newspaper accounts of Fritzl brutalising prostitutes in a brothel cellar in Linz were just as much fantasy.' However, the Austrian police confirmed it was true that Fritzl used local brothels and indulged in perverted practices there. His sexual appetite, it was said, was 'voracious'.

'His sex life can definitely not be classified as normal,' said District Governor Lenze. 'My information is that, on numerous occasions, he visited brothels where he indulged in various perverted activities.'

Another story emerged that Fritzl had dragged his wife

Rosemarie to a swingers' club, dosed himself up on a cocktail of pills and forced her to watch him having sex with other women. 'Fritzl said men of our age could have fun with sex,' builder Paul Stocker, now 65, told the newspapers. 'He said you needed to take three pills – Viagra, Levitra and Cialis. The pills kicked in one after another and you can go for it like a bull.'

A week after this conversation, Stocker said that another friend invited him to the Caribik swingers' club, near Amstetten, in 1977. 'An elderly couple came in,' said Stocker. 'They looked just like an old pair you might see in a park feeding the pigeons. I was speechless when I realised it was Fritzl with his wife.'

Stocker would have been 44 back then, while Fritzl would have been 52 and Rosemarie 48. The couple may have looked as if they were better suited to the park, but it was plain that Fritzl was in his element – although Rosemarie was thoroughly out of place. 'He obviously knew his way around,' said Stocker. 'Without a word, she went to stand in the corner. He treated her like a dog. She had to sit in a corner and watch as he did stuff with a young woman. He started on another visitor who was obviously not having a good time ... He made a good job of it. Then he left with his totally humiliated and degraded wife and went home.'

In all other respects, Fritzl seemingly lived the life of a respectable burgher. He enjoyed the annual get-together of his upstairs family, which often took place in his favourite restaurant, Bratwurstglockerl, in Linz. Then, in 2005, he threw a big 70th birthday party for himself at 40 Ybbsstrasse. Only feet away from the noisy gathering, Elisabeth and the subterranean children were none the wiser, the pleasure of human interaction with friends and family denied them.

In 2006, Amstetten honoured Fritzl and his wife on their 50th wedding anniversary. In the eyes of the town, he was still an upstanding family man. Amstetten Mayor Herbert Katzengrueber attended the celebration of their golden wedding; he said that Fritzl was well liked and that the discovery of what he had done came as a huge surprise. 'If you put 50 men in a line, he would be one of the last who could ever be suspected of committing such a crime,' said Herr Katzengrueber. However, Katzengrueber was aware that Fritzl had been trying to change the character of the town.

Amstetten was a small picturesque town of 23,000 in a region of daisy-filled meadows. It was mainly known for its local apple wine. The surrounding hills could be the setting for *The Sound of Music*. In the distance, medieval castles perch on craggy mountain tops. But Fritzl had planned to change all that by cashing in on the property boom that was sweeping Austria. He had bought several properties in Amstetten and planned to demolish them and build office blocks. That project also failed when planning permission was refused.

After that, he intended to make a fortune building a block of flats, again out of keeping with the character of the town. But to raise the money, he would have to remortgage 40 Ybbsstrasse. He was thwarted in this because, under Austrian law, the children, including Elisabeth, had an automatic right to inherit the property. She was listed in the deeds even though she was also officially listed as missing and it was unlikely, if not impossible, to obtain her consent. Austrian bankers are reluctant to remortgage properties under these circumstances because it makes them difficult to sell if the creditor defaults. After decades of legal wrangling, Fritzl managed to have

Elisabeth's name removed from the deeds in 2006, but this project also failed because, by then, Austria's property boom was over. He then tried to raise money to set up an Internet underwear business.

Fritzl took out a loan of €1 million and had mortgages amounting to €2.2 million, even though he was now retired. According to one legal source, he was having some problems in making the repayments. Keeping a second family underground was not cheap. Perhaps it was now time for Elisabeth to return to the land of the living.

There were other problems too. It seems that Fritzl was bored by the daily chores – the shopping, the rubbish burning, the upkeep of the dungeon cellar and the maintenance of his double life. At 73, he could no longer get around as he once did and he no longer found his daughter sexually attractive. The once-pretty Elisabeth was now anaemic, ailing and toothless. She resembled a woman the age of his wife, who he had gone off years before. Like Rosemarie, Elisabeth had had seven children, although with the meagre diet she was permitted in the dungeon she had not had the chance to fill out. However, there have been allegations that, by this time, Fritzl was now having sex with his sickly granddaughter Kerstin. Austrian police feared that he had turned the teenager into a second sex slave, though she, too, was pallid and practically toothless like her mother.

However, the police later said there was no evidence to suggest Josef Fritzl sexually abused any of the six surviving children he fathered with his daughter Elisabeth, although Kerstin was only brought out of her seven-week coma in early June 2008 and, consequently, still has the opportunity officially to confirm or deny these allegations.

'Only Elisabeth was abused sexually by her father,' said Chief Investigator Polzer, although this seems still to be mere speculation as he had no chance to question her. It remains to be seen whether Fritzl sexually abused Kerstin or her siblings, and details of the extent of his psychological and physical abuse will no doubt emerge in time.

At 73 years old, Fritzl had become aware that the situation could not go on for ever. He was an old man now, and it was becoming more and more difficult to keep up the double life. 'I was not so agile any more,' he said, 'and I simply knew that in the near future I would not have been able to provide for my second family in the bunker.'

In late 2007, Fritzl began preparing the end game. The following summer, he planned to stage-manage the release of Elisabeth and her children. People would be told that she had quit the obscure cult that had held her for the past quarter of a century and she would return to the house that she had, in reality, never left. Her shocking physical condition – and that of her children – would be blamed on the treatment inflicted on them by the religious cult.

It is ludicrous to think that he could have got away with this. Had the appalling state of Elisabeth and the children been perpetrated by the actions of the putative cult, they would have been liable to prosecution. Efforts would have had to have been made to track them down and arrest their leaders. But then, the authorities made little effort to trace the non-existent cult before. Perhaps if the family said they were unwilling to press charges, the police would drop the matter. Even if they did proceed with the investigation, they could hardly find a cult that did not exist. Everything depended on the co-operation of Elisabeth and the children. As it was their only chance to get out of the dungeon, Fritzl hoped they would go along with his story. 'Sure, that was my hope, however unbelievable it was at that time,' he admitted. 'There was always the risk that Elisabeth and the children would betray me.'

Deluded Fritzl seemed to think that, after his unspeakable maltreatment of them, his daughter and their children owed him a debt of loyalty.

Around Christmas 2007, Fritzl forced his daughter to write one last letter to prepare the ground for her liberation. In it, she said she wanted to leave the cult and return home, but that it was not possible yet. 'If all goes well,' she wrote, 'I hope to be back within six months.'

The letter was in the same hand as those delivered with the babies before. Later, DNA tests confirmed that Elisabeth had been the author. 'It just shows how perfectly he planned everything,' said Chief Investigator Polzer.

But how Elisabeth's heart must have soared. At last, there was light at the end of the tunnel. After nearly a quarter of a century, there was some prospect of escape. In just a few months, she could be free. She would see her mother again, and the children that her brutal father had taken from her at birth; she would breathe fresh air, see the sky and feel the sun and rain on her face. There was even a possibility that she could meet up with old friends. Then there were her brother and sisters to catch up with.

Her underground children would also be free. They would see the outside world for the first time and have the chance to run and play outdoors. Little Felix would be able to go to school. All three of them would have the opportunity to make new friends. Their other brothers and sisters would surely help.

Elisabeth may even have been willing to go along with her father's plan, no matter how unworkable it was. After 24 years and all the suffering she and her imprisoned children had endured, surely she would have been willing to agree to anything to be free.

But fate intervened. Before Fritzl could put his plan into action, Kerstin fell seriously ill.

8

INTO THE LIGHT

It is hard to fathom whether Fritzl really believed that he could get away with re-introducing his underground family to the world. However, he may well have been enjoying a growing sense of omnipotence. His cellar family were totally in his thrall. After all, they 'accepted me as the head of the family completely'. For them to have told anyone that they had been in the cellar, rather than with a mysterious religious cult, would have been a 'betrayal' of their '*Führer*'. They should be grateful. After all, he had given them clothes, food and shelter all these years. He had been generous with treats, gifts and appliances He had protected Elisabeth from drugs and spent his valuable time with their children. Now, out of the goodness of his heart, he was releasing them into the outside world – asking nothing in return, except their silence.

Rosemarie could be relied on to be completely compliant. She would just be delighted to have her daughter back, and there would be new grandchildren for her to enjoy. No one else in the family dared question or cross him. Friends and acquaintances had swallowed the lie about the sect before, they would again. And there was no reason to believe that the authorities would be any less cursory in their investigations than they had been before. In Catholic Austria, he might even have believed that God was on his side.

But Fritzl was suffering from hubris; he was about to play out the last act of an oddly inverted Greek tragedy. The truth was, he was not a god, or even a hero; he could not control everything. One thing he certainly could not control was the health of the children languishing in the cellar, the children whose health he himself had done so much to undermine. There were just months to go before he could relieve himself of the burden of his secret family when Kerstin fell seriously ill. It was about to spoil everything.

Again, Fritzl initially chose to treat her with aspirin and cough mixture. It did no good. He had no medical training and as, like the other bunker children, she had never seen a doctor, he had no medical history to go on. She had always been sickly, but she had previously pulled through. Now she was having cramps and biting her lips until they bled.

Fritzl must have known that, by siring children by his daughter, he was risking them being infected with genetic abnormalities. But Kerstin's illness was not something that he had encountered before; it was not obviously a hereditary condition – it seemed more like an infection. She was deathly ill, nonetheless. Her fits got worse, blood spewed from her mouth and she fell into a coma.

Now, with the prospect of release hanging tantalisingly before her, Elisabeth begged her father to take Kerstin to the hospital. She must have been full of foreboding. This could well postpone her father's plan to release her and the children that summer, if not finish it off completely. But what else could she do? Her daughter would die if she did not get proper medical attention quickly.

In the face of Elisabeth's pleas, Fritzl eventually relented. Was he exhibiting pity or compassion after so many years of cruelty? Or were there more practical reasons? As his plan to release his subterranean family that summer relied on his daughter's co-operation, he could hardly let another of her children die – Elisabeth would never have complied with his demands under those circumstances.

On the other hand, he might have been panicked at the thought of having to dispose of the dead body of a grown woman. To fit it in the furnace, he would have had to cut her up – a harrowing business for both him and her children, who would have had no choice but to be onlookers. And there would be some older people in Amstetten who already would be familiar with the smell of burning human flesh.

Taking Kerstin to the hospital involved considerable risk, but it was a risk Fritzl seemed prepared to take. While the 19-year-old was still unconscious, she was no threat. Once she came round, she might try and tell the hospital staff of her ordeal. However, her vocabulary was limited. She had no experience of the world beyond the cellar and would find it difficult to explain her plight. Even if she could put what she had suffered into words that the hospital staff could understand, who would believe her? The story would sound too fantastic. Perhaps Fritzl thought he could explain away anything she said by dismissing them as the ravings of a slightly backward child who had been kept in seclusion for her own good. It certainly seems that he planned to spirit her from the hospital the moment she was well enough to return to the cellar.

Another concern was not wanting to run the risk of his wife becoming aware of another of Elisabeth's children, especially a sick one. This time, she might not be so credulous – or so compliant. She would be bound to turn up at the hospital. Seeing her grandchild at death's door, she might unwittingly arouse the suspicions of the staff. Rosemarie would be another element that this time, perhaps, he could not control.

Although Kerstin was critically ill, Fritzl waited until his wife was away on a planned holiday to Lake Maggiore. Once Rosemarie was safely out of the way, he opened the door of the dungeon to let Kerstin out for the first time in 19 years. Now 73, Fritzl was unable to carry the unconscious teenager out on his own and Elisabeth had to help. So in the early hours of 19 April, a 42-year-old woman who had spent half of her life underground saw the outside world for the first time in 24 years. It was only for a few moments. Once they had got the comatose Kerstin above ground, Elisabeth was forced to return to her dungeon. She would only spend another week of captivity there, but when she went back downstairs, she did not know that it would not be for the rest of her life. Just at that moment, though, her primary concern was for her daughter – Kerstin's life must come first.

Ironically, although Kerstin, upstairs in the house, was out of the cellar for the first time in the 19 years of her life, she could not enjoy the fresh air or daylight. Deep in her coma, she could appreciate nothing of the outside world. She could not be roused and Fritzl called an ambulance.

At 7.00am, the local ambulance station received a call from a man who said that a young woman named Kerstin Fritzl was seriously ill. An ambulance and crew were despatched to 40 Ybbsstrasse to collect her. They rushed the ghost-like

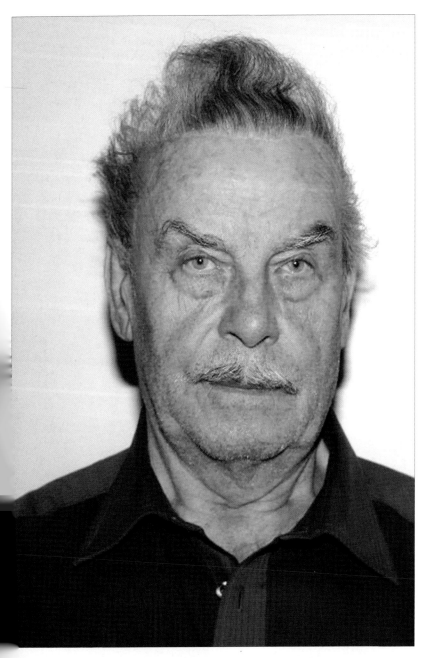

osef Fritzl, 73, confessed to holding his daughter Elisabeth captive in his ellar for almost 24 years and fathering seven children by her under his ouse in Amstetten, Austria.   © *REX Features*

Elisabeth Fritzl, pictured here as a teenager before she was lured into a cellar by her father Josef.

© REX Feature

The upstairs family.

Above left: Alexander Fritzl, 12, the surviving twin.

Above right: Monika Fritzl, 14, the second child to 'arrive' on Fritzl's doorstep.

Left: Grandmother Rosemarie.

Below left: Lisa Fritzl, 16, the first of Elisabeth's children to be 'abandoned'.   © *REX Features*

The House of Horrors – suburban respectability concealed its shocking secrets.

Above: The front door where the 'abandoned' children were found.

Below left: The entrance to the dungeon where Elisabeth was held.

Below right: The rudimentary bathroom and lavatory that Elisabeth and the three children used.

© *REX Features*

The narrow corridor that led from the bathroom in the cellar through to the bedroom that Elisabeth was forced to help dig out with her own hands.

© REX Feature

The world's media flocked to the small Austrian town of Amstetten as the shocking truth of what happened in that underground chamber of horror gradually came to light.

© REX Features

Above: The psychiatric hospital where Fritzl's wife Rosemarie, his abuse daughter Elisabeth, and her seven children, are all undergoing therapy.

Below: The courthouse of St Pölten, where Josef Fritzl is being held under arrest.

© *REX Featu*

teenager to hospital, where the staff did not know what to make of her.

Fritzl did not accompany Kerstin in the ambulance. He stayed at home and took a little time to rehearse his cover story, but this time it would not be enough to save his skin. The wall that he had so meticulously constructed between the normal world above ground and the secret underworld below had been fatally breached. No matter how hard he tried, he could no longer prevent the inevitable. That wall would come tumbling down, exposing both his quarter-century of lies and his hideous crime to the world. Later that morning, he made his way fatefully to the hospital.

When Fritzl arrived in the emergency room, he recited the tried-and-tested formula. He said his daughter had run off to join a strange religious sect and, for the fourth time, she had dumped one of her children on her grandparents' doorstep. But this time, he came up against a professional who was not prepared to swallow his story quite so readily. His strange version of events roused suspicions, when confronted by a sceptical doctor.

On the morning of Saturday, 10 April 2008, Dr Albert Reiter received the emergency phone call that would spark the beginning of the end for Fritzl. He was told that a critically ill teenage girl had been brought unconscious into the hospital. Also on hand was her grandfather. The physician rushed to the emergency room to examine the child.

'When Kerstin first came in to us, she was very pale,' said Dr Reiter, 'and she was bleeding from her tongue due to convulsions. Fritzl told us she'd taken some pills for a headache, nothing more. He seemed very correct. At the time, we had no idea what had happened to her. He claimed her mother was away, had left her at his house and asked him to look after her. That was his version.'

But on closer examination, Dr Reiter noted that her deathly pallor was caused not just by her illness; rather it suggested something more sinister. Then he noticed that the teenager had almost no healthy teeth left, which was most unusual for a girl of her young age. With no one else to turn to, he interviewed the patient's grandfather and quickly concluded that he was being told a pack of lies. 'Her grandfather came up with the story that he had found the girl on his doorstep,' said Dr Reiter. 'He said that she had been abandoned by the mother, who was part of a bizarre sect.'

This strange story set off alarm bells. 'I did not like his tone and something did not seem right,' said Dr Reiter. 'What made me particularly suspicious was that he did not seem to think it important to answer any of my questions, simply demanding we make Kerstin better so that he could take her away again.'

Fritzl produced a note which he said that his 42-year-old daughter had left with the child. It showed the depth of the mother's concern for her stricken daughter. But, although the child was plainly very ill, the note revealed she had only given her 'aspirin and cough medicine'. There was something wrong here.

At 10.37 that morning, the police received a call from the Mostviertel-Amstetten State Hospital to report the admission of a mysterious 'female person'. The patient was unresponsive and in a critical condition, and her symptoms suggested she had been severely neglected. A man had accompanied the woman, they were told. He was one Josef Fritzl of 40 Ybbsstrasse.

Naturally, the police had to follow this up and went to the house. During their subsequent interview, Fritzl told them that he had heard noises in the stairwell of his home. When he went to investigate, he had found a young woman leaning, apathetically, against the wall on the ground floor. She had been carrying a note, he told police. It was from his estranged daughter, Elisabeth, who wrote that the girl was her daughter Kerstin and that she urgently needed medical attention. For the time being, the investigation went no further, but questions remained.

The note itself was full of contradictions. 'Wednesday, I gave her aspirin and cough medicine for the condition,' it said. 'Thursday, the cough worsened. Friday, the coughing gets even worse. She has been biting her lip as well as her tongue. Please, please help her! Kerstin is really terrified of other people, she was never in a hospital. If there are any problems please ask my father for help ... he is the only person that she knows.' Then came the codicil, 'Kerstin – please stay strong, until we see each other again! We will come back to you soon!'

The note plainly came from a mother who was deeply concerned for the well-being of her child. But even someone with no medical training at all could see that the child was critically ill and, without prompt medical intervention, was likely to die. Why had the mother waited the four days from Wednesday to Saturday before she sought medical assistance? And if she was as concerned as she sounded, why had the mother herself not come in to the emergency room with the child to explain how her daughter had got into her wretched state?

Nevertheless, the note begged the medical staff to help

Kerstin. Why could the mother not have requested their help in person? What kind of parent would simply dump her sick child – who was plainly at death's door – on her grandparents and then not stick around to find out what happened? If she had the transport to get the comatose teenager to her grandparents' place, why could she not have brought the child direct to the hospital? Or even called an ambulance herself? It did not add up.

The child, the note said, had never been in a hospital. This, again, was unusual. In developed countries, most youngsters turn up at a hospital or clinic so that staff can check on their medical history and give them standard inoculations. The note also stated that she was 'terrified of other people' and that 'my father ... is the only person she knows'. This spoke of some psychological condition that might be relevant to the diagnosis Reiter was now seeking to make.

'If there are any problems please ask my father for help,' the note said. But Fritzl had been unco-operative and had fled the hospital at the first possible opportunity. Why would a loving mother trust her sick child to such an uncaring man? Then there was the touching postscript, 'Kerstin – please stay strong, until we see each other again! We will come back to you soon!' That was a clear indication that the mother loved her child very much indeed.

'I could not believe that a mother who wrote such a note and seemed so concerned would just vanish,' Dr Reiter said.

It is interesting to note that Sir Arthur Conan Doyle, the creator of Sherlock Holmes, was also a doctor. Holmes himself, Doyle said, was based on Dr Joseph Bell, who he had worked for as a clerk at the Edinburgh Royal Infirmary. A lecturer at the medical school of the University of Edinburgh,

Dr Bell emphasised the importance of close observation in making a diagnosis. Dr Reiter, as an experienced clinician, was similarly gifted. He paid attention to detail and realised that the style of the note did not tally with what Fritzl had told him about the mother and how she had simply abandoned the sick girl.

'I could not believe that the mother of a seriously ill 19-year-old girl would simply drop her off and disappear,' he said. 'From the tone of the letter the mum had sent it was clear that she cared very deeply for her child.' He knew that something was just not right.

As Kerstin's condition worsened, her body shut down. She suffered from multiple organ failure and was put on a respirator and a kidney dialysis machine. Dr Reiter grew concerned and called in specialists from Vienna. They, too, were puzzled. If the girl was to survive, they needed more background information on which to build a diagnosis. The patient was unconscious, so they could not question her to find out what they needed to know. What was really required were full details of her medical history, but as the child had not been to hospital before, there would be none on record. Unless her GP could be found, the only person able to supply the information needed was the child's mother. The woman may be under the control of some bizarre sect, but surely if she knew her child was likely to die without her help, she would get in touch.

So Dr Reiter pursued his hunch. In the face of Fritzl's opposition, he used the hospital's public relations department to launch a high-profile media campaign, urging Kerstin's mother to come forward with 'vital medical information' about her gravely ill child. 'I was certain of .

only one thing, that the mother was the only one that could help,' he said. 'I contacted the grandfather again, and told him we desperately needed to speak to the mother. I was convinced she had information that was the key to the mystery illness. I could not understand why he was so reluctant to help, but he did agree.'

Dr Reiter asked the hospital's public relations department to put out an appeal to the local media and even got Fritzl to provide a photograph of Elisabeth that had been taken before she went missing. Reiter was so concerned about Kerstin's condition that he even added the number of his own mobile phone at the bottom of the press release so that anyone with any information could get in touch.

Even though Fritzl had asked him not to, Dr Reiter again contacted the police, who saw where their duty lay. 'The man who claimed to be this young woman's grandfather said this was the fourth time his daughter, who had disappeared, had abandoned a child with him,' said Chief Investigator Polzer, who took over the case. 'We said to ourselves, it must finally be possible to find this woman. And that's not the hospital's job, it's a job for the police.'

The case of Elisabeth Fritzl, who was still officially classified as missing, was reopened. This time the police launched an extensive investigation. They wanted to locate Kerstin's mother, not just to aid Dr Reiter in his diagnosis and treatment of the sick girl, but also to find her and question her about what they thought might be a case of criminal neglect.

When questioned, Fritzl simply repeated his old story about Elisabeth running off to join a sect. Then he presented them with what was usually his usual trump card. It was another letter from his supposedly long-lost daughter, saying she was with a cult. In the letter, dated January 2008, she revealed that she had more children. She wrote that her son Felix had been very ill in September. He had suffered epileptic seizures and symptoms of paralysis, but had recovered. Kerstin, the letter said, had also had health problems, including stabbing chest pains and circulatory symptoms. However, she continued by saying that Elisabeth, Felix, Kerstin and another child, Stefan, would be coming home soon – perhaps they might even be home in time to celebrate Lisa and Kerstin's birthdays.

The police seized on this red herring. If such a seemingly poor mother had more children in her care, they need to find her fast. To Fritzl, it seemed that the same old lie had worked once again. In truth, it had only bought him a little more time.

The letter carried the postmark of the town of Kematen an der Krems, which was about 30 miles from Amstetten. Judging from the postmarks, Elisabeth's peripatetic sect never seemed to move more than a short drive from the Fritzls' home. Investigators descended on Kematen. Naturally, none of the doctors they questioned in the area had any recollection of a woman named Kerstin. No one had seen anyone matching the girl's ghostly appearance. There was no indication that Elisabeth Fritzl had ever been in the town, and no one knew anything about her mysterious sect either. The police became increasingly perplexed. Did this strange sect even exist?

On the morning of Monday, 21 April, the telephone rang in the office of Dr Manfred Wohlfahrt, the officer concerned with sects at the St Pölten diocese. Wohlfahrt was asked to come to the police headquarters in Amstetten immediately.

On arrival the police showed him the note that Fritzl had said Kerstin was carrying, along with the letter he said he had received from his daughter in January. Both were on blue notepaper. They asked Wohlfahrt whether the letters gave any clue as to which sect the woman who wrote them might belong to and where they might find her. Did the choice of words or phrasing, for example, suggest any sect he knew of?

Wohlfahrt studied the letters. He noted they were written in a very deliberate handwriting that looked almost like calligraphy. They had been composed in a deliberate, businesslike fashion rather than having been dashed off in the casual manner one would normally adopt when writing to a relative or acquaintance. He also noted that the words were assembled into 'oddly smooth, constructed and not very authentic' sentences. The letters, he concluded, were 'dictated'. There was no evidence of a sect, he said. Nor was there any indication that one had taken residence in the diocese or any of the other dioceses of Lower Austria. It was an assessment that might have been made 24 years earlier, had the police consulted him then.

Dr Reiter appeared on a news bulletin on ORF, Austria's public service broadcaster. 'What do you hope to achieve through our interview?' asked the presenter.

'I would like the mother to contact us,' said Dr Reiter. 'We will treat the contact with high discretion. And we will probably get a step further in our diagnosis and treatment.'

He feared Kerstin's mother might be afraid to come forward if she knew the police were involved – hence the 'high discretion'.

The appeal struck a chord. Journalists flocked to Fritzl's house, expecting his co-operation in the hunt for his daughter and they were surprised to be turned away. Reporters who knocked on his door were stunned when the retired electrical engineer reacted with anger at their questions. He flew off the handle when they mentioned Dr Reiter's attempt to trace his daughter.

'I was shocked,' said one journalist. 'Instead of being the concerned father I expected, he told me to clear off. He was shouting and swearing and really furious. He said he had wanted nothing to do with the appeal, but that the "bloody doctor" had forced him into it.'

Fritzl was getting rattled. For years, he had kept his hideous secret locked in the basement. The last thing he wanted was a gaggle of prying journalists looking into his affairs.

Other efforts were made to trace Elisabeth Fritzl. Dr Reiter stepped up the TV campaign with a direct appeal to Kerstin's mother begging her to get in touch, while police officers were dispatched to Vienna to comb through the records in an attempt to locate her. In the age of computerised bureaucracy, it is almost impossible to disappear completely.

'All the schools were written to,' said the District Governor of Amstetten, Hans-Heinz Lenze, who also had jurisdiction in the case. 'The central registry data base was searched; enquiries were made at the social security office. Every avenue was explored. There was not a shred of information about Elisabeth.'

They were hampered by the fact that, since her disappearance, no driving licence, passport or any other official document had been issued in her name. There were no photographs of her since she had been at school and no social welfare files in her name. And the births of Kerstin or the other children, Felix and Stefan, mentioned in the letter, had not been registered.

Having failed to find Kerstin's mother by the conventional bureaucratic route, the police changed tack. They went back to the family home and started to take DNA samples from the Fritzls, including the children whom Fritzl said had previously been abandoned by their mother.

'We wanted to have everyone's DNA samples in order to trace a possible father or fathers,' said Chief Investigator Franz Polzer. 'We always thought that a woman with so many children may have had more than one partner. One of them might have had a criminal record.'

Once they found the father, they reasoned, they would then have a possible link to the whereabouts of the mother.

The easiest way to isolate the father's part of the children's DNA was to screen out the maternal component, which they could deduce from the grandparents' samples. But, again, Fritzl was less than helpful. 'Herr Fritzl did not have time to give a DNA sample,' said Polzer. 'He kept postponing it because he had so much to do.'

While the police, the press and the public combed Austria for Elisabeth Fritzl, she was where she always had been – in her dungeon watching the TV. She saw Dr Reiter's appeal on the evening news, which he delivered with affecting sympathy. 'I can't simply look on,' he said. 'I am deeply distressed about this case. I have never seen anything like it.'

His evident concern touched Elisabeth and gave her the courage to beg her father to release her – 'temporarily', she said. He agreed only on the condition that she did not betray him to the authorities. She was put on an oath to maintain the fiction that she had been away with a religious sect, just as they had planned for her summer release. She promised. By then, she would have promised anything.

On Saturday, 26 April, Josef Fritzl decided that there was only one way to save Kerstin and preserve his cover. He allowed his daughter and her children out of the cellar, this time, perhaps, for good. Elisabeth, Stefan and Felix were to resurface as planned, only the schedule had been advanced.

In a way, Kerstin's illness and the broadcast appeal might have seemed like a blessing. It provided the perfect excuse for Elisabeth to leave her fictional sect and return home. What mother would put her religious views before the life of her child? It made the story of her return all the more convincing.

When Rosemarie and the other children were out of the house, Fritzl brought Elisabeth, Stefan and Felix out of the dungeon, and the two boys saw daylight for the first time in their lives. The police are unsure of what happened in the house during the next few hours. It seems that Fritzl briefed his daughter once again on how she was to explain the last 24 years, as he was still worried that his evil secret would be revealed. There are indications that he and Elisabeth visited the hospital several times, but Dr Reiter was not there.

'As far as I can remember, they even went to the hospital twice as the main doctor was not there,' said Chief Investigator Polzer.

That evening, they were going to try again. This time, Fritzl called ahead to Dr Reiter and said, 'Elisabeth has returned. I am bringing her to the hospital and she wants to see her daughter.' Then he added something even more disturbing. 'We do not want any trouble,' he said. 'Do not call the police.'

But the police were already involved. Naturally, Dr Reiter called them immediately and alerted them to his suspicions. When Fritzl led the disoriented Elisabeth into the hospital to see Kerstin, they were already waiting for him.

'When they got there later on, the police had already heard they were coming,' said Polzer.

In a dramatic scene, officers swooped on the couple. It was Elisabeth they wanted to question, but Fritzl seems to have put up some kind of fight. He could simply have been seen to have been defending his daughter. The police handcuffed him and forced him into a police car. The two of them were then taken to the police station, where they were separated. But it was not Fritzl that the police were interested in.

For there was no indication that he had committed any crime, although he might have known more than he was saying. Their investigation concerned Elisabeth Fritzl's criminal neglect of her daughter. With her obstreperous father safely out of the way, they began their interrogation.

'The questioning focused on this woman, where she had actually been and why she had neglected her children like that,' said Chief Investigator Polzer. But, like her father, Elisabeth Fritzl was unhelpful.

'It was not all that easy for the police as Elisabeth did not want to talk,' said District Governor Lenze, who was now overseeing in the case.

Naturally, Elisabeth was more interested in being with her sick daughter than talking to the police, but they were insistent. This woman, they thought, had cruelly abandoned three children on their grandparents' doorstep, and neglected and mistreated another to the point where she might very well die. And they knew from the letter that Fritzl had already showed them that she had two more children who might be similarly in danger.

At first, Elisabeth stuck to the story that she had run off to join a bizarre religious sect that had little time for children, but that did not explain her appearance – or the terrible condition of her daughter. Although she had initially been arrested on suspicion of maltreating her own child, it seemed evident to the police interviewing her that she had suffered the same ill-treatment herself. Like her daughter, she had no teeth and a deathly pallor. As the questioning continued, Elisabeth became 'greatly disturbed', the police said. But they took it slowly and, after two hours of careful persuasion – and repeated assurances that neither she nor her children would ever have to see her father again – she began to tell them her incredible story.

'She was given this assurance,' said District Governor Lenze. 'It was quite late, around midnight, that she revealed that she had not abandoned her children, but had been incarcerated for 24 years. And then, without a break, in a mere two hours, she gave an account of the 24 years she had spent in the cellar.'

At 12.15am, when the officers completed the first three full pages of notes from the interrogation, they knew that the enigma they had been working on so far had suddenly evolved into the highest-profile case of their careers.

At first, it was difficult to comprehend, but then, over the next two hours, Elisabeth spilt out the entire story of her 24 years in captivity. She told the police that her own father had imprisoned her from the age of 18 in a purpose-built cellar; he had raped her repeatedly and she had given birth to seven children. It seemed utterly incomprehensible, but the evidence was there, sitting right in front of them.

'The first detective was presented with a strange picture,' said Polzer. 'He looked at this woman, at her physical appearance. I don't want to go into too much detail, but looking at this woman you could believe that she had been imprisoned for many, many years.'

HOUSE OF HORRORS

It was all too clear that the young woman had gone through some appalling ordeal and it became more and more plausible that the terrible story of imprisonment, rape and incest Elisabeth Fritzl had told them was true.

'It still sends shivers down my spine,' admitted Lenze.

This was all the more uncomfortable for the District Governor as he had had contact with Fritzl whom, until then, he had believed to be an upstanding citizen. 'For me, personally, it was an experience,' said Lenze, 'especially because the perpetrator telephoned me 24 hours before the crime was discovered and he thanked me profusely for, during the week that Kerstin was in hospital, assigning a crisis intervention team to support the family.'

9

'IS GOD UP THERE?'

The police were shocked by the story Elisabeth Fritzl told them; they could hardly believe it. Until she spoke out, there had been no indication that Herr Fritzl was anything but an upstanding pillar of the community. At the time, the authorities did not know that he had a background of violent sexual assaults, which had been expunged from the record.

'We knew nothing and I can't investigate matters of which I know nothing,' said District Governor Hans-Heinz Lenze. 'In Austrian law, there is a statute of limitations.'

Even without that vital piece of information, Elisabeth's extraordinary allegations had to be investigated. The following day, police frogmarched Fritzl to his house, where he was forced to show them the cellar. The secret dungeon was so well hidden that, when the police searched the property, they failed to find it. Eventually, Fritzl gave in and showed them where it was. After passing through five different rooms in the cellar – including a room containing a furnace and a small office – and eight locked doors, they reached Fritzl's workshop. There, hidden behind a shelving unit in the workshop, he showed them a 1 metre-high reinforced concrete door. It was so small the building inspectors had failed to spot it. Fritzl then handed over the remote control and the code that opened the dungeon door, and they squeezed through.

Chief Inspector Leopold Etz, the head of Lower Austria's murder commission, was the first officer to set eyes on the frightened, ashen-faced Fritzl boys, who had spent their whole lives underground.

'They both looked terrified and were terribly pale,' he said. 'The two boys were taken upstairs from the underground bunker and appeared overawed by the daylight they had never experienced before. The real world was completely alien to them.'

Etz told a German newspaper he was 'staggered' to watch the siblings' initial bewilderment and shock as they now found themselves in a world they had only known before on a television in their dungeon and from their mother's descriptions about the life she had lived up until her own incarceration at the age of 18.

The boys were said to be able to communicate quite well in German, although their use of language and speech was far from normal. Pointing to the sky – having seen it for the first time – Felix asked a policeman, 'Is God up there?'

Their mother had always told him that 'heaven was "up there"'. This was a poignant thought from a woman who had spent most of her adult life in subterranean gloom but knew that a world of fresh air and freedom existed above their heads. It was all the more poignant when you think that her life above ground with her father had been anything but heavenly.

The older boy walked hunched over as the ceilings in the cellar were so low he could not stand upright. The other boy preferred to crawl, though he could walk with a strange, simian gait. Between themselves they babbled in their own coded tongue. However, they did understand German but spoke it in a unique accent gleaned from years of watching TV in the windowless bunker.

The police who liberated Stefan and Felix were the first strangers the boys had ever seen. 'Everything was new,' said Chief Inspector Etz. 'The only idea they had of the real world was from the television.'

Although the two boys were strange and, in some ways, feral, it was plain that Elisabeth had done a good job in bringing them up. 'We were very surprised at how well-mannered and educated they were,' Chief Inspector Etz said. 'We know that the mother did her best to give the children an education, given her limited resources. She was also the only one that could treat the children when they were ill.'

Once the children had been discovered, Fritzl was taken away. Elisabeth was then brought to the house to ease the boys' daunting passage into the outside world. Now it was a question of getting the boys to a place of safety where they could begin to move on from their ordeal. They waited quietly with their mother to be transferred by car. When it turned up, five-year-old Felix grew alarmed.

'He found it so strange that he clung to his mother in panic as the door opened, as if he was fearful of what would come out of it,' said Etz.

The first stop was the hospital, where the boys were to be given a comprehensive check-up. They had never received any professional medical attention before, although Elisabeth had done her best from the medical books that Fritzl had brought her. As they were unused to sunlight, it was thought best to delay the trip until dusk.

'Later on that evening, we had to drive them to hospital,' said Chief Inspector Etz. The two boys had never been in a car and whooped with excitement as the vehicle set off, as if they were on a fairground ride. But it was also scary. 'We had to drive very slowly with them because they cringed at every car light and every bump,' said Etz. 'It was as if we had just landed on the moon.'

But soon, they got to enjoy the thrills. 'They were amazed at the speed and really excited,' Etz said. 'They had never known anything like it – they had only ever seen cars on TV in the dungeon. Little Felix was beside himself with excitement. He was shrieking with pleasure when he saw cars coming the other way. He and his brother braced themselves whenever a car went past. They kept thinking there was going to be a head-on crash.'

They had problems with distance perception, having never seen anything more than a few feet away. Their only other visual experience was of the two-dimensional world of television. Now all sorts of real-life, three-dimensional experiences awaited them, each of which the two cave-dwellers greeted with genuine pleasure.

'Driving to the hospital, Felix made excited gurgling noises when he saw a cow,' said Chief Inspector Etz. When he saw a stream, he asked what it was, but above all it was the mobile phones of the police officers that grabbed his attention. 'The ringing tone flummoxed him at first, then later it made him curious,' said Etz. 'He was completely bowled over when one of the policemen spoke into his phone.'

However, it was plain that the two boys were bewildered by the world they were seeing for the first time. They hardly spoke at all – except when little Felix said that it was wonderful.

'What was wonderful?' Etz asked.

'Everything,' Felix replied.

At the hospital where their older sister lay comatose, the two boys were given a full medical check-up and their state of health was said to be surprisingly good under the circumstances. However, they were extremely pale and suffering vitamin D deficiency – vitamin D is made in the skin by the action of sunlight. As in their mother and older sister, this had led to the loss of their teeth. All four were anaemic, too. Damage had also been done to their immune systems and doctors found that young Felix's joints and muscles had not developed properly in the cramped bunker, possibly due to malnutrition. It seems that in latter years, when Fritzl did not find his daughter so beguiling and sought his sexual outlet elsewhere, he no longer visited so regularly with food supplies. As a result, the little lad walked like a monkey.

When the boys came out of the hospital after their check-up, it was dark. 'They were fascinated by the headlights and were shouting and hiding behind the seats,' said Chief Inspector Etz. 'Everything was new and amazing. But the best bit was when they saw the moon. They were just open-mouthed with awe and nudged each other and pointed. I've seen a lot, but nothing like this.'

Felix repeatedly hummed an unknown melody which gave him some comfort. The police believe it was a tune his mother used when putting him to sleep.

'It can't be called a good-night song really as there was never any night in the cellar,' said Etz. In the gloom of the cellar, artificial days and nights were created by a timer switching the lights on and off so the hours of relative darkness could be called a 'night' of sorts, but there were certainly never any good nights in the cellar.

Now that Elisabeth was on hand to supply the vital medical information needed by the doctors, Kerstin's treatment could be started in earnest and it was decided to keep her in an induced coma until her condition could stabilise. Her breathing was controlled by a respirator. The doctors feared that a lack of oxygen caused by her severe cramps might have led to brain damage. The teenager's immune system had collapsed and she suffered kidney failure. The doctors hoped that keeping her in a coma would help her body recover; they intended to give her time to regain her physical strength before they tried to wake her.

The hero of the moment was Dr Reiter. Not only was he looking after Kerstin, but it was his gut feeling for something that simply didn't make sense that set off the chain of events that had freed Elisabeth and the children from their dungeon. But no one was more surprised about how things turned out than him.

'I am amazed this all finally came out,' he told the press later. 'I obviously had no idea this would be the end result – who could have predicted that? – but I'm glad I followed my instincts.'

He was just as shocked by the story his suspicions had uncovered as anyone else, although his main concern, as always, was for his patient.

'It's a horrible story,' he said. 'Although Kerstin is stable, we don't know if the prognosis is good. She's in a severely life-threatening condition which we can't explain. All we know is that she had a headache, took aspirin, then started suffering convulsions every hour. Her immune system may be hit. In addition to nearly 20 years underground with no sunlight and 20 years of psychological stress come factors such as infection. We're just happy that she and her family are free at last.'

Psychologically, it was Elisabeth Fritzl who had suffered the worst. The children's mother had known life outside the cellar and therefore had something with which to compare their life below ground. She had seen the possibility of good in the world and knew that others did not have to live as they did; she had also endured life as a captive and victim of sexual and psychological abuse longer than any of the others – at first in darkness, chained, then for four long years on her own. She had been raped by her father thousands of times and sexually humiliated in front of her own children. For 8,516 days of her life, the comforting cycle of dawn and dusk had been replaced by the switching on and off of an artificial light. One day was indistinguishable from the next or the day before, the passing of time only recognisable by the transient nature of life – her children growing older, her pallor deepening and her own hair turning grey until, on the day of her liberation, it was completely white.

Little is known about the aching hours of boredom the family suffered below ground as the police declined to reveal details of their everyday life in the cellar. 'These unfortunate people deserve a right to privacy about the intimate details of their life,' said Chief Investigator Polzer.

It is a miracle that Elisabeth did not lose her mind during those interminable days of captivity underground. Many victims suffering lesser fates have succumbed to the unravelling of their sanity, something she had somehow managed to avoid. 'I have rarely seen such a strong woman,' said Dr Reiter. 'I wouldn't be surprised if she had superhuman powers.'

Although Dr Reiter's actions had essentially solved the case, there was plenty more for the police to do. Chief Investigator Franz Polzer, head of the Lower Austrian Bureau of Criminal Affairs, was put in charge of the investigation. As his enquiries began, he called a press conference and told the assembled journalists, 'This is one of the worst cases in Austrian criminal history. We've never seen anything like it before; it's beyond comprehension. The suspect was very authoritarian and in control of those around him. Nobody dared go against his word; there was no escape. He deceived everyone, including his wife. Nobody knew what was going on. It's impossible even to begin to imagine what the mother and children have gone through. The cellar is so small there was only just enough room to survive. The mother is extremely weak; the children were born into a jail – they knew nothing else.'

Polzer outlined the lengths that Fritzl had gone to in order to dig out much of the low basement with his bare hands, making regular trips to suppliers for materials, and described the basic facilities and layout. He also pointed out that there was foam insulation throughout to sound-proof any noise made by the captives and that the basement labyrinth also contained a padded cell. 'We're not talking about a prison designed to hurt its prisoners,' he continued, 'but something built to fulfil their basic human needs. He got planning permission and gradually built the various rooms in which the children were born and lived. Fritzl went out at night to buy groceries for the cellar-dwellers and banned his wife and the other children from entering the basement. He then passed the food through a hatch to be cooked on small hot plates.'

Chief Investigator Polzer then revealed to a shocked press conference the full horror of Fritzl's crimes: 'He admitted that he locked his daughter in the cellar, that he repeatedly had sex with her, and that he is the father of her seven children.' He added that three of the children had 'never seen sunlight'.

Fritzl, Polzer said, had a 'very high sex drive and libido' which saw him father seven children with his wife Rosemarie, as well as the seven with Elisabeth, who, he said, had not just endured rape at his hands but 'sexual abuse at a completely different level'. But a high sex drive was not enough to explain – and certainly not excuse – Fritzl's depraved actions. 'He was driven somehow to this behaviour,' Polzer added, 'but we don't know why or how. He hasn't given a motive.' Nevertheless, the case was 'by and large, solved' as Fritzl had confessed to 'everything', Polzer said.

But he made this announcement before Fritzl had seen a lawyer, before any evidence had been examined and before other witnesses had been properly interviewed. Journalists asked Polzer why he was so sure that Fritzl, who had lied and dissembled for years, was suddenly telling the whole truth.

'There can be no doubt,' came Polzer's inscrutable reply.

Clearly, a man who had deliberately manufactured a series of elaborate lies to conceal his crimes from the authorities, his children, his neighbours and even his own wife for nearly a quarter of a century might have more cards up his sleeve.

'This man led a double life for 24 years,' admitted Polzer. 'But now he was a pathetic figure, a broken, aged man in his declining years, and far from the tyrannical despot he was described as being for so many years. 'Fritzl was an extraordinarily sexually potent man,' said Polzer. 'If you look at him today, you would hardly believe he was capable of doing these things.'

He even gave Fritzl credit for finally allowing his secret to be uncovered after Dr Reiter had appealed on television for Elisabeth Fritzl to come forward and help her daughter. 'Josef Fritzl then, for once, showed he had a human side and allowed his daughter Elisabeth out of the cellar to join his daughter Kerstin,' Chief Investigator Polzer said. 'Perhaps he was aware that he couldn't keep the thing going for ever. Maybe he sensed that his strength was waning,' something that Fritzl himself had also admitted.

Polzer also maintained that Fritzl had worked alone. 'We are not conducting an investigation into a crime involving accomplices,' he told the press. Strangely, though, he mentioned that the Fritzl case had come to police attention due to an anonymous tip-off. 'Knowing about a crime is not the same as being an accomplice,' he said. 'The informant asked for anonymity and we will respect that.'

Later, he admitted, 'We think Fritzl acted alone but cannot exclude the possibility that someone else was aware of what was going on downstairs.'

He then refused to elaborate as he was bombarded with questions from the media. How could he be sure that Fritzl's wife Rosemarie knew nothing, when she had not yet been questioned?

'Do you think any wife in the world would be able to accept that kind of behaviour?' he asked. He suggested that it simply 'defies logic' that anyone could have remained silent under those circumstances. 'What woman would stay silent if she knew that her husband had seven children with his daughter and was holding her prisoner in the cellar?' he asked.

When journalists balked at this, Polzer said, 'Let me ask you a question: how can you be sure she knew?' He was apparently irritated that a lady's honour had been brought into question. 'Frau Fritzl's world has imploded.' It is inconceivable that she could have known, he argued, therefore she did not know.

However, Elisabeth's school friend, Christa Woldrich, believes that at the very least Rosemarie Fritzl is guilty of negligence by not making more of an effort to discover what had happened to her daughter. 'I don't understand why she did not take the opportunity at some point – maybe while he was away on one of his four-week holidays – to take action and say, this is my child and I want to know where my child is,' said Christa. '"Why did my child leave one baby, or even three babies, on my doorstep?" She did not take action as a mother. I don't understand either the authorities or the mother.'

Local journalist Mark Perry, who covered the case early on, thinks that Rosemarie, as a loving grandmother, sought to present a picture of the perfect family, a strategy that, ultimately, proved counter-productive. 'If Rosemarie Fritzl had not kept the family together for so long, it might have come out much earlier,' he said. 'But she tried, on the outside, to present the idyllic family with three lovely children, and adopted them and was the perfect grandparent, and gave them the love their own mother couldn't give. So actually, unwittingly, she was an accomplice in her husband's tyranny. But who could blame her? All she wanted to do was to give their grandchildren – who had apparently been dumped on their doorstep – a nice childhood.'

While maintaining that Rosemarie was not a suspect in the case, the police announced that she was not in a fit state to be questioned. She had been sent to a psychiatric hospital – along with Elisabeth and her grandchildren – where they were undergoing therapy as a family. Then Polzer began to hedge his bets. 'Up until now, no one has been ruled out as a suspect,' he said. 'We always categorically stated that our investigations have, so far, given us no reason to suspect anyone else. It may be hard to comprehend, but we must accept that a woman bringing up seven children can't take care of everything or pay the amount of attention to her husband [that] she would, if she had a smaller family.'

DNA samples taken from the dungeon indicate that no one else was present in the sound-proof cellar, except for Josef Fritzl and his captives – although that did not rule out someone else knowing about what had gone on underground. But Fritzl was a meticulous and secretive man who could have run his second life in the cellar without anyone being any the wiser.

'Up to now, we are only looking at a single suspect and I have to add that there is a certain logic to the fact that his man did not tell anyone else about his affairs,' said Polzer. 'Because it was the only way, through secrecy and iron self-discipline, that he was able to keep it hidden from everyone for such an incredibly long time.'

On 2 June, the prosecutor Gerhard Sedlacek ruled out the possibility of Fritzl having any accomplices. However, beleaguered Chief Investigator Franz Polzer was forced to admit that the case raised 'a' million-and-one unanswered questions'. Faced with the international outcry, Polzer promised they would all be resolved, a task which would involve piecing together every detail of Fritzl's depraved past.

'IS GOD UP THERE?'

With the case against Fritzl apparently tied up, journalists then began to ask a whole stream of questions about the conduct of the Austrian police in cases involving missing persons. Above all, why had the police, social services, doctors and teachers at the schools attended by the Fritzl children failed to detect anything was amiss for nearly a quarter of a century? The local authorities also had to fend off criticism that they ignored suspicious signs from the house.

District Governor Hans-Heinz Lenze was able to show reporters documents that proved that his council's go-ahead for the adoption and fostering of three of Ms Fritzl's children was perfectly legal. 'I have inspected the adoption files and see absolutely no reason for an investigation,' said Lenze. Defending the welfare staff who checked on the children, he said, 'We hadn't a clue anything was wrong. They had no reason to suspect.'

He dismissed criticism of the authorities for giving custody of three children to Josef Fritzl, considering his criminal record. The records had been searched and no trace of his previous sex crimes could be found. Social welfare teams had seen Josef and Rosemarie Fritzl regularly after they took custody of the children and had visited the house 21 times. They insist they noticed nothing unusual during routine visits. True, they had never looked around the house, but Lenze had an explanation for that: 'Herr Fritzl was a patriarch, very authoritarian, so certain areas within his house were exclusively for his use,' he said. 'But why would this lead to suspicions that there was a second family being kept down there? Who gets such an idea into their head? I ask you – it's like the former tenants now talking ... it's all too easy to be wise after the event.'

HOUSE OF HORRORS

Of course there was good reason to be suspicious of the Fritzls. The family had, in the space of a decade, registered one missing person and made the claim that three babies had been dumped on the doorstep. These matters were on the record.

'There was no reason not to believe their story,' said Lenze.

Josef Schloegl, the head of the Amstetten district court whose duty it was to oversee the children, agreed with Lenze. 'There was no reason to suspect that something was wrong,' he said. However, Schloegl admitted that rules had been broken because the youngsters had been formally handed over to Fritzl without the approval of their missing mother Elisabeth. He conceded there had been questions over the whole procedure at the time but it had been finally approved after they found no irregularities; it seemed the best alternative at the time.

'The grandmother took loving care of the children,' said Lenze. 'Lisa, Monika and Alexander – these three children were very well brought up. They were doing very well at school. They were integrated into the community and the notes in the records about all the meetings with the grandmother, Frau Fritzl, suggest that the atmosphere was normal.'

There was even sympathy for the elderly couple who had suddenly acquired a new young family. 'Only the first child, Lisa, was adopted,' said Lenze. 'The other two were officially raised as foster children. This option was chosen as the State does not pay support for adopted children, whereas in the case of foster care, child support ranging from €397 to €410 is paid per child per month, depending on the age of the child. In hindsight, and to an outside observer, it is almost inconceivable that this man claimed support. It is a legal provision in Austria and citizens are entitled to it.'

Although he vehemently defended himself and his town in public, in private Dr Lenze was distraught. 'I can't sleep,' he admitted. 'As a father, I can't begin to imagine what that poor young family suffered. I've resorted to sleeping tablets – I just can't get the suffering out of my head. I'm totally shocked.'

Professor Max Friedrich also understood why the Fritzl family raised no suspicions. 'In the world upstairs, and everyone who knew them said so, everything seemed right,' he said. 'The children went to school, they did their homework properly and were brought up strictly by this father. So, after some time, people would have said, "This is an honourable man." He is strict – but, as we say in Austria, a little bit of strictness never hurt anybody, so all this certainly played a part.'

But the signs were there for everyone to see, according to Hedwig Woelfl, the director of a child protection centre in Austria. 'Elisabeth ran away from that house as a girl; police searched for her, brought her back and delivered her back into the violent embrace of her father,' he said. 'Running away from home was a clear sign of unhappiness, but nobody apparently showed any interest in the fate of this girl.'

Questions about the conduct of the authorities were not just being asked by Austrian journalists; the international press corps had descended on Amstetten and the story quickly became such big news worldwide that the government in Vienna was forced to step in. 'We are being confronted with an unfathomable crime,' said Interior Minister Guenther Platter, seeking to divert criticism from the administration. Even the Austrian President, Alfred

Gusenbauer, intervened, announcing a global PR campaign to save his country from being tarnished as the 'land of the dungeons'. This was particularly apposite after the Natascha Kampusch case and the discovery, in February 2007, that a lawyer in Linz had locked up her daughters for three years in almost complete darkness.

The girls' ordeal started when they were 7, 11 and 13. Their parents had divorced and the mother won custody of the children, but subsequently suffered a nervous breakdown. She took them out of school, saying she wanted to teach them at home, but instead kept them hidden away in rooms lit by a single lightbulb. All they had to play with were mice.

When finally freed, they could not cope with sunlight. They had been isolated for so long that they developed a language of their own. It was said their mother escaped child welfare visits because she was a lawyer. When their father tried to see the children, his ex-wife told him they were either ill or visiting their grandparents. The three – Viktoria, Katharina and Elisabeth – were only freed when the authorities acted on a neighbour's suspicions.

'How can the authorities be duped so easily?' a reader asked Austria's daily *Wiener Zeitung*. 'One can only hope that these poor creatures get adequate psychiatric help.'

The daily *Kurier* came up with another 'dungeon' case where a Viennese couple kept their adopted daughter, who had learning difficulties, caged in a cold room like an animal. The apparent frequency of these cases was as damning an indictment of Austrian society as you could get and the headlines were unambiguous: 'THESE CASES SHOCKED THE NATION'.

But the Fritzl story plumbed new depths. 'After this latest

case, it will be impossible to carry on with business as usual,' wrote leading columnist Petra Stuiber in Austria's daily *Der Standard*. 'An entire nation must ask itself what is going fundamentally wrong.'

The front-page headline in Austria's *Kronen Zeitung* referred to the Fritzl case as 'MARTYRDOM IN THE HOUSE OF HORROR'.

'HOW CAN IT HAPPEN HERE?' asked Austria's *Die Presse* daily, while readers of Austria's *Wiener Zeitung* wanted to know, 'How is such a thing still possible today and how many people may be still living in such circumstances?'

Neighbours quoted by *Die Presse* said the family shut itself off so much that some people who had lived in the same street for a long time thought the 'old man' might even have died. Such a lifestyle was unusual in a community where most neighbours knew each other, the paper reported.

But President Gusenbauer wanted to keep the focus on the Fritzl case. 'We will not allow our country to be held hostage by one man,' he said. 'Austria is not the perpetrator. This is an unfathomable criminal case, but also an isolated case.'

However, the local politicians in Amstetten were not so sanguine. 'What happened in that cellar is now inextricably part of the history of this town,' the town spokesman, Hermann Gruber, said.

When Natascha Kampusch heard of the Fritzl case, she issued a statement saying she wanted to contact Elisabeth Fritzl to offer emotional and financial help. 'I can imagine that it is very difficult both for the mother of the children as well as for the wife of the perpetrator to get through this,' she said.

The two cases are now inextricably linked in the public imagination. Asked whether he thought there might be other men like Fritzl and Priklopil who imprisoned children in secret bunkers, Chief Investigator Polzer said, 'It is a real possibility.'

Not only were the inhabitants of the picturesque town of Amstetten shocked to discover that they had a depraved monster in their midst, the community also became the centre of world media attention, with journalists from all over the world stalking the streets, asking anyone who would speak to them how this outrage could have happened right under their noses.

'Fritzl was always friendly – that's why this is so unbelievable,' said 56-year-old Franz Redl, who owned a shop across the street. 'I'm sure the authorities did all they could. He planned everything so perfectly.'

Another neighbour in Ybbsstrasse, an elderly woman named Maria, said, 'I just don't believe it. They were nice people. I used to watch them taking their three children to school.'

Certainly Fritzl seemed to tick all the boxes of the good, upstanding family man. 'You would see him two or three years ago with the children and they would play in the garden,' said another resident. 'Sometimes you would see Josef's grown-up children there, too.'

This seemingly model, middle-class Austrian family often used to go for a lunchtime pizza at their favourite Italian restaurant, the Casa Verona in Amstetten, just a short walk from 40 Ybbsstrasse. 'They just seemed so very normal,' said the owner, Wael Sahan. 'The two teenage girls and their younger brother were smartly dressed and really polite, unlike some kids we serve. And there was lots of laughter from their table, particularly when the father cracked a joke.'

Generally, the population looked on in stunned disbelief as the investigation unfolded. Neighbours who milled around the three-storey Fritzl house were disgusted and wondered how such an atrocity could have occurred in their own community, while others reacted with a mixture of bewilderment and horror. 'It's a catastrophe,' said one. 'It makes my hair stand on end.'

Neighbours said that Fritzl and his wife's five other children were all respected members of the community and had families of their own. 'One cannot comprehend the dimension of this,' said 34-year-old Doris Bichler, a neighbour who was walking down Ybbsstrasse with her own daughter two days after the secrets of the cellar had come to light. 'Natascha Kampusch was bad, but this is of a totally different scale.'

While Natascha Kampusch's captivity was possible because of the anonymity of the suburbs, Elisabeth Fritzl and her children were prisoners in a small, close-knit community of grape-growers. Neighbours talked of how Fritzl's wife Rosemarie used to take her three grandchildren for walks and how Josef always gave a cheery greeting. 'I would see the old lady almost every day, taking the children to school,' said another neighbour. 'They seemed a lovely family.'

'Amstetten is a close community,' added resident Sabine Ilk, 'and it's just unbelievable nobody knew what was happening for all that time.'

Günther Pramreiter, who ran a bakery next door to the Fritzls' building, said, 'You're amazed that something like this could happen in your neighbourhood.' He said the couple, or their adopted children, would come in every other day to buy rolls.

Among those in the Fritzls' neighbourhood, there was a disquieting sense that more could have been done. 'I think the authorities are overworked and weren't able to follow up every lead,' said 50-year-old Franz Jandl, who owned a shop across the street from the apartment. 'For a little country to have this kind of thing happen a second time is a catastrophe. It's just very sad.'

Joachim Wasser, 75, added, 'This is like the Kampusch case but much worse. It must never happen again.'

Matthias Sonnleitner, who managed a hardware store on Ybbsstrasse, said his children had taken martial arts classes with the Fritzl children. Rosemarie Fritzl occasionally came to his store to buy curtains, he said. He suspected nothing.

And while some Amstetten residents speculated on the perfectly normal, unremarkable behaviour of the Fritzl family, others were puzzled as to how Fritzl's dungeon could go undetected for so long. 'How is it possible that no one knew anything for 24 years?' asked Anita Fabian, a local teacher. 'This was not possible without accomplices.' The police were confident that Fritzl had acted alone, however.

Forty-two-year-old Guenter Haller, who worked across the road from the Fritzls, was also stunned. 'It's a complete shock,' he said. 'This is the friendliest town I've ever lived in. How the other tenants did not see anything escapes me.'

But someone must have suspected something and the police began their investigation with those closest to the scene of the crime. 'In the past 24 years, around 100 people have lived in the house,' said Chief Investigator Polzer. 'We want to talk to all of them – possibly one of them observed something out of the ordinary, or something that may not have seemed too important at the time, but could be of relevance knowing what we do today.'

The police began to track down all the tenants who had rented rooms in the house since 1984. Sabine Kirschbichler, who recently lived in the house for two years, told reporters that she frequently saw Herr Fritzl carrying heavy bags of shopping into the cellar after dark. 'Now, I realise why we weren't allowed to rent cellar space,' she said.

Kirschbichler, who is now in her mid-twenties, lived in a second-floor apartment with her brother Thomas for two years until 2003. They thought something was a little strange at the time, but Fritzl's odd behaviour failed to spark any significant suspicions. 'Mostly, you only saw him in the evening, often with shopping bags,' said Sabine. 'I thought, "Something's not right in his marriage if he's always doing the shopping."'

Her brother Thomas added, 'At least now we know why we couldn't rent a storage room in the cellar.'

Others think this is being wise after the event. 'In hindsight, you can always claim that you heard something like knocking,' said tenant Georg Friedrich. 'But that simply isn't the case. I can't ever recall hearing knocking or anything at all. And if I had heard something, what could I have done? It could have been children playing, you don't know.'

The police also interviewed the rest of the family to see what they knew. What emerged was a portrait of a man who was brutal, not just to the family he kept locked in the cellar and his other incestuous offspring that he kept upstairs, but to his original family as well.

'We have spoken at length to Elisabeth's brothers and sisters,' said Chief Investigator Polzer. 'All said their father wasn't just very strict, aggressive, dominant and power-mad, he was a "real tyrant". They weren't ever allowed to address him or ask him anything. That was why every child except one son left the house as soon as they could. But one son wasn't allowed to leave, just like Elisabeth. He is very slow and has a few problems and difficulties. Josef kept him, using this son as his slave and house-boy. I believe it was Josef's youngest son. He had to wait on his father hand and foot, and skivvy for him.'

There have been some questions about how much Josef Jr knew. Sabine Kirschbichler said he had a key to Fritzl's cellar, where the door to the dungeon was concealed behind a cupboard. Elisabeth's brother was fat and usually drunk, she said. 'He was the caretaker and if anything was broken he would go straight to the cellar to fetch a replacement,' she said.

The other Fritzl siblings, Elisabeth's brothers and sisters, were traumatised when the secret of the House of Horrors came out. 'They are trying to take in the terrible truth about their father while dealing with media,' a relative said. Even Elisabeth's doting big brother Harald, now in his 40s, who left home when his sister vanished, believed his father's lie that she had joined a religious cult.

Horst Herlbauer, the husband of Elisabeth's older sister Rosemarie, now nearly 50, said his wife was stunned by the revelations about her father. Herlbauer and Rosemarie were frequent visitors to Fritzl's home in Amstetten, while sister Elisabeth was being held captive in the cellar. 'Although Rosemarie left home with me more than 25 years ago, we went back for family occasions,' he said. 'But we never suspected anything was wrong and never had any reason to think anything had happened to Elisabeth.'

They, too, had fallen for the lie that Elisabeth had run off to join a cult. 'Nobody could have imagined what had really taken place,' said Herlbauer. 'Josef seemed to be a normal dad and family man. He was always working hard in his job or on the house and there never appeared to be any problems at home. He was outgoing, friendly and popular with the neighbours. We always believed Elisabeth had run away and not come back – everybody did. We didn't question it, even when some of her children appeared and were adopted into the family.'

The family were completely unprepared for the revelations that followed. 'We were shocked to learn what he had done,' said Herlbauer. 'That wasn't the man we knew.'

But their thoughts were with Elisabeth. 'It's impossible to describe the mental torture and anguish she's been through,' Herlbauer continued. 'It's a terrible ordeal beyond words. It's unreal.'

The family were trying to keep themselves out of the public eye. Since the disclosure of her sister's abuse, Herlbauer's wife has left their home in Traun. Meanwhile, the small chalet-style home in Amstetten where Elisabeth's younger sister Gabrielle lives with her husband Juergen Helm and their child has a sign outside that reads, '*Reporter nicht erwunscht*' – 'Reporters not welcome'. Similar signs went up outside houses around Amstetten as the small Austrian town tried to cope with the media's insatiable demand for details of one of the most extraordinary and shocking crimes in the country's history.

10

A FAMILY
REUNITED

No one, it seems, was more surprised to discover what was going on in the House of Horrors than Rosemarie Fritzl – who, some argue, should have known all along. She was on holiday when the terrible truth began to come out.

'Rosemarie was away when Kerstin was taken outside and to hospital,' said family lawyer Christoph Herbst. 'Every year, she takes a week away in Italy.'

It seems that Fritzl deliberately waited until his wife was away before he brought Kerstin above ground, even though the child's condition was deteriorating rapidly. Her absence was confirmed when a postcard from Italy arrived at the Fritzl home in Amstetten after the cellar nightmare had been exposed. It carried a picture of an island in the idyllic setting of a lake in northern Italy and was addressed to the 'Family Fritzl'.

Rosemarie wrote, 'Dear family, my holiday has been lovely. Although I'm really busy every day, I fall into bed dead tired, but I'll soon be home. Love Mama.'

As usual, Rosemarie had travelled alone, leaving the children to the tender mercies of their father. She was blissfully unaware of the drama unfolding at home. However, she could not be kept out of the loop for long.

'She returned as soon as she heard about Kerstin,' said attorney Herbst.

Ironically, the picture on the postcard is a photograph of Isola Bella, a small rocky island in Lake Maggiore, where a palace was built by a local aristocrat in the 17th century. Local legend has it that the ladies of his household asked him to build the new palazzo on the island, away from his castle on the mainland, so that they would not have to hear the prisoners screaming in his dungeons.

Fritzl took advantage of his wife's absence to remove the critically-ill Kerstin from the bunker and it is thought that he was trying to get her treated in hospital and back into the house – and the cellar – before Rosemarie returned, but the publicity generated by Dr Reiter's TV appeal wrecked this plan.

Word of the incredible developments in the life of the Fritzl family soon reached Rosemarie in Italy and she raced home. It is now feared that, had Fritzl acted sooner and not waited until his wife went away, Kerstin might not have suffered multiple organ failure, risking her life. When Kerstin arrived at the hospital, she was in a critical condition. She did not react well to treatment and the prognosis was not good. 'The young woman is suffering from multiple organ failure,' a spokesman for Mostviertel hospital said. 'That means her chances for survival are very low indeed.'

Prosecutors said they would press for murder charges to be brought against 73-year-old Fritzl if Kerstin did not recover. 'If the young woman dies, we will look at bringing charges against the accused for murder through negligence,' said a spokesman for the authorities.

While Kerstin remained in the care of Dr Reiter at the hospital in Amstetten, Elisabeth and her two other cellar-children, Stefan and Felix, were taken to the Amstetten Mauer Landesklinikum psychiatric clinic where, they were cared for by Dr Berthold Kepplinger, head of neuropsychiatry there. Along the way, DNA samples were taken. Tests soon confirmed Elisabeth's story – and Fritzl's admission – that the children had indeed been sired by her own father.

Reports from the clinic said that Elisabeth remained surprisingly robust. According to psychologists, she is one of those 'unbreakable' people who can be exposed to unthinkable horrors and, miraculously, come away seemingly unharmed. The phenomenon is well known to psychologists. It seems there are some people whose lives are not destroyed by post-traumatic stress disorder. They appear to have the capacity to separate themselves from the horrors that were inflicted on them, as if they had been spectators to their own suffering. In the dungeon, Elisabeth had no support in her ordeal. Now she has teams of professional carers and interested onlookers on her side. 'Perhaps Elisabeth Fritzl will be strong enough to save her own family,' wrote Der Spiegel, 'and to bring together the two halves that her father had separated into two worlds, even to cope with the suspicion that her mother, Rosemarie, or perhaps someone else in the family, might have known something after all. Who, if not Elisabeth, could rise above this abyss?'

Stefan and Felix found the outside world alien. Initially, they were terrified of rustling leaves, traffic and the blue colour of the sky. They had never seen anything like it. They remained fascinated by the moon, gazing 'open-mouthed with awe' at it. However, Chief Inspector Etz soon noted a change in five-year-old Felix as he got used to the daylight. 'The sun fascinates him even more than the moon,' said Etz. Felix would put his hand in front of his eyes and then take it away again, as if he was not able to believe what he saw. Afterwards, he kept covering his face with his hand once he realised that he could not look at the sun directly.

Initially, Elisabeth and the boys had to wear dark glasses and were plastered with sunscreen as their skin had almost no tolerance to sunlight – something the boys' skin had never seen. 'When the sunbeams struck Felix's face, he squealed loudly,' Etz said.

Doctors said that trying to tackle the health effects of the incest, the isolation and the lack of medical care in the bunker family was a huge and unprecedented task. After spending their entire lives locked in the twilight of a dungeon, it is thought that the family face years of intensive therapy before they can hope to live even a relatively normal existence. Their life underground left them so traumatised that doctors reportedly built them a windowless chamber similar to the dungeon where they were raised so the children could retreat to its safety whenever the strange new world around them became too overwhelming.

Light levels were kept low throughout the clinic so that the boys could gradually get accustomed to normal light. Even though Elisabeth was once used to the sunlight, after 24 years in the dark, she could no longer handle it and doctors had to cover windows, fearing light could damage the family's fragile health.

'They have to develop a tolerance for daylight and also to develop a sense of spatial awareness,' said Dr Kepplinger.

Until they came above ground, Stefan and Felix had never seen an object at any distance. It was something that took some adjusting to. The children also had to learn about everyday objects – everything from telephones and cars to computers, trees and fresh air. Felix, it was said, continued to be confused by various mobile phone ring tones.

There were other things to get used to as well. Although the children knew they had siblings upstairs, it is not clear what this meant to them. Locked away in a cellar for their whole life, they could not easily grasp the concept that there *was* an 'upstairs' – or any world outside their windowless dungeon. Their mother had never told them the truth about their terrible plight. Instead, she invented a fantasy world for them by filling their heads with wondrous adventure stories featuring princes and princesses. The children's only exposure to anything approaching real life was through storylines of daytime soap operas.

'It seems they may have created their own illusory world,' said Professor Rotraud Perner, a psychiatry professor from the Danube University at Krems who examined them.

Now, gradually, they would have to get used to the real world – a world of sunlight and space, a world where they had brothers and sisters, a world full of strangers and new possibilities. But however much opportunity this new world holds for them, the sad truth is that both of them may have suffered permanent damage, emotionally and mentally, as a direct result of their isolation.

'Psychologically, a lot depends on what their mother has told them over the years, whether she has explained the reason for their imprisonment or whether they have come to accept it as a normal condition,' said Professor Perner.

After it was confirmed that the 'foundling' children were also the offspring of incest, they, too, were subjected to detailed medical scrutiny. They were found to be relatively healthy, though there is some suspicion that they suffer from heart problems, but their condition could hardly be compared to that of their siblings who lived below ground.

'There is a vast difference between those who had a normal life and those who lived up to 24 years in this dungeon,' Dr Kepplinger said. But Lisa, Monika and Alexander also had a lot to come to terms with. Alexander, particularly, had already been unsettled when he was told that the people that he thought were his parents were, in fact, his grandparents and that his mother had run off to join a sect. Then he was scared that she might come back and get him.

Now they had a new and much more terrible story to deal with. Their mother had not abandoned them at all, but had been incarcerated and abused only metres beneath their feet – and they had never known that she was there. The strict patriarch in their household, who they loved after a fashion, was in fact, an evil and sadistic monster, the stuff of nightmares. They had three siblings they knew nothing about and Alexander had had a twin who was now long dead. Every emotional certainty in their lives had been destroyed. The full horror of what had happened in their own home would take years to sink in.

'Each child will need individual therapy and we should be careful not to overdo it,' said Dr Kepplinger. However, for the moment, the cellar-children had to be the priority. They had suffered even more trauma.

'The children took some items from the cellar with them … for example, toys,' said Dr Kepplinger. 'Physically, they are in quite good condition. And they love the clinic food.'

The children raved about the first dinner they were served by the hospital staff. At last, they could taste what fresh food was like. Elisabeth had striven to give her offspring the best she could under the circumstances, but she had neither the ingredients nor the facilities to produce anything more than just palatable. Fritzl bought cheap food in bulk, with only an eye for storage. Even when there was no holiday in the offing, he did not want to make too many late-night trips to outlying stores, with the attendant risk and the suspicions his nocturnal deliveries engendered. Elisabeth had to make do with what she was given. If her father did not care about the state of the air she and the children breathed, he was hardly going to worry about the standard of nutrition he provided.

While the boys soon got used to their new-found freedom, there were reminders of the terrible conditions they had endured. Both boys panicked when faced with confined spaces, particularly the hospital lifts, fearing they would get trapped inside. Felix particularly was terrified.

'Felix was scared of the elevators,' said Chief Inspector Etz. 'When using one, he didn't stop clinging on to his mother as the floor moved.'

The boys had a rudimentary grounding in German and could make themselves understood, but they could not speak 'normally' and their ability with words was not well developed. They were particularly inarticulate when compared to their brother and sisters who had been reared upstairs. 'The children who grew up in the cellar are as you'd expect them to be, considering what they've been through,' said Dr Kepplinger. 'They can speak and make themselves understood, but they're far from being in a normal state.'

Despite Elisabeth's heroic efforts to make life as normal as possible for them, she had problems of her own and they had to conserve both energy and air. 'They did not speak much in the bunker,' said Kepplinger. 'Most of the speech they heard came from a television that was on in the cellar almost non-stop day and night. The result is that there are massive gaps in their knowledge.'

Chief Inspector Etz had been the first to speak to the boys after they were released from the cellar and he went out of his way to correct any misapprehension. 'When the media write that the children speak, then this is just half true,' he said. 'Among each other, they communicate with noises that are a mixture of growling and cooing. If they want to say something so others understand them as well, they have to focus and really concentrate, which seems to be extremely exhausting for them.'

Dr Kepplinger concurred, 'They communicate among each other, but this is far from a "normal way" of expressing yourself.'

However, with the aid of doctors, they could construct proper sentences, but the effort left them exhausted and they quickly reverted to their secret, animal-like language when talking among themselves.

Etz also noted Felix's infantile behaviour. 'The boy prefers to crawl but he can walk upright if he wants,' he said. 'He mostly uses a mixture of the two – half-walking, half-crawling.'

Felix also found comfort in clutching the teddy bear his father had given him, while Stefan was soothed by the sight of tropical fish. 'Felix spends hours clutching the bear and it's like a comfort blanket to him,' said a hospital source. 'Josef gave them goldfish while they were down there and Stefan has been given an aquarium to help him. You would think the children would want to forget their time in the cellar, but it's all they've ever known.'

In time, the doctors hope that substituting the so-called 'luxuries' provided by Fritzl during their time in the cellar will help the pair adjust to their new life of freedom. Doctors believe it will take years for the family to recover completely – though it is thought that the 18-year-old Stefan will never lose the stoop that his years underground have given him. A source at the clinic spoke of the pitiful sight of 5 foot 7 inch Stefan unable to stand up straight. 'His head is constantly bowed because he never got out of his cell ... It was only 1.7 metres [5 feet 6 inches] high, and, if Stefan could stand up straight, he would be 1.72 metres [5 feet 7 inches]. It is impossible to say if this operable.'

Elisabeth, too, is hunched like an old woman as, for the last 24 years, she has never been able to extend herself to her full height. This adds to the impression that she is 20 years older than her actual age. A police artist who sketched her said, 'Her complexion belongs to someone much older – she could be 65. Her hair is grey, turning white. There's no spark left.'

But that spark does not seem to have been extinguished completely. 'The one thing she wants more than anything,' said a member of the family, 'is to feel drops of rain on her skin.'

Although they might be restored to physical health, it is feared that Stefan and Felix may never lead a normal life. 'Felix is younger so he has more of a chance to start again,' said a spokesman. 'It is not so easy for his elder brother.'

Their care will also cost millions. Medical bills at the Amstetten-Mauer clinic alone are expected to top €1 million. Austrian celebrities have donated thousands of euros to the fund for the Fritzls, and former kidnap victim Natascha

Kampusch alone donated £20,000 to the Fritzl family to launch the fund-raising appeal.

The day after Elisabeth, Stefan and Felix were released, doctors arranged a reunion with their above-ground family. After 24 years, Elisabeth was to be reunited with her mother; she would also see Lisa, Monika and Alexander, from whom she had been separated soon after birth. And the separated siblings would meet for the first time. Some psychologists expressed fears that such a reunion, so soon after Elisabeth and the boys had been freed, might prove traumatic, but it did not turn out that way.

'It was astonishing how well the reunion went,' Dr Kepplinger said.

There were also fears that the upstairs and downstairs children would shun each other. 'But it was not like that,' Kepplinger continued. 'It was amazing how easy and natural this first encounter was.'

Rosemarie broke down in tears at the sight of her daughter, whose ordeal had aged her out of all recognition. Reunited again, mother and daughter hugged for a long time.

'They cried and didn't want to let each other go,' said an observer. As Rosemarie embraced her long-lost, prematurely white-haired and now toothless daughter, she offered a simple apology. 'I had no idea,' she said.

As if realising her long ordeal was finally over, 42-year-old Elisabeth broke down in tears in her mother's arms and said, 'I can't believe I'm free – is it really you?' The tears came in floods. 'I can't believe I'm out,' sobbed Elisabeth. 'I didn't think I would ever see you again; it's all too much for me.' And as for her father, she added, 'I don't ever want to see him again.'

Mother and daughter hugged each other for a while, and the two women sobbed uncontrollably. It became clear to observers that Rosemarie was innocent of any complicity – conscious or unwitting – in the horrendous incarceration of Elisabeth.

'The wife of the accused man clearly had no knowledge of the terrible fate of her daughter,' said Dr Kepplinger. 'The two women fell into each other's arms and just wept bitterly. They held each other and did not want to let go. They said they loved each other and pledged never to be separated again, with the mother repeating, "I am so sorry – I had no idea."'

Dr Kepplinger's assessment confirmed Frank Polzer's assertion that Rosemarie knew nothing of what had gone on in the cellar. According to Polzer, she collapsed emotionally when she was told what had happened to Elisabeth. 'When she found out her daughter was in the cellar, she had a nervous breakdown,' said the investigator.

Rosemarie's younger sister Christine was also concerned about her emotional state. 'My sister is apparently doing very badly,' she said. 'I know my sister and when something is wrong with her children the world collapses ... For sure, the world has collapsed for her.'

As well as meeting her mother, Elisabeth was reunited with three of her children, who had been taken from her as babies. When she saw them, she said, 'My babies ... you are so beautiful.' She held them close and stroked their faces.

Stefan and Felix were greeted warmly by their upstairs brother and sisters, Alexander, Lisa and Monika, who, before then, they had only seen on video.

'It was a genuinely happy occasion, not forced, as was the very moving meeting between Rosemarie and Elisabeth,' Dr

Kepplinger said. He told journalists that the family members interacted very naturally, even though the three children who lived above ground had never known of their siblings in the dungeon. The children, he said, were doing 'relatively well'.

'It was a very touching moment – very dramatic and emotional for all of them,' a police source said. 'There were tears and the ones who had been in the cellar were afraid. It was very hard for them.'

While Stefan and Felix knew they had brothers and sisters above ground, they were still afraid of strangers. On the other hand, the upstairs children had known nothing of those in the dungeon, but they coped better because they had benefitted schooling and social interaction.

During the reunion, Dr Kepplinger said, it was clear that the vocabulary of the downstairs children was very limited. They stumbled and searched for words. Elisabeth had done her best, but with no social intercourse beyond Fritzl and their fellow captives in the airless cellar, there were few opportunities to develop language skills. 'Their mother taught them some reading and writing,' said Dr Kepplinger, 'although Elisabeth herself lost much of her childhood knowledge because of the years of sexual abuse that began when she was 11, and her imprisonment from the age of 18. And there were no books in the dungeon. The main source of education, over the years, has been the television.'

This left them intellectually stunted, though Dr Kepplinger said Stefan could read and write in a 'reduced form'. He also said Elisabeth had spoken 'quite a lot' about what she went through in captivity, but he would not provide details. 'It was definitely dreadful for her and for her children,' he said.

While Stefan and Felix were not as articulate as Lisa,

Monika and Alexander, it was said that 'they were able to express themselves'.

Despite the communication problems, the meeting between the two sides of the family was a success, though stressful for all concerned. 'As you can imagine, they were all very distressed and extremely worried about meeting each other for the first time. However, the family came together naturally,' said Dr Kepplinger. 'The one who seemed most distressed was Felix. He'd jump and start at the slightest disturbance and held on to his mother the whole time. It is not surprising he was so scared. Now the novelty of being free from the cellar has worn off, he needs some peace. After all, in his whole life he had only ever seen four other people.'

Although five-year-old Felix was said to have clung nervously to his mother's legs, terrified, doctors say that, because of his age, he has the best chance of being integrated into society and living a relatively normal life. For the moment, though, Felix crawled rather than walked and squeaked with excitement when confronted with anything new.

Although things seemed to be going well on all sides at the outset, psychologists warned there were still massive psychological hurdles to overcome. And there were other precedents available to guide and inform some of the treatment now being administered. Cases such as the Fritzls' are not outside the scope of psychological literature, especially in Germany. The Fritzl cellar-children have been compared to the early 19th-century case of Kaspar Hauser, a feral child who suddenly appeared in the German city of Nuremberg in 1812 at the age of 16, claiming to have spent the whole of his life locked away. Nowadays, 'Kaspar

Hauser' syndrome is a recognised psychiatric term for those suffering social isolation.

But the priority currently for the entire family is to assess each individual's needs and to make the transition from former to current living conditions as painless as possible. 'We are looking after all of them with a large team of child and adult psychologists, therapists, neurologists, speech therapists and physiotherapists,' Dr Kepplinger said. 'Each of the patients is traumatised in a different way and we are giving them individual therapy.'

In the meantime, there were numerous medical problems to sort out. Kerstin, Elisabeth, Stefan and Felix all had badly decayed teeth. They had never seen a dentist, so this was a priority. There was, of course, the possibility that Felix could develop a proper set of adult teeth. To do that, the effects of his vitamin D deficiency would have to be reversed. While this can be boosted medically, the root of the problem will only be overcome once he has developed a tolerance for sunlight; the exposure of his skin to its UV rays will begin his body's own production of the missing vitamin.

Vitamin D deficiency will have contributed to Felix's walking difficulties as well. It seems as if his joints have not developed properly. He is also known to suffer breathing difficulties and spasms, which would have the same cause. Lack of vitamin D would have retarded his growth too.

This deficiency in vitamin D would also have been a factor in Elisabeth and Stefan's stooped posture as it leaves bones deformed and softened. Stefan was also tested to see if his sight and hearing have been permanently impaired by 18 years of confinement, and all three were anaemic.

The cellar family have to be monitored closely for other

conditions, as there is some evidence to suggest that vitamin D may help to prevent diseases such as cancer, diabetes, tuberculosis and heart disease.

It also seems that the two boys may have defective immune systems. This is not surprising as the development of a healthy immune system does depend to some extent on the body being constantly challenged by new infections and allergens. A childhood spent in virtual isolation in an enclosed, unchanging environment would prevent this from happening.

Professor Robert Gaspar, a specialist in paediatric immunology at Great Ormond Street Hospital in London, said the information released by the Austrian authorities did not reveal much about the precise nature of the immune problem and the true extent of this would become clear over the coming months. 'A healthy immune system isn't just created by nature,' he said, 'but also by the environment that a child lives in – there could be a lack of exposure to the normal repertoire of challenges that other children would face.'

He suggested the children's immune system might also be compromised in some way by lack of vitamin D, which plays a key role in enabling immune cells to clear the body of potentially harmful debris and infection. If their immune systems are permanently damaged by their captivity, then they could face a lifetime of increased vulnerability to a range of infections and illnesses. In any case, they will have to have all the inoculations that other children are given as they are growing up.

Naturally, the children reared above ground suffer none of these problems. They were brought up on fresh milk and were used to playing in the garden. However, Lisa has a heart problem that may derive from the genetic composition of her parentage. Monika, too, may suffer a milder form of the same congenital condition, for the same reasons. Otherwise, the upstairs siblings were reported to be healthy. Despite the abnormal circumstances of their birth, they were brought up to enjoy a relatively normal life. All six of Elisabeth's surviving children fathered by Fritzl seem to have escaped the worst of the genetic defects caused by inbreeding.

Quite apart from the social stigma associated with incestuous relationships, there are good biological reasons why they are to be avoided. If a family harbours a genetic defect, there is an increased risk that a child of an incestuous relationship could inherit two, rather than one copy of the defective gene, making a health problem inevitable. This could be the cause of Kerstin's epilepsy as well as Lisa's heart problem. However, there is little or no data about the precise nature of the threat of genetic abnormality caused by incestuous relationships between father and daughter because when such things occur, people usually keep quiet about it. Scientists estimate that the risk of defects is roughly doubled in first-cousin marriages, so the risk in a father-daughter relationship would be considerably higher.

While the upstairs children were relatively privileged, they may also have suffered psychological damage, too. Twelve-year-old Alexander, particularly, has to cope with the fact that he had a twin brother that he had not been told about, and that his twin, now named Michael, died three days after childbirth due to the neglect of the man whom Alexander first thought of as his father, then his grandfather – and he now knows is both his father and grandfather. His dead brother was then burnt in the household incinerator by the man who was supposed to be protecting and nurturing his family.

According to a hospital spokesman, there are problems all round. 'All sides have had a lot to come to terms with,' he said. 'The above-ground children have to accept that, two floors below, members of their family were hidden away – and their grandfather is also their father. The stories they were raised with – that the mother had joined a bizarre sect and abandoned them at birth – have also been exposed as lies, and that, in fact, she had been imprisoned in the cellar for 24 years.'

Another psychologist tried to sum up the scale of the family's suffering. 'How do you greet your brother who you didn't even know existed, and who you have just learned has spent his whole life until now imprisoned in a dark dungeon, only two floors below your own bedroom, locked up by your grandfather, who, you discover, is also your father? And how do you greet your mother, who you've always been told had fallen into the arms of a devilish sect and given up her children when they were still babies, but who you learn also had to vegetate in the cellar for 24 years?'

The upstairs children are also likely to suffer from 'survivor's syndrome', like Holocaust survivors who feel guilty for remaining alive when so many others perished. Their bunker siblings suffered while they were picked by their father, for some arbitrary reason, to live their life in daylight. They will also have to get used to the idea that their mother had not abandoned them – a falsehood they had found it hard to come to terms with not so long before – but had, in fact, been suffering her own terrible ordeal, only metres beneath their feet.

Psychologists asked to comment on the case were almost

unanimous in their view that the ordeal suffered by Elisabeth, Kerstin, Stefan and Felix would mark them indefinitely. 'The four will never be able to live normal lives. I am afraid it is too late for that,' Bernd Prosser, a clinical psychologist, told Austrian television.

However, those closer to the family see cause for hope following the 'astonishing success' of the meeting of the two sides of the family. 'The reunion went incredibly well,' said Dr Kepplinger. 'They got along very well and it was far more successful than anticipated. It was astonishing how the grandmother and Elisabeth immediately came together; it was a very emotional scene.'

It was therapy in itself. 'It was astonishing how easy it was,' said Dr Kepplinger. 'This will help their recovery and we'll try to ensure they stay together from now on.'

The clinic set aside a space of around 80 square metres (860 square feet). It was reserved as a living area for Elisabeth, Stefan, Felix, Lisa, Monika and Alexander – along with grandmother Rosemarie – who were to spend time there together while they got to know each other.

'The family is pleased with the surroundings, but it's going to take a long time to re-introduce them to some kind of a normal life,' said Dr Kepplinger.

While the cellar family were still kept in a relatively confined space, they were allowed to stretch their legs. Later, they would be permitted to walk further afield under supervision. 'In the clinic area, the children can shout, play and will eventually get to know their siblings from outside of the cellar,' said Dr Kepplinger. 'They can be themselves here, undisturbed by anyone. The young people have space to play, they can run around.'

It seemed to be working. 'The members of the family talk a lot,' he said. 'They are very happy to be together. They enjoy the food especially. The kids are playing, jumping about, moving around as they wish; they've got their toys with them and there are people there for them round the clock.'

Kepplinger said Felix was the liveliest, but he was also very clingy, never letting his mother out of his sight. However, he was soon making remarkable progress and, within a few days, found he could make friends. 'We are proud Felix trusts us more and more,' said Chief Inspector Etz, a regular visitor. 'We are almost friends already.'

Sadly, the police had to visit repeatedly to debrief the victims. 'It makes us extremely sad to hear more and more of what the boy had to endure,' said Etz. 'So far, we have met him a couple of times. He was always happy about seeing us again and waves and smiles … He is full of joy and excitement, he slaps the air with his hand when he can't control his excitement.'

On 31 April, hospital staff put on a party for Alexander's 12th birthday – and that of his twin brother Michael, whose body Fritzl had incinerated. 'They were delighted with it and thoroughly enjoyed the cake,' the staff said. No one missed the presence of the father of the two respective families who had, fortunately, been detained elsewhere.

No matter how well things seemed to be going, doctors say the road to recovery could take years. Elisabeth and her six siblings were receiving legal advice as they tried to comprehend how they were deceived and maltreated for 24 years by their tyrannical father. It is possible they may seek compensation, though loans made to their father have been called in and he is now bankrupt. Meanwhile, the clinic did everything it could to keep the family well away from the media pack that had descended on Amstetten.

11

THE MONSTER
SPEAKS

While the Fritzl family were beginning their recovery in the Mauer clinic, their tormentor was on suicide watch in prison. He had been remanded in custody in jail in St Pölten, the provincial capital of Lower Austria, while being investigated for alleged rape, incest, kidnapping, wrongful imprisonment, cruelty, coercion, enslavement and murder.

After the remand hearing, prosecutor Gerhard Sedlacek said, 'He's completely calm, completely without emotion.'

But Fritzl's defence lawyer, Dr Rudolf Mayer, one of the best-known advocates in Austria, painted a different picture. Fritzl, he said, was distraught. 'He's really hit by this,' said Mayer. 'He is a shattered and ruined man. He is emotionally broken.'

While Fritzl has confessed to fathering seven children by Elisabeth, Mayer remained adamant. 'The allegations of rape and enslaving people have not been proved,' he said. 'We need to reassess the confessions made so far.'

On 8 May 2008, Rudolf Mayer released a statement on

behalf of his client. It was the confession that Fritzl had made to the Austrian prosecutors and was passed to the media at his request. Although the man was plainly trying to explain – if not excuse – his monstrous behaviour, it gives a glimpse into the dark impulses that drove his actions.

'I grew up in a poor family,' said Fritzl. 'My father was a no-good scoundrel who always cheated on her and my mother threw him out of the house when I was four – and she was quite right to do so. After that, it was only the two of us.

'My mama was a strong woman. She taught me discipline, order and diligence. She enabled me to get a good education and job training and she constantly worked hard and would take difficult jobs only to support the both of us.

'She was as strict as it was necessary. She was the best woman in the world. And I was her husband, in some way. She was the boss at home, but I was the only man in the house.'

This begged an obvious question – was there anything sexual about the relationship between Fritzl and his mother? When he was asked whether he had been sexually abused by his mother, he said, 'No, never. My mother was decent, most decent. I loved her over everything. I have admired her. I admired her very much. But I have naturally not done anything. There was nothing there.'

Asked whether he had sexual fantasies about his mother, he said, 'Yes, probably, but I was strong, almost as strong as my mother, and I have therefore managed to suppress my urges.'

Otherwise, as a young man, he insisted that his sex life was perfectly normal. 'Later, I got older and I started going out and I had several amorous affairs. And then I found Rosemarie. She had nothing in common with my mother, but, however, there were some similarities. She was also wonderful, but wonderful in a different way. She was much more shy and weaker than my mother.'

Speaking of his family, he said, 'I always wanted to have many children. Not children that would have to, like I had, grow up alone, but children that would always have someone to play with. I had a dream about a large family ever since I was a little boy. And Rosemarie appeared to be a suitable mother. That motive [for marrying her] was not a bad one. And it is true: I always loved her and I will always love her.'

The prosecutors then asked what happened when he raped a woman in 1967. He replied, 'I don't know what came into me. But this is also true: I always wanted to be a good husband and father.'

It was then that he began to blame his crimes on his Nazi past. 'I admit I have always valued decency and good behaviour,' he said. 'I grew up in the Nazi era and strictness and discipline were very important then. I have probably subconsciously picked up some of that, which is only normal, but I am not the beast the media make me out to be.'

When asked what he would think of a man like himself, he admitted, 'Seen from the outside, I would probably think he was a beast or a monster.'

He also rejected the allegation made by his daughter that he started abusing her when she was 11. 'That is not true,' he said. 'I am not a man who would molest children. It only started later, much later, when she was already down below.'

He admitted that he began planning the imprisonment of his daughter a long time before he lured her into the cellar. 'It was approximately two, three years before,' he said. 'It must have been 1981 or 1982 when I started to turn a room in my cellar into a cell.'

The police now think that it was 1977 or 1978, soon after Elisabeth said he started to sexually abuse her.

'I brought in a heavy door of steel and concrete and equipped it with a remote-controlled electrical motor, which would open it only after a numeric code was entered,' Fritzl continued. 'I isolated the whole bunker to become sound-proof. I installed a washbasin, a toilet, a bed, a cooker and a refrigerator. Electricity and light were already installed.

'Perhaps someone noticed the construction works, but it would have not made any difference whether they did or not. The cellar of my house belonged to me and to me alone ... it was my kingdom to which only I had access. Everyone who lived there knew that – my wife, my children, my lodgers – and no one would have dared to enter my realm or even to ask me what I was doing there ... I told everyone that my office was there, full of private files that were my business alone and that was enough – everyone adhered to my rules.'

Speaking about incarcerating Elisabeth, he said, 'Ever since she entered puberty she did not adhere to any rules any more ... she would spend whole nights in dingy bars, drinking alcohol and smoking. I only tried to pull her out of that misery. I got her a job as a waitress but she would not go to work for days. She even escaped twice and hung out with bad people during this time and they were not good company for her. I would bring her back home each time, but she would try to escape again. That is why I had to do something; I had to create a place where I could keep Elisabeth, by force if necessary, away from the outside world.'

He denied keeping his daughter in handcuffs, in chains or on a dog leash as she alleged. 'That would not have been necessary,' he said. 'My daughter had no chance of escape. It was a vicious circle, a circle from which there was no exit – not only for Elisabeth, but also for myself. With every passing week in which I kept my daughter captive, my situation was getting crazier. I really was thinking about whether I should let her go or not, but I was not able to make that decision, although – or maybe exactly because of that – I knew that with every passing day what I had done would be more severely judged. But I was afraid of being arrested and of having my family and everyone out there find out about my crime – and so I postponed my decision again and again. Until, one day, it was really too late to free Elisabeth and take her upstairs.'

It was only when Elisabeth was locked away in the cellar that he began to compare his daughter to his mother, he said. Gradually, he started to have sexual fantasies about her, which he claimed he tried to suppress. 'But the urge to have sex with Elisabeth was growing stronger and stronger,' he said. 'I knew that Elisabeth did not want the things I did to her; I knew that I was hurting her, but the urge to finally be able to taste the forbidden fruit was too strong. It was like an addiction.'

Not only did he want to have sex with his daughter, he wanted to have a second family with her. 'In reality, I wanted to have children with her,' he told the prosecutors. 'Elisabeth naturally had a fear of giving birth, but I brought her medical books to the cellar, so she could prepare for the Day X. I brought her towels, disinfectants and nappies.

'I was looking forward to the offspring. It was a beautiful idea for me, to have a proper family, also down in the cellar, with a good wife and a couple of children. I made preparations for all possibilities. Every time I left the bunker, I would activate a time-lock, which would make sure that the doors to the dungeon would open if I would not return after a certain period of time. Had I died, Elisabeth and the children would have been freed.'

Fritzl also boasted of acts of generosity. 'After Felix was born at the end of 2002, I even gave Elisabeth a washing machine so that she could wash the clothes and bed sheets of the children and not have to handwash them in the basin,' he said. 'I always knew during the whole 24 years that what I was doing was not right, that I must have been crazy to do such a thing, but still it became a normal occurrence to lead a second life in the cellar of my house.'

Asked whether he saw his captives as a second family, he said that that was exactly how he viewed them. He also said that Elisabeth never told the children that they were a product of her father's imposed incestuous relations with her. The children in the dungeon always had to call him 'Grandpa', even though they saw him raping her.

'Elisabeth has always taken care of things for the sake of the family,' he said. 'I have tried to provide for my family in the cellar as best as possible. Whenever I went to the bunker, I would bring my daughter flowers and cuddly toys as well as books for the children. I would watch an adventure film on video with them while Elisabeth would prepare our favourite food and then we would all sit together at the kitchen table and eat together.'

He also admitted the children were often suffering from infections, coughing attacks, chest pains and epileptic attacks – though he took no effective action to relieve their suffering. When Kerstin became ill, he said, 'She tore the clothes from her body and threw them in the toilet.' It was then that he realised that he must get her proper medical attention, he said.

Fritzl claimed he was already planning to free his secret family and integrate them into his upstairs family. 'I wanted to take Elisabeth and the children to my home,' he said. 'I have grown old in the meantime, I was not so agile any more and I simply knew that, in the near future, I would not have been able to provide for my second family in the bunker. Elisabeth and the children were supposed to tell the story that they had been at a secret location with a cult until they were set free.'

By this patently transparent device, he said that he hoped he would have been able to get away with his crime, but he knew the risks. 'Of course this is what I hoped for, even if that hope was weak,' he said. 'There was always the danger that Elisabeth and the children could have betrayed me but I accepted that risk and I have done that as the tragedy [with Kerstin] escalated.'

When asked how he had managed to prevent his daughter and her children from escaping, he said, 'It was not difficult. I did not need to use physical violence. Elisabeth and the children fully accepted me as the supreme head of the family … they would never have dared to attack me.

'Apart from that, they also knew that I was the only one who had the numeric code for the remote control that could open and close the doors to the dungeon.'

The prosecutors asked Fritzl whether he had threatened them with gas poisoning if they attempted to escape. He denied it. 'I have only explained to them that they should not fiddle with the dungeon door or else they could receive an electrical shock and die,' he said.

When asked why he had taken three of his children upstairs to be brought up relatively normally by his wife, Fritzl said it was because they were 'cry-babies'. They got on his nerves in the confined cellar and he was afraid the noise they made would lead to the dungeon being discovered.

However, the police now believe that that may not have been the reason at all. While Lisa was formally adopted, the other two were registered as foster children – entitling Josef and Rosemarie Fritzl to child support which helped supplement the family income. He racked up over £2,000 a month in various State benefits – €600 (£480) a month for Lisa after she was adopted and €1,000 (£800) each for their foster children, Monika and Alexander. As Fritzl's businesses were in financial difficulties, this income helped pay for his lavish lifestyle – his clothes, his flashy car, his brothel visits and the holidays in Thailand. The police have suggested that this was the real motive for him to bring the children upstairs. After examining his financial records, they found that Fritzl was in constant need of cash to service his debts.

'They were cash cows for him,' said an investigator in Amstetten. 'Everything he did was not out of concern for them, but to get money.'

When asked whether he was now looking forward to death he said, 'No, I only want redemption.'

In the meantime, Fritzl faced public contempt. In jail, he constantly watched coverage of his case. Despite everything he has owned up to, he sought to complain about his treatment by the media. His attorney Rudolph Mayer said that his client felt that he was being unfairly treated. 'He feels the reporting on his case is unfair,' said Mayer. 'It is totally one-sided.'

Fritzl protested that he was being portrayed as an ogre. 'I'm no monster,' he told Mayer. 'I could have killed them all, then nothing would have happened to me. No one would ever have known about it. I would never have been caught.'

Instead, he had saved the life of Kerstin, he claimed, while putting himself at risk in the bargain. 'Without me, she would not be alive any more,' he said. 'I was the one who made sure that she was taken to a hospital.'

He even claimed he was kind to the family he kept imprisoned underground and that he'd been sorely misunderstood. 'He is very depressed ... It is certainly hard for him in jail,' said Mayer.

Given the facts surrounding Fritzl's decades of planning and executing his demented strategy, as well as the sexual, physical and psychological abuse meted out by him on his own family members, it is hard to sympathise. Prison guards have revealed that his fellow inmates constantly yelled at him and made threats. 'Satan, come on out,' they shouted. 'We're going to kill you.'

A recently released inmate said, 'At night, the other cons shout out, "We're going to get you, Satan, come out and play," and they bang on the door when they walk past his cell.'

Mayer said that Fritzl was 'very quiet and humbled' – not the arrogant egomaniac the police said they had to deal with. His client, he said, understood the 'anger of the people outside' and was prepared to accept his punishment. 'I only want one thing now,' Fritzl said, 'and that is to pay for what I did.'

But it is plain that he is building up to an insanity plea. 'I knew I must be mad for doing such a thing,' he said. He claims that he was driven by addiction that 'got out of control'.

His lawyer concurs. Speaking from his office opposite Vienna's Central Criminal Court, Mayer said, 'My client is psychologically ill and, as a result, is not responsible for his actions. He is not a monster ... he is just a human being.

Locking him up in jail is not the right thing to do. He needs proper psychological care.'

There was outrage in the Austrian press when it appeared that Mayer was angling for a lighter sentence by claiming his client was mentally ill, but he remains unconcerned. 'Every case that has a psychological background is interesting,' he said. 'We defence lawyers believe that there are good souls.'

Rudolf Mayer considers himself both a 'therapist and lawyer'. Throughout his career, he has been attracted to cases with a 'psychological-psychiatric background,' he says. Indeed, his plush offices are just around the corner from where Sigmund Freud used to practice.

'Josef Fritzl is being portrayed as a horrific monster and sexual tyrant,' said Mayer. 'My job is to show him as a human being.' Obviously, he is going to have his work cut out.

Mayer went on to explain his methods: he said he always uses his first ten-minute meeting with a client to get a feeling for the individual. 'I turn off my rational brain, switch on my gut instinct and concentrate on the person's eyes,' said the lawyer. 'It's a tried-and-tested tactic – the eyes reveal 90 per cent of a person's psyche.'

To most people, the pale eyes they have seen in photographs of Josef Fritzl appear faintly satanic, but that may be because anyone who knows anything about what he has admitted to doing already has a biased opinion. Even his lawyer admits Fritzl has a 'Jack Nicholson look' – that of the murderous madman the actor plays in *The Shining* presumably.

Putting aside his gut instinct and what he read in his client's eyes, Mayer thought he got through to Fritzl when they first met. 'The first 30 seconds of a meeting is crucial for establishing psychological contact,' he said. 'I believe that, in this time, I succeeded in bonding with Herr Fritzl.'

His overall impression was that his client was 'a paterfamilias, a patriarch, with good but also bad sides'. While Mayer claimed Fritzl was 'very seriously affected and emotionally broken', in interrogations he was found to be 'unresponsive'.

Throughout their second meeting, Mayer said, 'I just let him talk and I listened to him.' Fritzl spent two hours speaking about his life and giving his version of things, but Mayer refused to reveal any details of the conversation and he has also asked his client to be more circumspect in future. 'He has already said too much,' said Mayer, aware that Fritzl's detailed confession is going to tie his hands in this case. He need not have worried, though. When prosecutors threatened to charge him with murder over the death of Michael, Fritzl withdrew his co-operation.

Mayer said he knew little about Fritzl's early life or why he destroyed the life of his child in such a hideous way. 'That is exactly where my task begins,' said Mayer. 'Who is Josef Fritzl? Why is he the way he is?'

Those are the questions he was seeking to answer as he got to know his client better, and he believed he would discover why Fritzl decided to imprison his own daughter. 'After three decades' professional experience as a defence lawyer, I am convinced of one thing,' he said. 'There is an explanation for every deed, for every criminal act.'

Like the police, Mayer was convinced there were no accomplices in this case and he did not know if his client was going to be charged with more rapes or other crimes, such as the unsolved murder of Martina Posch in 1986. 'I am waiting for the coming conversations with my client to see if he mentions anything,' he said.

He also said that he was not put off by the severity of the crimes that Fritzl has committed – by his own admission – or the circumstances of the offences. 'I wasn't shocked,' he said. Indeed, he was pleased to have been appointed to the case. 'Herr Fritzl was asked if he wanted me as his defence lawyer,' said Mayer, 'and he said, "Yes, I know him from the TV!"'

Mayer first hit the headlines in 1996 when he defended two neo-Nazis accused of sending a series of letter bombs and succeeded in securing an acquittal for them. His chances of negotiating any kind of light sentence for Josef Fritzl look slim, but that did not seem to deter him. Indeed, he revelled in the limelight. 'Even a Colombian radio station has asked me if I am prepared to do a live interview,' he said.

It seemed as if an insanity plea was Mayer's only option, given Fritzl's confession and the charges that the prosecutors were preparing against him. 'They want him jailed for the rest of his natural life,' said Mayer. As Fritzl is already 73, he is hardly likely to suffer anything like the length of imprisonment he subjected his daughter to.

Mayer was particularly concerned with the possibility that Fritzl might be charged with murder over the death of baby Michael. 'He has admitted Elisabeth had the twins on her own in the cellar and that he did not see her until three days after the birth,' continued the lawyer. 'He told me that when he found one of the babies was dead, he put its body into his furnace. Elisabeth says her baby developed breathing difficulties and Fritzl failed to get medical attention that could have saved its life. Police now say he is guilty of first-degree murder because he did not allow the child to be treated and it died as a direct result.'

Mayer said Fritzl had stopped talking to police after they accused him of murdering the child by neglect and that Fritzl will not say another word to authorities. He also told his attorney that he will now never reveal why he imprisoned his daughter. A second murder charge hung over him if Kerstin did not recover.

'The maximum sentence for murder in Austria is 15 years, but everything possible is being done to maximise my client's sentence,' Mayer complained.

Elisabeth's school friend Christa Woldrich voiced what she considered a more fitting retribution for Fritzl. 'If I had to decide what happened to him, I would fling him into the same hole Elisabeth and the children were in,' she said.

But his lawyer pleads in mitigation, 'Herr Fritzl admits he raped and imprisoned his daughter, but he does regret what he did … he is emotionally destroyed. He thought he was protecting his family and said that was his job as the patriarch.' Mayer even hinted he would ask a judge to free Fritzl at his next court hearing.

Despite Mayer's insistence that his client may be insane, the police insisted that Fritzl was 'composed and rational' and in a good mental and physical condition. But Mayer said Fritzl has been examined by prison doctors who have diagnosed him as suffering from schizophrenia.

The court appointed Austria's leading forensic psychiatrist, 46-year-old Dr Adelheid Kastner, to determine whether Fritzl was fit to stand trial. 'I am conducting exploratory conversations to get to know every possible part of the defendant's personality,' she said. 'The court wants me to probe several questions and has given me a deadline but if I need longer, then the court will have to wait.'

Mayer said that Fritzl had told him, 'I had a breakdown from which there was no escape, not only for me, but also for Elisabeth. The longer I kept her prisoner, the more insane my situation became, the worse it seemed to get. The desire for her became stronger and stronger. I've known for 24 years that what I was doing was wrong, that I must be insane to do such a thing. But I was driven by these forbidden desires. They were just too great for me.'

Mayer said his client was under psychiatric care, but he refused to say if he showed any remorse. In what appears to be an indication that he did not, Mayer replied only, 'I cannot say at this point.'

When District Governor Hans-Heinz Lenze visited, he found Fritzl unrepentant. 'When I met him again in his cell, I said, "It was you, Herr Fritzl. I am appalled by you. How can anyone do such a thing?" To which he replied, "I am very, very sorry for my family, but it can't be undone." I replied, "You should have thought of that earlier."'

Like his client, Mayer is furious about the coverage of the case. He put out Fritzl's statement saying that he was not a monster on the grounds that he could have killed Elisabeth and the children, but didn't. But what he didn't do hardly mitigates what he did.

Nevertheless, Rudolf Mayer agrees with Fritzl. 'The media coverage is completely over the top,' he said. 'So part of my job is to move it away from the monster, back to the human being. Because it is a human being on trial, not a monster.'

But the question put to the court will not be whether Fritzl is a monster or not. More likely it will be whether or not he is sane. In his confession, he said, 'I always knew … that what I was doing was not right.' He said he had a strong sense of 'decency' inculcated into him by the Nazis and the strictness of his mother. Indeed, he even claimed that he initially imprisoned his daughter to keep her away from the wickedness of the world. Knowing right from wrong is the standard legal test for sanity. It was only later that Fritzl said, 'I knew I must be mad ...'

Doctors have already provided an initial assessment of Fritzl's personality. Austria's top criminal psychiatrist, Reinhard Haller, whose analysis of defendants is used by the courts, said, 'Fritzl appears to have been driven by pronounced narcissism and a need to exercise power over others – and that may help explain how he got away with the abuse for so long. This man must have been insane and must have felt he was far superior to others.'

Haller also suggests that, although Fritzl sexually abused Elisabeth as a child and repeatedly raped her in the cellar, he was not motivated by sex. 'It was a drive for power. He's probably a person with one very weak spot which he compensates for through sadism. He wants to have 100 per cent control over his victims. That is his kick – the absolute power of the patriarch. He probably would have carried on doing this until he no longer had the power to control his hostages if nothing had gone wrong.' He contends that Fritzl's power complex may have resulted from his being abused by his mother.

Kidnapping victim Natascha Kampusch was not slow to speak out on the subject and lend her insights into the mind of the abductor. She admitted to feeling 'relieved' when the story broke. There were parallels, she thought, between her case and that of Elisabeth. 'Priklopil's mother,' she said, 'was blind with mother-love. It was the same with Josef Fritzl. He idolised his mother to an abnormal degree and that's what my abductor was like. He was very attached to his mother. Before she came over to tidy up, I'd have to clean the whole house so that she thought he was this proper, upstanding person. Regardless of what I did, he would always say, "My mother does it better."'

After Kampusch escaped and Priklopil committed suicide, his mother told a journalist that she hoped that Kampusch had, in some way, loved her son. His mother said that subtle changes in his home led her to believe that her son had a girlfriend. She noticed there were two pillows on his bed, tiny cactus plants in the living room and the smell of cooking in the kitchen – when she knew her son never cooked.

'I have no contact with her,' said Kampusch. 'At first, I thought that it would be a good idea to meet her to help her to deal with her bad conscience, because she hadn't noticed anything, and to help her come to terms with her situation, because she'd not only lost her son but she'd lost the son whom she thought was a well-behaved, well-adjusted, nice man. But I don't see it the same way. I don't really want to meet her.'

Kampusch's insights may well be used in court in the Fritzl case.

While Haller believes that Fritzl was driven by a high degree of narcissism arising from his omnipotence over the situation, other psychologists have identified another form of narcissism that could have been relevant in this case. It is the narcissism of the art collector who buys stolen paintings so that he can have them for only himself. Fritzl kept Elisabeth and his three children in his vault as such trophies. Each time he went to see them, to spend an hour or two with them, or to bring them food and medication at night, he was able to reassure himself that the uniqueness of his property made him all the more unique.

'There are no comparable cases worldwide,' said Haller – not even that of Natascha Kampusch. She was kidnapped by a stranger, as was Colleen Stan. In the other Austrian cases where family members were imprisoned, there was no hint of sexual abuse. Abductors who have kept sex slaves rarely want to have children with them.

However, in 1988, Gary Heidnik was convicted of kidnapping six African-American prostitutes to set up a 'baby farm' in the basement of his Philadelphia home. Two of his captives died and he was executed for murder in 1999. But, again, his sex slaves were not relatives.

Sigrun Rossmanith, another Austrian court psychiatrist, concluded that Fritzl developed two personalities, one of which was dominated by the need to exert total control over others. Elisabeth was a victim of his power complex. 'She was a slave that he could use at any moment of his choosing,' she said. 'He made her submissive and used her according to his needs. He exercised absolute control over her.'

Fritzl's double personality was even reflected in the design of his – at first sight – ordinary-looking, three-storey house on Amstetten's Ybbsstrasse. The light-grey façade of the building which looked out on to the main street is a normal, turn-of-the-century provincial townhouse with net curtains hanging in the front windows, but the back of the house, which was extended out over Fritzl's notorious cellar, looked not unlike the kind of massive Second World War bunkers that were built by the Nazis to withstand air-raids. Passers-by were confronted with solid, windowless concrete walls at ground level. The only windows at the back of the building were on the top floors, and the garden was hidden behind a row of evergreen trees and a hedge.

Despite Dr Rossmanith's assertion that Fritzl had developed two personalities, Reinhard Haller concluded that he was not insane. 'Fritzl is no way crazy or mentally ill, otherwise he would have made mistakes,' said Haller. 'He is a technician who very carefully carried out one step after another. He must have unbelievable self-confidence ... His main motivation was the exercise of power. It is not a sign of mental illness, but rather of an extreme personality disorder.'

It is plain that the authorities plan to fight any insanity plea and will seek to prosecute Fritzl to the limit of the law. After all, the eyes of the world are on the case and Austria's national honour is at stake.

Amstetten District Governor Hans-Heinz Lenze dismissed the idea that Fritzl was insane. He was, Lenze said, 'intelligent, a strategist, an almost-perfect criminal of the worst kind'.

Since taking on the Fritzl case, Mayer said he had received death threats and hate emails, but he is obdurate. 'I will not be swayed by a lynch justice mentality,' he said. 'Every accused person has a right to a defence and the lawyer that fails to do his best for his client is failing in his duties.'

For him, it is a matter of integrity. 'Lawyers who refuse to defend certain acts contradict my view of professional ethics,' he said. He sees the hate emails as an occupational hazard and was not worried about the possibility of being physically attacked. 'I may be 60,' he said, 'but I am an enthusiastic member of my local boxing club and I know how to look after myself. Having any other protection such as a security guard is pointless. If people want to get you, they will manage it.'

He has no qualms about taking on the case and is sanguine about talking to the accused. 'What impressed me was that I could not detect the sort of negative vibes I get with, say, a car thief,' said Mayer. 'He is in a very bad way psychologically but he does not complain. His biggest fear is how his children are faring without him.'

In prison, Fritzl was held in relatively luxurious conditions, especially when compared to those Elisabeth and the children endured in their dank cellar. His cell measured 10 feet by 12 feet and had a ceiling 10 feet high – allowing more than enough room to stand upright. It was lit by a large window. Along with a TV, he had a bedside lamp and pot plants which flourished in the natural light that streams through the glass. There was a smart, self-contained bathroom area with a hygienic toilet and hand basin. The jail bedding was bright and clean, and was worlds away from the cellar's damp and mouldy mattresses. Magazines were provided so he had something to read; prison nutritionists made sure he got three healthy, balanced meals a day. This contrasted with the stale food served up to his dungeon family. He was allowed to eat in his cell and shower alone. As a concession, he was permitted the use of a private shower to protect him from other inmates. Even so, Fritzl complained about feeling bored and isolated in jail.

'We have isolated the inmate Fritzl from other prisoners for his own safety,' said Friedrich Wallner, head warder at St Pölten jail. 'He goes to the shower on his own and goes for walks in the prison courtyard sometimes. But, most of the time, he sits in front of the TV, watching reports about the case.'

An insider said, 'He wants to see every word written about

the case and watch every TV report. It's like a game to him – he has become obsessed. The warders are under strict orders to maintain his safety.'

Already Fritzl has received numerous death threats. 'The inmates are well aware of what he's done,' said the source. 'There's even a contest to be the first to attack him – and some want him dead. There are also fears Fritzl could kill himself, but no one wants him to die without explaining what he did.'

Prison staff were said to be 'keeping a very close eye on him'. He was being especially protected for two reasons, they said – first, so he won't 'pass judgement on himself' and try to commit suicide, and second because 'he doesn't have a particularly good position in the hierarchy of prisoners'.

'He seems a bit afraid,' says Günther Mörwald, the prison governor at St Pölten. Fritzl was not speaking much but, according to Mörwald, he was slowly understanding 'what he did to his family'. The prison governor said he was seeing the 'first signs of regret'.

Although Fritzl is kept away from the other prisoners, for his own safety he has been given a companion. His cellmate is a 36-year-old career criminal, accused of shooting someone. The man was hand-picked to ensure Fritzl does not commit suicide.

'The guy is doing time for violent offences,' said a prison source. 'The staff picked him because he's not the sort of man you mess with; he's a heavy thug. He's there to alert wardens if Fritzl looks unstable or if he's about to kill himself. You could call it a kind of in-house suicide watch.'

When Fritzl was examined by a psychologist and a psychiatrist on 29 April 2008, both concluded there was no suicide risk. Afterwards, Governor Mörwald said he seemed 'calm and collected'. 'He's in good shape physically,' said Mörwald. 'He will undergo a medical examination today but doesn't appear to have any health problems.' Nevertheless, he remained segregated from the other prisoners for his own safety.

However, concerns about his health surfaced again later. It seems the 73-year-old has a heart condition and doctors wanted to test him for an unspecified blood disease. An inmate released from St Pölten jail in early June 2008 said, 'He really looks unwell. He's lost a lot of weight and hasn't left his cell for fear of being attacked. He is suffering.'

The case could take two years to come to court, and it is thought that Fritzl may not last that long. The police fear he might die in prison before he explains exactly why he imprisoned his daughter and their children.

Meanwhile, despite everything that's happened, Fritzl is begging the prison authorities to allow his wife to visit him, although there is no indication that she would want to. He also wants to see Elisabeth. Apparently, he began to cry himself to sleep in prison, overcome with remorse. He told his legal team he was worried about how they are coping without him. A source at St Pölten prison said, 'Fritzl's mood has changed dramatically in the past three weeks. When he first arrived, he was arrogant and unrepentant but he's now a broken man.'

At first, jailers were shocked by his cold, unrepentant attitude. After a few weeks' reflection, there was an outpouring of remorse. Then all he talked about was seeing his family so he could apologise and make sure that all was well with them. Fritzl then sank into a deep depression. He refused to leave his cell for his hour a day of fresh air and exercise, afraid his fellow inmates would attack him. He would weep all through the night and lost a lot of weight. There were fears he was wasting away.

Despite everything that's happened, Fritzl wants to see Elisabeth, the children and his wife Rosemarie. He told his legal team, 'I want to see my family to explain things and find out how they are. I am worried about them.'

'It's ironic that a man who kept his family trapped in a cellar for so long is now suddenly concerned for them,' the source continued. But Elisabeth had already said she never wanted to see her father's face again. Fritzl had just one visitor as he awaited trial in jail, an unidentified family friend.

In his cell, he has been swamped with over 5,000 items of hate mail, but among the post he was said to have received over 200 love letters from women offering him affection and understanding. They maintain he was misunderstood and 'good at heart'. He did, after all, only lock his daughter Elisabeth away in a cellar for 24 years to prevent her from straying and to keep her safe from drugs and booze. Some were even said to excuse the fact that he fathered seven children with his daughter by saying he only wanted to teach her about the 'joys of motherhood'.

It was not unusual for criminals to receive letters of support, said Dr Mike Berry, a psychologist at Manchester Metropolitan University. Even sex murderers such as Peter Sutcliffe receive love letters and offers of marriage, he reveals. 'Writers often feel they can help or change the prisoners, usually without much success,' he said. 'But there is a risk of the writer getting conned and emotionally hurt by the prisoner.'

As well as investigating Fritzl's possible involvement in the murders of 17-year-old Martina Posch in 1986 and Anna Neumauer, also 17, in 1966, the police are also looking into the possibility that he was involved in the unresolved murder of a Czech prostitute. According to the German newspaper *Bild*, the police were trying to establish a possible connection between Fritzl and the murder of Gabriele Supekova, a 42-year-old prostitute whose body was found near the Austrian border in August 2007, where Fritzl is said to have spent time on holiday. And they have reopened the case of 16-year-old Julia Kuehrer, who disappeared from Pulkau, 60 miles from Amstetten, in June 2006.

12

MOTHER'S DAY

Mother's Day in Austria is celebrated on the second Sunday in May, as it is in the USA and Canada. In 2008, it fell on 11 May, just three weeks after Elisabeth Fritzl and her two boys were freed from the dungeon. For the first time, Elisabeth could celebrate Mother's Day with the three children who had been taken from her at birth. A source at the clinic said, 'If ever a mum deserved a Mother's Day hug, Elisabeth does. But as they're all still getting used to the simple things in life, it wasn't a huge party.'

Nevertheless, Elisabeth's children gave her flowers and they all sat down for lunch together as a family at a flower-strewn table.

'It was a touching scene,' said an insider, and hospital staff were optimistic about the future. 'There are signs of a happy unit beginning to form,' the clinic source said.

For the first time in 24 years, Elisabeth herself was able to spend Mother's Day with her own mother. However, there were still concerns about her health. At that time, she was still not well enough to talk to the police, who were eager to firm up murder charges against Fritzl. Officers believe there is sufficient evidence to hold him responsible for the death of Alexander's twin brother Michael.

In her initial eight-page statement, given when she first emerged from the dungeon, Elisabeth said she had given birth to twins Michael and Alexander alone. But by the time Fritzl visited three days later, Michael was dead. Fritzl then burned the child's corpse in the household incinerator and Alexander was taken to be raised upstairs. The police said they were still keeping an open mind as to whether there was enough information to decide if his neglect of Elisabeth and her baby constituted murder. To bring a murder charge, they would have to prove that Michael would have survived had Fritzl not denied the child appropriate and timely medical attention.

Meanwhile, Stefan, Felix and Kerstin were issued with birth certificates and proof of Austrian citizenship, which means that, at last, they officially exist. Until then Kerstin, Stefan and five-year-old Felix were not registered because their father had kept their births a secret, but Elisabeth managed to record the dates of their births, which she provided to the authorities.

Given her condition, it is thought that Elisabeth will remain in the clinic for months and she will need treatment for many years to come. However, their solicitor Christoph Herbst, a regular visitor, said that the family live a 'more or less regular life' in the Mauer clinic. 'They rise at about six or seven in the morning,' he said, 'then they have breakfast together. They get the breakfast from the hospital. Then they sit together at a large table and talk, discuss and make jokes.'

Afterwards, the cellar-children enjoyed activities denied them in the cellar, aided by their above-ground siblings. 'Then everybody does their own thing,' said Herbst. 'They play on the computer, they read books, do some drawings, whatever they want. It's very amazing to watch the family because they behave like a normal family.'

He was also full of praise for Elisabeth. 'Elisabeth is a tower of strength. She's happy now for the first time,' he said. 'Her biggest wish now is to have the family together. They need time to heal and to grow together. Everything else is secondary for her.'

Herbst also praised her efforts to bring some semblance of normality to her children's lives in the cellar. 'Elisabeth tried to educate the children in the dungeon,' he said. 'They had lessons, they learned grammar, they learned the language, mathematics. So they have been raised very well, they are very well behaved; it is really astounding. If you meet Stefan, he is a very polite and educated person. I think Elisabeth tried to give them a structure and a good life under the circumstances in the dungeon.'

He said that Elisabeth was reacting well to her belated return to life outside the cellar. 'Elisabeth is very happy to be rediscovering the world,' he said. 'She is very keen to go outside and feel the rain on her skin. But it is important for them to adjust slowly. For now they just talk to each other.'

Elisabeth and the children who lived in the cellar have no concept of time or of the future, he said. 'Some people who hear the story think Elisabeth is like something from a horror film but rumours that she has no teeth and cannot talk are not true. If you met her, you would not realise what she has been through, as she seems just like every normal person. She tells her family that all she longs for is a normal life – or as normal a life as they can get. That's her only wish.'

Herbst also complained of misreporting and said that huge strides had been made since the family first emerged. 'There are a lot of things that have been reported badly or wrongly. I mean, first, the children speak normal German; they communicate as anybody does; they walk as anybody does. And also what has been reported about Elisabeth ... I mean, she is a normal-looking woman, a very attractive person, if you meet her and see her. You know, the most important point right now is that she has the feeling that the kids are happy, that they feel comfortable and that gives her the best relief.'

Since Elisabeth Fritzl was imprisoned 24 years ago much has changed, but she still retains a basic knowledge of the world that she can build on. 'Elisabeth, let's say, is let back out into a world she once knew and which she can remember and which has been reflected on television,' said Professor Friedrich of Vienna University. 'The others, the children, will be let out and will have to be taught how to live. And those senses that weren't stimulated downstairs will have to be stimulated. For example, rain makes a swishing sound. You can hear how the wind rustles the leaves in the trees. And when you go for a walk in the woods on a rainy day, the earth gives off a certain scent. So all sorts of completely new sensations hit you.'

Christoph Herbst has witnessed this with his own eyes. 'Some days ago it rained and Felix said, "I want to see for the first time rain because I have never experienced that,"' he recalled. 'If you hear that you realise, yes, he didn't see that before. So I think he still has a lot of things to experience.'

Life was also difficult for the three other children, who were living upstairs, because they now had to live in semi-darkness with their mother and brothers at the clinic.

However, they were coping well. 'They are all happy and there is a lot of laughter, which you might not expect,' said Herbst. 'Felix makes everyone laugh. They are teaching him to run because inside the cellar he could not run. It is really brilliant how Elisabeth has reacted to the outside world. They are all rather fine. Elisabeth is really an impressive person; she is very strong.'

Elisabeth had also been visited by local priest Peter Boesendorfer, who was impressed with her progress. 'Elisabeth is seeking out staff to speak to in the hospital,' he said. 'It is a good sign that she is looking to chat to new people. No one can believe how normal she appears, but I suspect it hasn't really hit her yet.'

However, Rosemarie was not coping so well. It was hard for her to take in the enormity of what had happened. Up to this point, she had been unable to speak, formally, to the police. As a loving mother and grandmother, it was impossible for her not to be affected by their suffering.

And there is another burden that she must bear; although she had been officially exonerated, people were still asking how it could be possible that she did not know what her husband had been up to all those years – a question that she must have asked herself many, many times. With the benefit of hindsight, she must have realised that there were a hundred telltale signs that she could have followed up on, had she not been so intimidated by Fritzl.

However 'healing' the immediate post-release period appears to have been for the family, some doubt the sense in putting mother and daughter back together again. 'I have the impression that the doctors and therapists are reviving a family system that has proven to be damaging for Elisabeth Fritzl in the past,' said Helene Klaar, a Vienna lawyer specialising in family law. 'It is difficult to understand why Elisabeth Fritzl must now live with her mother, the same woman who never helped her as she was abused by her father.'

As the first few weeks of freedom ticked by, Elisabeth was desperately worried about Kerstin, who was then still critically ill in the hospital's intensive care unit. Her condition had stabilised but doctors were waiting to discover the effect of total organ failure on her brain and, after a month-and-a-half, it was reported that they were slowly beginning to bring her round from the coma by gradually reducing the dosage of the drugs used to keep her in an artificial sleep.

A hospital spokesman said, 'The doctors are very optimistic about the future development but, at this stage, it is impossible to say how long it will take before she actually wakes up.'

Otherwise, Elisabeth was preoccupied with the day-to-day business of raising her family.

'Doctors are controlling the family's treatment,' a clinic source said. 'But Elisabeth is the figurehead who gets them together for three square meals a day. She had the kids in a routine during their time in the cellar and she won't let that go. There's actually a lot of laughing and joking.'

For the first few weeks, the family spent much of their time watching Disney DVDs together and reading letters of support from around the world. Even though they had emerged from the dungeon weeks before, Elisabeth and her youngest son Felix still had to wear dark glasses because their eyes were so sensitive to light. However, one source said, 'Their skin is getting better and getting darker and they're growing accustomed to the light.'

Elisabeth still had to calm the boys, who both suffered panic attacks sparked by the grim memories of their long incarceration and years of being starved of oxygen. They also suffered from ringworm, a fungal skin condition caused by living in dank conditions.

Felix was progressing well, because of his youth. He learnt to run about freely inside the sprawling hospital complex. The staff were delighted to spend time with him because, for Felix, everything was new and exciting. 'They are teaching him to run,' said Christoph Herbst. 'He delights in every new discovery. This week, he saw rain for the first time. He was fascinated by it. Elisabeth is really happy in the pleasure he has in his new freedom. All she wants is for the family to heal and grow together.'

But Stefan was struggling to cope. After 18 years in a cramped cellar, he was left battling motor-skill difficulties. In the outside world, he encountered problems with co-ordination. It was suspected that he was suffering from serious motor neurone problems and has difficulty in moving as a result.

Psychologically, he was having difficulties, too. He would choose to sit by his fish tank all day in the family's darkened quarters inside the hospital – much as he did in the cellar.

Despite claims from the clinic that the family were interacting well and recovering faster than expected, experts have voiced fears that the decision to place all family members together may not necessarily turn out to be the best solution in the long term. 'Placing the family together can only be the very first step, until the beginning of the process of dealing with the conflicts within the family,' said Eva Mueckstein, the president of the Austrian Association of Psychotherapists.

There were bound to be conflicts between children brought up above ground, who led a relatively normal life, excelling at school and playing musical instruments, and their siblings who lived in the dungeon and who were only starting to adapt to the outside world. The upstairs children were now receiving private tuition, but were finding life locked away in the hospital frustrating.

'It is very difficult right now for Alex, Lisa and Monika, who lived together with their grandma upstairs,' said Christoph Herbst. 'They cannot see their friends; they cannot meet their classmates. They even miss school. And this is something that is very hard for them. They are just asking when can they meet them again, when can they go to school again. And we all hope this will happen pretty soon because they have to have their normal life again.'

For the moment, though, they were being strong. 'Lisa, Monika and Alexander are keen to see their friends again,' said a visitor. 'They are being as positive as possible, but it's been very hard for them to adapt to life inside. Despite their joy at being with Elisabeth and the rest of their family, it's almost like they are now in a prison themselves. They are being very good but it's tough.'

The upstairs children handed their mobile phones in when they first arrived at the clinic and have not spoken to anyone outside since. The plan was to send them back into the outside world in September, but it still had to be decided whether they would return to their old schools or begin afresh elsewhere. The family lawyer, Christoph Herbst, has looked into the possibility of providing them with new identities to allow them to get on with their lives. There were also rumours that they planned to relocate to a nearby country – even England was mentioned – to get away from anyone who knew them so that they could live life in relative anonymity.

But it has also been pointed out that rifts could well become acute between the upstairs and downstairs children who have had to cope with vastly different pressures and upbringings. Several psychologists pointed out that the above-ground 'foundlings' are well educated, sophisticated and sociable, while those from the cellar have yet to learn even the most basic life skills, such as crossing the road, using the telephone or buying something in a shop.

Dr Kepplinger defended the treatment of the children in the clinic. He said that each member of the Fritzl family was receiving a treatment that had been tailored to their individual needs. 'The team of therapists is trying to adapt to the special needs of individual family members but I would like to emphasise once more that the family will need a lot of time.'

The rambling, wooded grounds of the Landesklinikum psychiatric hospital in Amstetten-Mauer were to be the setting for Elisabeth, Stefan and Felix's introduction to the world. When doctors believed they could cope with the kaleidoscope of colours they had only seen previously on TV, they were let out of the darkened clinic and finally emerged into the light. Dr Kepplinger had given his consent to the expedition after closely monitoring them. Their first steps into the outside world were in a secret garden protected by dense foliage. The doctors let Elisabeth and the two boys spend some time outdoors, walking around in daylight as part of their tentative steps towards recovery.

'The light sensitivity has almost disappeared,' said a source in the clinic. 'None of them are wearing goggles now – they are ready for daylight.'

The two boys were amazed at the world they saw around them. They marvelled at the sunshine, woodland and fish in the pond. It soon became a daily routine for Elisabeth to go out for walks with Stefan and Felix. But despite the evident progress they were making, the doctors decided that the Fritzls would not be ready to return home any time soon.

'What is now clear is that the family will need to remain here for several more months,' said the clinic head Dr Kepplinger. 'To give them a good start in their new life, they all need to be very carefully protected and very slowly reintroduced to the real world, and to each other. In particular, Elisabeth and her two children from the cellar need to have further therapy to help them adjust to the light after years in semi-darkness. They also needed treatment to help them cope with all the extra space that they now have in which to move about.'

However, their forays into the outside world soon caused problems because of the intense media interest in the family. Since they had been released from the dungeon, the clinic had been besieged by journalists and TV crews all hoping to catch a glimpse of them.

Dr Kepplinger complained that the family was unable to walk freely outside because of the huge number of journalists who had descended on Amstetten from all over the world. In effect, he said, the Fritzl children had been 'imprisoned for the second time' following their trauma in the cellar. During the first week, the hospital management complained that 22 paparazzi had to be escorted from the premises after sneaking into the clinic to try and get exclusive pictures of the Fritzls. Since then, it had been necessary to call in an élite police force, police dogs, and local volunteer firefighters, as well as a private security firm to guard the hospital.

Some of the photographers had even constructed bird-watcher's hides. 'The paparazzi dig holes in the ground, cover them with aluminium foil to fool infra-red detectors, then hide in them with their cameras, covered in army camouflage blankets,' said hospital security chief Richard Riegler. 'Until now, we've caught all of them but I don't know how long this will last.'

Photographers from around the world camped outside the clinic hoping to snatch the first pictures of the Fritzl family then in residence. The asking price for a picture of the unseen Elisabeth Fritzl rose to $1 million, according to Austrian media, and the paparazzi became desperate to claim the prize.

'The greed of some reporters clearly knows no bounds,' said District Governor Hans-Heinz Lenze.

One night, a photographer managed to climb the 19th-century façade of the clinic to reach the third-floor balcony next to the rooms where the family were being kept, but the screams of a nurse alerted security officers who apprehended the man after a short struggle. During the altercation, one of the security officers fell from the balcony and was injured.

Another paparazzo tried to take pictures of the Fritzl family through the clinic fence as they played in the garden. He was chased away by a security guard, but the photographer then hid behind a tree and, when the guard caught up with him, hit him across the neck and shoulders with a stick. The 30-year-old guard was knocked out and sent to hospital with minor injuries but the photographer escaped.

Starved of news, speculation took over. According to *Österreich*, doctors hid the Fritzl kids in groups of other children so they could go out in the open. The newspaper also claimed their mother Elisabeth had been disguised as a nurse so that she could have a walk outside unnoticed.

'Otherwise they cannot go outside because there are so many paparazzi who want to take photographs,' said Christoph Herbst. 'This is something that imposes on them again, the feeling of being captured.' Dr Kepplinger then issued an urgent plea to the media to stop staking out the clinic and to leave his patients in peace. 'The family needs time now,' he said. 'They clearly have no desire for publicity and have a right to privacy after the terrible ordeal they have gone through.'

Amstetten's District Governor Hans-Heinz Lenze rode to the rescue again. He said he had instructed police to take down the personal details of all photographers caught trying to get into the clinic and, where possible, to make a complaint to the relevant press regulation bodies. Lenze said British photographers were being singled out because they were the main perpetrators, although journalists from other countries have also been stopped from trying to gain entry to the clinic. He added that he was looking into making a formal complaint about the activities of UK photo-journalists to the Press Complaints Commission.

'We have been in touch with the Press Complaints Commission, who have said they can accept complaints about British journalists operating abroad,' said Lenze, 'and that sneaking into hospital dressed as cleaners or policemen would definitely fit in their remit. From now on, names will be passed on as soon as we have them.'

However, publicity did bring its benefits. Along with the cards and letters, well-wishers have sent piles of gifts. One of them sent Felix a scooter which he quickly learnt to ride.

'Felix loves his new scooter the most,' said a hospital source, 'and is endlessly spending time whizzing around the grounds.'

He was also taken to McDonald's by his carers. Hospital staff said that Felix was thrilled to travel the three miles to visit the restaurant where he enjoyed a Happy Meal. 'He loved it,' a source said.

Although he had seen their ads on television, Felix did not believe McDonald's really existed. To manage his expectations in the cellar, he had been told that the burger chain was fiction. His secret trip to sample a burger and fries was the five-year-old's first outing from the psychiatric clinic since he had been freed from the dungeon. He was accompanied by nurses and wore sunglasses to protect his eyes from daylight.

'Felix is loving his freedom,' said a hospital source. 'He's made so much progress since he arrived at the clinic three weeks ago. He loved going to McDonald's but is also fascinated by cars and loves going out in them.'

His above-ground siblings Alexander, Monika and Lisa joined him on the outing. They were also said to have been making signs of 'real progress'. At that time, Stefan had yet to leave the clinic and it was thought that it would take some time before he was up to it.

Elisabeth was visited in hospital by her big brother, Harald, who tried to comfort her. He had left home when his sister vanished, after falling for his father's lie that she had joined a religious cult. Her closest sibling, Harald has been left guilt-ridden and shattered.

Elisabeth's younger sister, Gabriele Helm, now in her late thirties, broke down when she met her sister and joined the rest of the family in therapy to cope with the shock. 'None of us can believe how normal Elisabeth seems,' said

Gabriele. 'She is healthy and very chatty and doing very well; every day she gets a bit stronger. I can't say what the family is going through. It is more than anyone can believe; it has devastated us. We are working together to support Elisabeth. She is overjoyed to see her children. She told them they were beautiful and she is spending all the time getting to know them.'

Her husband Juergen Helm was equally shocked by what had happened. 'I have lived in the house for three years and have been in the cellar at least once,' he said. 'It was scattered with junk and I had no idea this family was living a few metres away. It's incredible.'

Family friend Elfriede Hoera said she now hoped the family would be able to rally round in a desperate attempt to rebuild their shattered lives. She put her faith in older sister Ulrike to pull them together. 'Ulrike is the strong one,' Elfriede said. 'She stood up to Fritzl as a child and I believe she will help pull everyone through.'

However, sources close to the family said, shockingly, that Elisabeth still loved her father in what may be a version of the Stockholm Syndrome, where hostages come to identify with their captors. While Elisabeth has vowed that she will never again come face to face with the monster who raped and abused her for years, like it or not, he is still her father.

The other residents of Amstetten were also struggling to deal with the enormity of the crime as more details of the so-called 'House of Horrors' unfolded. As the world's media filled the streets, a vigil was planned in the town as a show of solidarity towards Elisabeth and her children. On the night of 29 April – three days after Elisabeth and her two boys had been freed – some 200 people gathered in the quaint market square in Amstetten in the rain, holding candles and umbrellas. Flowers were laid outside 40 Ybbsstrasse by sympathisers. Many were shocked. Until the previous weekend, the pretty Austrian town's main claim to fame was its apple wine; now it would for ever be associated with the Fritzl family. The supporters were angry with the authorities for not having noticed that something was going terribly wrong; they also felt guilty because they had not spotted anything themselves.

In the town square, they unfurled banners, carrying message of sympathy for everything Elisabeth and her children had suffered. A speaker at the vigil expressed the 'bewilderment, shock, paralysis and speechlessness' of the people of Amstetten, who asked 'to be informed and look for answers'.

A young mother named Stefanie explained why they were there. 'We need to show the world we are not bad,' she said. 'We do care about each other.'

When the Fritzl family, recovering in the nearby Mauer clinic, heard of the town's sympathetic response, they showed their gratitude for the support with a large hand-made poster, which was exhibited in a shop window in the centre of town. The central message read, 'We, the whole family, would like to take this opportunity to thank you for your sympathy for our fate. Your compassion is really helping us get through this difficult time and shows us that there are good and honest people out there who care for us. We hope that the time will soon come when we can find our way back to a normal life.'

The thank-you message was encircled by outlines of their hands. Each had an individual message inside expressing what they wished for and what they missed.

Stefan wrote, 'I miss my sister. I am enjoying freedom and my family. I like the sun, fresh air and nature.'

His younger brother Felix simply listed some of the things he was enjoying in the outside world – 'Sleigh rides, driving in a car, playing ball, swimming ... Playing with other children, friendship, running in the meadows.'

Lisa wrote, 'Wishes – health, that everything turns out well again, love, happiness. Misses – Kerstin, school, friends, fresh air, Class 1C.' Monika wrote, 'Wishes – that Kerstin gets better, lots of love, that everything is soon past. Misses – fire brigade [an Austrian youth group], music school, friends, school, Kerstin.'

And Alexander's wishes and misses read, 'I wish for freedom, power and strength, and the sun. I miss fire brigade, school and my sister Kerstin.'

The adults also made a contribution. Rosemarie – grandma – wrote, 'I wish to live with my children in peace with the help of God. I miss my kind friends and my freedom.'

Elisabeth said, 'Wishes – my daughter Kerstin's recovery, my children's love, protection for my family, people with warm hearts and understanding.'

The poster was completed with a heart-shape to represent Kerstin.

Family lawyer Christoph Herbst explained, 'The initiative for the public address in a form of a poster came from the family themselves. It is their wish to thank the community for the support.'

Although the people of Amstetten were touched, the poster did nothing to stop their relentless self-examination. On the May Day bank holiday, the day the town traditionally set aside to celebrate the beginning of summer, families stayed inside, haunted by the shadow of Josef Fritzl.

MOTHER'S DAY

A neighbour watching as forensic scientists removed boxes of belongings from the underground prison told reporters that the community was gripped by guilt at having let Elisabeth languish in an airless cell for so long. But what could they have done? 'Had we noticed anything, we'd have said something,' he said, refusing to give his name.

One neighbour recalled Fritzl's 'immaculate cravat', another his 'decent posture'. But the discovery of the crimes of retired grandfather Josef Fritzl – until then the epitome of upright Austrian life – had shattered every illusion. A painted sign left on Fritzl's garden fence said it all: '*WARUM? Hat es keiner gemerkt?*' – 'WHY? Did nobody notice?'

Twenty-six-year-old Edison Rafael said, 'It's essential these questions are asked. How on earth can a man carry out such a complex, harmful operation for so many years without anybody in a tight-knit neighbourhood having a clue? We have to start talking about it and stop brushing things under the carpet.'

But Wolf Gruber, one of Fritzl's neighbours, struck back at any implied criticism. 'Much has been made of the neighbours failing to notice anything funny going on,' he said, 'but the fact is that you can't see anything that's going on in the Fritzl house from the outside. Everything is concealed.'

It seems that Fritzl was lucky in his choice of immediate neighbours. On one side there was an elderly lady who eventually went into care, leaving the house empty. Beyond that lived a couple who spent their weekdays in Vienna. Fritzl's nearest neighbours were Herbert and Regina Penz, who lived three doors away and they saw nothing.

'Nobody in this street noticed anything at all,' said Herbert Penz.

'What are you meant to spot around here?' said his wife Regina. 'All the gardens are open, while Herr Fritzl's is all concealed, built up and the few open spaces are covered by trees and bushes. You can't see anything.'

And Fritzl guarded his privacy.

'A neighbour wanted to prune the hedge last year,' said Regina Penz, 'but Herr Fritzl said, "No, leave it." And if someone doesn't want people seeing into their garden, you have to accept it. Other than that, you can't see anything.'

The Fritzls kept themselves to themselves.

'The Fritzl family never came to any of the garden parties we used to have around here,' said Herbert Penz. 'They never came. So, in the end, basically, people stopped inviting them because everyone knew that the Fritzls would never come to any kind of party.'

It was known that Josef Fritzl had been a successful and respected engineer and that DIY was his hobby. 'Herr Fritzl was always hard-working,' said Herbert Penz. 'We often heard the noise of the cement mixer. I think that Herr Fritzl did most of the building work himself. We thought he was adding on an extra room to rent out, or something like that.'

The neighbours also knew of his reputation as a disciplinarian. 'I did hear talk among the neighbours that Herr Fritzl was very firm with his children,' said Herbert Penz. 'And that absolute obedience to Herr Fritzl prevailed. His wife, too, was very submissive towards him; we all knew it. He was very domineering with his family.'

His wife Regina concurred, 'He was very strict.'

'He was strict and people discussed it and knew about it,' said Herbert Penz.

Even though Fritzl's harsh behaviour was widely known, he

was not condemned for it. At the time, in the eyes of the neighbours, Elisabeth herself was to blame. 'Apparently, Elisabeth had already caused trouble before,' said Regina Penz. 'She had disappeared once before and then turned up again. But if there are seven children, one of them is bound to be trouble. You have to accept that these things happen. It doesn't mean you've done anything wrong as a parent.'

Number 40 Ybbsstrasse is now an attraction for ghoulish sightseers. Hordes of tourists from across Austria, Germany and Hungary have turned up outside the property, with some posing for pictures. Locals complained to police about the numbers arriving but officers said they were powerless to act.

'It is bad enough that journalists and TV crews have beleaguered our town,' said one Amstetten resident, 'but now there is this ghoulish tourism with people coming to Amstetten just to see the house in Ybbsstrasse. It is appalling … we just want to be left in peace.'

The three-storey Fritzl home facing one of Amstetten's main roads has also been put on the route of a sightseeing bus tour which now routinely stops in front of it. One tour operator was said to be handing out mock business cards with Josef Fritzl's address and work details as a sick souvenir.

'There are more and more tourists turning up to have their picture taken in front of the house,' said the police. 'It has become a sort of pilgrimage site.'

Even one of Monika Fritzl's teachers turned up with Monika's classmates to see the goings-on around the dungeon. 'The children are desperate to see it for themselves,' she explained. 'There's no point keeping it from them, that will only make it worse, and they'll find out anyway because it's all anyone's talking about.'

After the initial shock, other people who knew Fritzl in Amstetten spoke up about their suspicions. Franz Haider, now 58, who worked under Fritzl for three months in 1969 at a local cement and building supply company, Zehetner Baustoffhandel und Betonwerk, was unsurprised. He believed he was the sort of man capable of keeping a secret for years, even a monstrous one. 'It's the kind of thing he would do,' he said.

Although Haider insisted that he would never have believed a crime like Fritzl's to be possible in Amstetten, now that it had occurred, he said, he cannot imagine anyone more capable of concealing such a secret for 24 years. As well as being secretive, Fritzl had all the necessary technical expertise. 'Concrete technology was Fritzl's specialty,' said Haider. 'He could have built anything himself.'

When Haider worked with Fritzl, their department was developing a machine to pour concrete pipes, such as those used in sewage systems. Fritzl was the technical director of the project and spent months developing a large and complicated machine, 5 metres tall, 3 metres wide and 3 metres deep to do the job. Haider joined the project later as an assistant. He said that, in the time he worked with him, all that he learned from Fritzl, other than matters concerning the machine, was that his boss was married. Other than that, Fritzl remained tight-lipped about his private life. He never had any personal phone calls and there were no family photos on his desk. He did not even tell Haider that he had children.

Gertrud Ramharter, a neighbour who lived across the street on Ybbsstrasse, said that she repeatedly heard hammering and construction noise coming from the Fritzl property. She did wonder what was going on, she admits today. 'What's he building? And how big is it going to be?' she would ask herself. Unfortunately, she did not ask anyone else, or complain about the noise or the building work.

Others who have come forward to say they knew 73-year-old Fritzl were also being questioned. 'We're casting a wide net. It's a lot of work,' Chief Inspector Etz said.

But the police remained puzzled by the case. 'We still find it hard to believe that no one – no neighbour, family member or acquaintance – noticed anything,' said Chief Investigator Polzer, who headed up the police investigation. Meanwhile, around the world, people were saying exactly the same thing.

13

BACK IN THE CELLAR

As Fritzl refused to answer any further questions and neither the family, tenants nor the neighbours knew anything more, the police had to turn to forensics to piece together the story of what had happened below ground for the past 24 years. Their job was gruelling. Doing forensic work in the cramped cellar was 'oppressive', admitted Chief Investigator Polzer. Officers could only work one hour at a time below ground because of the lack of oxygen in the windowless dungeon.

'There is so little oxygen that the victims would have had to spend nearly all their time lying or sitting down,' one officer stated.

The forensics team said that the atmosphere underground was so lacking in oxygen that if any more than four officers were admitted to the bunker at any one time, they had great difficulty in breathing.

Other investigators stayed away but, as head of the investigation, Colonel Polzer had to visit the scene of the crime. 'I went to see this dungeon – this prison – for myself once,' said Polzer. 'I went through it and was very glad to be able to leave. The environment in this room where the ceiling was kept very low, less than 6 feet at the highest point, was anything but pleasant. Everyday living, personal hygiene, etc., must have kept the level of humidity high.'

Visiting the cellar played tricks with the imagination – it was all too easy to visualise the horror of being locked in, and not knowing if you would ever see daylight again. If police forensics experts could only work down there for an hour at a time, what must it have been like to live down there for days, weeks, months and years on end?

'If we sat down and attempted to capture those years in a few lines, or a brief report, or even a documentary, we would not succeed,' said Polzer, 'because I believe that, in those 24 years, life must had felt as if it lasted ten times as long as real time.'

There can be no doubt that for the captives being sealed in this airless vault, barely able to move, time must have hung heavy on their hands.

Investigators found two heavily-reinforced concrete doors that could only be opened by remote control. When closed, they were hermetically sealed and the only air came in through a small ventilation shaft. But even when they were opened, the air inside remained fetid and the investigators looked for some other way to ventilate the bunker.

'We are trying to find another way out of this room because the working conditions in this prison are so exceptional,' said Polzer, going on to compare entering the cellar to climbing into an old submarine and then submerging. He said that officers with years of experience of crime scenes have been shocked to the core on entering one of the tiny rooms and being confronted by the reality of what it must have been like to live under those conditions. 'What the officers had to look at down there was terrible,' said Polzer.

The police said the cellar was damp and covered in mildew and that, as a result, its inhabitants were suffering from fungal infections. But what most affected the investigators was finding the pitiful drawings made by the three children kept in the tiny, dark space since their birth.

The dungeon where Elisabeth and the kids lived was impossibly remote from the world outside. It lay deep below ground at the end of a labyrinth – you had passed through the five different rooms in the cellar and eight locked doors even to reach its entrance. Fritzl had installed a number of complex electronic locks. It was the sort of security you would expect to see on a bank vault.

On reaching Fritzl's subterranean workshop, the entrance to the dungeon was not immediately obvious. It was hidden behind a shelving unit stacked with tins of paint. This had to be moved to one side to reveal the entrance to the dungeon, a one-metre-high reinforced concrete door. The steel frame of the door had been sprayed with concrete, making it so heavy that it took four firemen to shift it. Fritzl only moved it with the aid of an electric motor. If that had failed, the cellar family would have been trapped, sealed in their tomb for ever.

No casual visitor would even have got as far as the workshop; it was out of bounds. Fritzl's son-in-law Juergen Helm admitted he had been down to the cellar, but he had no reason to suspect that there was a hidden doorway behind the shelves. Fritzl's son also had access to the cellar, but – according to all reports – he was rather slow on the uptake and, anyway, he was completely under the thumb of his father. Otherwise, the entire cellar area and workshop was strictly off limits to Fritzl family members, friends and the tenants who lived upstairs.

'Whoever enters it will be given immediate notice,' one former tenant was told.

This was also made clear to Joseph Leitner, Alfred Dubanovsky and Sabine and Thomas Kirschbichler, who had all lived in the house.

The secret door was electronically locked and could only be opened with a special code and a remote control, which Fritzl carried with him at all times. To get through the tiny entrance, you had to bend double. From the doorway, there was a narrow passageway leading into a series of rooms with an area of approximately 650 square feet (60 square metres). The floor was bumpy and uneven. Nowhere was the ceiling more than 5 feet 6 inches (1.7 metres) high. A narrow corridor, barely a foot (30 centimetres) wide and 16 feet (5 metres) long, led to an area where there were cooking facilities and a small bathroom with a shower. A tube connected to the living area provided some barely adequate ventilation for the four people living 24 hours a day, seven days a week down there.

The entire cellar was small, stifling and dark, lit only by dim electric bulbs. Exposed pipes lined the moisture-drenched walls. There were scant furnishings and possessions apart from the television, video player, a radio and the children's paintings and posters were hung on the walls. From the very first room containing the kitchen and bathroom, investigators were left feeling sick. The shower was covered in mould, and the toilet was in a 'catastrophic' state, investigators said. With the doors hermetically sealed, no fresh air could get in and no stale air or moisture could not escape.

BACK IN THE CELLAR

The small bathroom contained a tiny hip bath with a shower decorated with pictures of an octopus and a flower. On the other side of a short partition was a hand basin, with a cupboard above holding a toothbrush and other toiletry items. Next to it was a hand towel. A red hot-water bottle also hung there. There was a peg on the wall where Elisabeth hung a white bathrobe, and a small table that she covered with a bright orange plastic tablecloth. Nearby were small hot plates for cooking.

A further corridor led to two bedrooms, separated by a thin partition; each contained two beds. The Austrian police have refused to release pictures of the victims' sleeping areas or possessions to the press, saying they wished to protect their privacy. However, it is known that no door or curtain separated the bedrooms – or any other room – which confirmed that Fritzl sexually assaulted his daughter Elisabeth in clear view of their children. He was totally without shame. With no door or screen around the bathroom and lavatory, all other bodily functions had to be conducted in full view of the other occupants.

At least part of the dungeon appeared to be padded and the whole vault was well sound-proofed, but it made no difference. It was so far underground that no sound could be heard. No noise from the outside world could penetrate the thick concrete walls and no scream, however loud, could escape. The ventilation shaft was of the type designed for nuclear bunkers, so it had baffles to deaden the blast and filters to prevent fall-out passing down it with the air – which also meant that sound could not travel along it. The dungeon was totally isolated, an enclosed, silent world, completely detached from anything going on around it.

The filtration system in the ventilation shaft would have restricted the air flow running through it, depleting the oxygen supply. But then nuclear shelters were only designed to be occupied for a couple of weeks before the occupants were to venture outside – not months and years on end. With little airflow and insulated walls, the heat generated by four bodies, cooking, hot water and even the fridge and freezer and other electrical appliances would have made it unbearably hot. Add to that the humidity produced by washing, bathing and cooking, and it is not hard to imagine that it was like living in a sauna.

The rooms were described as being neat and tidy, the police said – a tribute to Elisabeth's housekeeping skills. However, officers complained that the stench in the cellar was 'almost unbearable'. There was nothing she could have done about this; there was no way to vent the smell of cooking or human habitation. With no windows, only artificial light, no fresh air and no room to exercise or run around, it was no wonder Elisabeth and the children were ill. Doctors said the lack of oxygen may have contributed to Kerstin's condition.

The forensic team had to comb the scene for weeks on end, their work-rate hampered by the lack of oxygen. 'Investigators wearing special clothes and masks can work there for only one hour,' said Polzer, 'and during this hour they try, one team after the other, to gather everything available in this living space and search particularly for DNA traces to establish if the alleged criminal really committed this on his own. Not until then can we start with technical investigations like sonar probes, cavity and sound measurements, and also to comprehend all the electric and electronic systems.'

DNA analysis of samples taken from the cellar eventually

confirmed that Fritzl had worked alone. Gerhard Sedlacek, a prosecution spokesman, later said that forensic experts found no traces of DNA in the cellar prison belonging to anyone except Fritzl and his captive family, and that Elisabeth told detectives that she never saw or suspected anyone else to have been in the cellar. But plenty more was to be done.

Even a week after its discovery, Chief Investigator Polzer said, 'There are still areas we haven't found inside the dungeon and I expect it to take at least two weeks before we have answered all the questions we need to about how Fritzl controlled the areas and imprisoned the children.'

It soon became plain to the investigators that Fritzl's building work was not yet over. The police searched the earth- and rubble-filled rooms adjacent to the 60-square-metre windowless living quarters they already knew about. 'Areas of the dungeon appear to have been under construction and it is possible Fritzl may have been planning to expand it even further,' said Polzer, possibly belying Fritzl's claim that he intended to release his captives all along. 'The man is evil beyond words,' Polzer continued. 'The misery he has inflicted on his family is unimaginable.'

Even three weeks into the investigation, officers were breaking through old walls underground to reach the hidden rooms. Forensic experts also examined the electrical, plumbing and security features of the dungeon to see whether Fritzl could have built it himself or had help from someone else. In the end, they concluded that he had acted alone, although his unfortunate daughter had been forced to help with the manual labour, despite her frail condition. Together with her father, they had dug out 200 tons – 17 truckloads – of earth which he had somehow disposed of.

The police remain baffled. They also want to know how Fritzl was able to take two beds into the cellar in 1993 without his wife or neighbours noticing. He later took a large washing machine underground, again without raising suspicions. Freezers, fridges and food were also shifted without inviting questions. And the 'plumber' who Alfred Dubanovsky said he saw going down into the cellar has still not been identified or come forward.

As Fritzl was the subject of a murder investigation, police teams wearing T-shirts bearing the legend 'Trained to search for human bodies' were brought in. They used sniffer dogs to search the site for human remains.

'If there's anything down there, our dogs will find it,' one of the handlers said. 'We will keep them working until we're satisfied the job has been done.' They were unable to find any traces of bodies or leads to other victims.

Forensic archaeologists were also called in. They used sonar and ground-penetrating radars to probe the area around the house, looking for graves and buried body parts in the garden. The police also used sonar probes to discover the full extent of the underground bunker complex. They suspected that there were further hidden rooms under 40 Ybbsstrasse and the surrounding area, although none were found. In wartime, it was common to knock through cellar walls into adjoining basements to provide an escape route if a building was bombed.

Detailed searches were also made of the other buildings that Fritzl owned in case they, too, had secret dungeons. However, it is thought that looking after his second family underground at 40 Ybbsstrasse took up so much of his time that it would have been impossible for him to have maintained more captives elsewhere. This time, though, they had to be sure. After all, the police had turned down two earlier opportunities to search 40 Ybbsstrasse after Fritzl's bogus fire-damage claims, not including the time they overlooked searching his home when Elisabeth Fritzl was first reported missing.

According to the police, Fritzl had been planning to build a dungeon in readiness for his daughter for many years. They believe he began his hideous plan as early as 1978 – six years before he imprisoned Elisabeth in the cellar and soon after she alleged that he began sexually abusing her. Despite his protests that he imprisoned her to save her from the world of drugs and was only overwhelmed with the desire to have sex with her later, it seems clear to the police that he intended to imprison her as his sex slave all along. He wanted her all to himself.

When she was a child, he could have sex with her because she could be intimidated into silence and she was his alone. But as Elisabeth grew to womanhood, she would naturally become interested in men her own age, and they would return her interest. Fritzl knew that he would have to face this one day so, by that time, he would need to have a dungeon ready. His wife was living at the guesthouse at the time and so he could work on the construction of the bunker unhindered.

It was no accident that Fritzl imprisoned Elisabeth at the time when she met her first serious boyfriend and had decided to have sex with him. Fritzl prevented this. Indeed, Elisabeth has never enjoyed the innocent pleasures of sex with someone of her own age or someone she cared for. Nor has she known what it is like to have sex voluntarily. All she has ever experienced is the selfish brutality of her callous father. The joy of sexual love which, for most people, is one of the most precious things life has to offer, has been denied to her. It was stolen from her along with freedom, light, fresh air, social interaction and almost everything that makes life worth living.

Amstetten authorities authorised the building of a cellar in 1978. Inspectors examined the project in 1983 – the year before Elisabeth went missing – and did not notice anything suspicious. Afterwards, Fritzl abandoned the plans he had shown the building authorities and secretly expanded the cellar area but the building inspectors did not visit again.

'Today, we know for certain that part of the old cellar and the old house was kept back as a reserve, so to speak,' said Chief Investigator Polzer, 'and that this new house suddenly gained a small space of 30 to 35 square metres [320 to 375 square feet] without anyone noticing. We are now proceeding on the assumption that he had already settled on the plan to build his own personal "*Reich*" as early as 1978 and start a relationship with his daughter Elisabeth in the cellar.'

As well as his reputation for being interested in DIY, Fritzl had another good excuse for his building work, even after the completion of the authorised nuclear air-raid shelter. It was well known locally that he took in lodgers, so his cover story was simply that he was building an extension to the family home in order to take in tenants.

The underground complex the police were now examining was practically palatial compared to the original underground dungeon where Elisabeth was first incarcerated. Until Lisa was born, she was confined to one tiny room. She had lived there alone to start with, then with Kerstin and Stefan. Then, gradually, the dungeon was enlarged over the years. It was thought that Fritzl may also have broken through into a disused cellar and planned to expand out under the garden. Somehow, he managed to carry out this construction work secretly, as well as deliver food and clothing to Elisabeth and the three children without being noticed.

To begin with, she had no cooking area and no facilities for storing food, so she was completely dependent on her father's visits – and the attendant price she would have to pay. The cooking area, where the walls were adorned by children's drawings, and the bedrooms were only added later. Before that, Elisabeth and the two children would have had to eat, sleep and live in a single room with a low ceiling and a floor space of just 20 square metres (215 square feet). That's just 4.5 metres by 4.5 metres, or 14 feet 6 inches by 14 feet 6 inches – smaller than the front room in a standard central London flat and little larger than some prison cells.

Extending the dungeon with Elisabeth and the children captive inside would have only made the nightmare worse. Their tiny living area would have been filled with dust and rubble, and the task itself must have been debilitating due to the lack of oxygen. It took years to extend the dungeon to the modest size it is now. Despite all the difficulties, it is not hard to see why Elisabeth went along with her father's plan. After nine years in the tiny room, helping to extend their living quarters was the only way she could make life better for herself and her children.

14

THE ROAD TO
RECOVERY

Elisabeth Fritzl, Kerstin, Stefan and Felix are now out of the dungeon and in the care of the medical profession. Their imprisonment and ill-treatment at the hands of the monster – a word Fritzl does not like – have left them debilitated, scarred and ill-equipped for life in mainstream society. So what is the long-term prognosis for their recovery? An international team of experts have convened to give their assessment.

According to the British general practitioner Dr Julian Spinks, the children may have been left with deformed, thin and weak limbs due to being starved of sunlight and having no room to run around and play. They could also be at an increased risk of diabetes. 'They've not been exposed to sunlight which will have affected their ability to make vitamin D, the nutrient allowing bones to absorb calcium,' he said. 'This means they could have thin, bendy and pliable bones. It would be similar to osteoporosis but the bones will tend to bend rather than break. They may also have deformed limbs.

The children's muscles will be weak as they've not been able to run around and build strength.'

There are other long-term consequences of vitamin D deficiency. 'We don't know why, but people who have been deprived of vitamin D also tend to be more likely to suffer from type-1 diabetes later in life,' he said, 'and they're also at risk from skin conditions like psoriasis.'

However, Dr Spinks is optimistic about the children's future. 'It's a horrible situation but one which can be remedied,' he said. 'They're still young and can make a recovery if they are given a good diet, the chance to run around and build up strength and are re-introduced slowly to society. With a bit of luck, there will be no permanent damage.'

The cellar captives emerged with the skin of a baby, untouched by sunlight and pure white. Initially, they had to wear sunscreen of at least factor 30 every day when venturing outside to avoid sun damage. According to Doctor Manu Mehra, a skin expert from the cosmetic surgery firm Transform, 'Anyone who has been kept away from sunlight would be very pale and more prone to sunburn and sun-related skin damage.'

On the other hand, there are advantages to not being exposed to the sun. 'They would not have any moles or freckles, which are signs of sun damage,' said Dr Mehra. 'There should be no difference in skin thickness but they would need to wear at least factor 30 suncream every day, even when it is cloudy, until the skin adapts to sun exposure. This could take months. The skin would be the same colour as when they were born as there would be no melanin produced or pigment created.'

Shut off from daylight for years, the children's eyesight

could also be permanently affected. For example, they may never be able to do everyday activities such as driving a car. According to Doctor Rob Hogan, president of the College of Optometrists, 'They are likely to have very large pupils as the size is created by the amount of light received. This means at first they will need sunglasses to go outside as their eyes won't be able to adjust. They will never have had eye examinations, so they may have sight problems and they might not have full visual capacity, meaning they won't be able to drive. And when the brain and eye don't work together properly, it can cause a lazy eye.'

The older children, particularly, may have problems. 'Eyes mature with the brain until the age of about seven,' said Dr Hogan. 'After that, if they are in a situation like this, the visual cortex may not mature to the same degree as normal children.'

Being deprived of light and living on the meagre rations that Fritzl provided would have caused iron-deficiency anaemia, which would leave the children malnourished, underweight and suffering from stunted growth. According to Dr Denise Parish, a dietician from the University of Wales Institute in Cardiff, 'If they've been malnourished, it will show in their growth and weight gain. They could be shorter and underweight compared to other children of their age.'

However, Dr Parish believes the prognosis is good. 'Once they are started back on a normal diet they should recover fairly quickly. Given a balanced diet – three meals a day, five portions of fruit and veg, three portions of carbohydrates, three of protein and some dairy produce – they should catch up with others of their age.'

Though physically the captives should recover quite well,

they may well suffer more profound problems. It was noted when Stefan and Felix emerged from the dungeon that they communicated between themselves in a series of grunts and growls and found conversation with others very difficult. Experts believe that Stefan may never be able to talk properly and, though Felix is young enough to perfect his language skills, his early life may have left a permanent scar. 'We don't know enough about it yet so any diagnosis is speculative, but extreme emotional trauma may mean that they cannot speak properly,' said Professor Susan Edwards, head of clinical language sciences at Reading University. 'If their mother taught them how to talk and they had a TV, you would imagine they could talk. But it may be Fritzl banned them from talking, so they created their own means of communication.'

There are other factors to be considered in the development of language. 'To be able to speak you need to have adequate hearing, intelligence and emotional stability, so one of those could be missing,' said Professor Edwards.

Some research has suggested that once children get past the age of 11 or 12 and cannot speak, they will never be able to master language fully. 'There is a claim that their brains lose the ability to learn grammar – while they will be able to pick up vocabulary they will not be able to fully speak their native tongue,' said Professor Edwards. This may leave Stefan permanently debilitated. Those under the age of 11, however, fare better. 'Young children like Felix have more potential for recovery,' she said.

Prolonged exposure to television as a sole means of experiencing the outside world is also liable to leave its mark. According to Frank Furedi, professor of sociology at Kent University, 'The meaning of anything is specific to our

252

circumstances ... the mother [Elisabeth] would have known what a television was before she entered the cellar. She would have gone into the cellar understanding a TV to be a means of communication and entertainment – she may have even known that it was something used by mothers as a kind of digital babysitter. But for the children, the television would have been very much an artefact, an empty map which they could fill in according to their imagination.'

In such extreme circumstances, this could have profound consequences. 'If your whole life is spent in a cellar, and you've never been outside nor had any contact with other people, then the idea of there being a difference between your reality and an outside reality would be very difficult to conceptualise,' said Professor Furedi. 'There is no point of comparison and therefore, even if you saw people standing outside houses on TV, it would be something that you would not understand.'

Television would have left the children ill-equipped to deal with life outside the dungeon. 'They will be quite bewildered by the world,' said clinical psychologist Ron Bracey. 'They've been used to a very narrow focus to their lives and environment. They now have to learn to expand their horizons and understand the wider world. They will also be very frightened and confused about what happened to them – it will be hard for them to come to terms with what's been going on.'

Many experts also agreed that dealing with other people would be particularly difficult. 'They will be withdrawn socially as they've been away from other people for so long and more likely to cling to toys and each other,' said Dr Bracey. 'It will be worse for the elder children as their sense of reality and the world will be completely skewed compared to their contemporaries.'

Dr Bracey also pointed out that, after witnessing the repeated rape of their mother by their grandfather/father, the children may also consider such behaviour to be 'normal'. 'These traumatic events may represent normality to them,' he said. 'But they will have a sense of distrust for men and male figures.'

However, he believes they may be able to put the horror behind them with time and therapy. 'It is possible but there will be constant reminders for them,' he said. 'They will always be known as "those children" and have to put up with constant reports, books and even films about the events but there is a chance they could adapt and adjust and lead normal lives.'

Then there is the plight of Elisabeth Fritzl herself. Psychologist Anne Carpenter, a specialist in helping adult survivors of childhood sexual abuse, considered her case in the *New Statesman*. A consultant forensic clinical psychologist employed within the Forensic Mental Health Directorate of Glasgow and Clyde Health Board, Carpenter has worked for over 20 years with victims of child abuse, female offenders and mentally disordered offenders. She has also worked extensively with Victim Support Scotland and is a member of the Parole Board for Scotland. 'The story of Elisabeth Fritzl, the 42-year-old woman who was imprisoned in a cellar and raped by her father over a 24-year period, is so shocking it is inconceivable to most of the public,' she said. She saw Fritzl's treatment of his daughter as an extreme case of sadistic emotional and sexual abuse.

However, child abuse is widespread and the treatment of its

victims commonplace in the mental health field. Progress has been made in this area, Carpenter said. In the last 30 years, academics and clinicians have developed a greater understanding of the complicated psychology of survivors of abuse. 'Clearly, this woman is likely to require extensive help and support to come to terms with her dreadful ordeal,' she said. 'However, those involved in her recovery will need to be cautious and sensitive, particularly as she will have grown used to her emotional and physical needs being over-ridden by her abuser. In fact, she may be unable to articulate or even recognise them.'

According to Carpenter, Elisabeth Fritzl would be feeling a range of conflicting and confusing emotions – shock, disorientation, anger, guilt and sadness, as well as happiness and relief at having been rescued from her long ordeal. It was likely that she would shift rapidly from one emotion to another in the early stages of resolution and would need gentle support from those caring for her.

'Ms Fritzl will have to be gently encouraged to express her own needs and make her own decisions,' said Carpenter. 'Living in a cramped cellar away from normal social contacts will mean she has lost many basic life skills – meeting people, shopping, using a telephone, even crossing the road – all will be strange and daunting tasks.'

But Carpenter warned against heavy-handed intervention. She believed that intensive psychological therapy was often inadvisable in the immediate aftermath of extreme trauma, particularly at a time of extensive police and media interest. Recent research undertaken on the subject of counselling demonstrated that, in the immediate period after distress, probing too deeply and too quickly into feelings can be counterproductive. 'Any disclosure of abusive experiences can lead to the individual feeling that they are being abused all over again,' she said. 'People often describe traumatic "flashbacks", where they feel as if they are being pulled back into the past and are being abused again.'

No one would want to put Elisabeth Fritzl through that.

'They may experience sounds, smells or sensations which can feel distressing, as if they are losing their minds. Such experiences are quite normal and are the mind's ways of rationalising and understanding the incident. They are, however, very alarming.'

Because of the prolonged sexual nature of her abuse, Elisabeth was likely to be extremely sensitive emotionally. After all, the whole world knew what she went through and, in such cases, the disclosure of the details of the abuse was particularly difficult where the victim was unaccustomed to being treated with respect. Having grown up in a strong Catholic tradition, she might even expect to be punished or blamed. As she had been accustomed to abuse for most of her life, Elisabeth Fritzl may even expect to be abused again by those looking after her.

Having been completely in the power of her tyrannical father for so long, she would have lost all individual initiative. She would expect her therapists to tell her what to do in every particular – where to go, what to eat, who to speak to, and when. Consequently, at the preliminary stage she would need gentle support, which would be crucial in helping her resolve and understand her feelings, Carpenter continued. At this stage, all those involved should be telling her that they believe her and know it was not her fault.

Survivors of sexual abuse often express feelings of extreme

guilt. They feel guilty because they did not stop the abuse – even though, as in this case, they were in no position to do so. Although people rarely voice such feelings, in the back of their minds, they ask, 'Why didn't I stop it?' Even though the question should never be put so bluntly to Elisabeth, it would always be hanging somewhere in the air.

Victims of sexual abuse also feel guilty because they 'let' it go on for so long. This would be particularly difficult for Elisabeth Fritzl. She suffered seven years of abuse before she even entered the dungeon. But it started at an age where she was much too young even to known what was going on, let alone stop it. Then, when she grew old enough to understand what her father was doing to her and might have been mature enough to put an end to it by fleeing, she was incarcerated. For years, she must have cursed her stupidity in allowing herself to be lured downstairs. Early on, while chained up and kept alone and in the dark, she was forced to make that terrible compromise. As she put it herself, 'I faced the choice of being left to starve or being raped.'

Under such circumstances, she may still have the nagging doubt that she might have been in some way complicit in her own sexual abuse. Elisabeth could also be feeling additional guilt because she was forced to submit to her father in front of her own children.

Victims also, perversely, feel guilty because the abuser has been arrested. After all, Elisabeth put her own father behind bars. She had promised to maintain the fiction that she had run away to a cult so that she could go and see Kerstin in hospital. And, at first, she did her best to be as good as her word. It took several hours of police interrogation before she 'betrayed' her father. Of course, what Elisabeth Fritzl did, by any standards, was entirely justified but in her fragile emotional state, she was likely to reflect some of the burden of guilt on herself.

Working with abuse survivors and sex offenders has helped clinicians understand the very complex relationships that exist between them and Carpenter believes that Elisabeth was likely to suffer from Stockholm Syndrome. 'Identified in the 1970s, Stockholm Syndrome recognised that, where a victim is dependent on their abuser for their very survival, a curious, almost infantile attachment can develop,' she explained. 'The victim may hotly defend the perpetrator and even apportion much of the blame to themselves; particularly where they have been told by the abuser that they are to blame.'

In Elisabeth's case, such an attachment would be reinforced by the fact that the hostage-taker was her father. She would need to be reassured that such feelings are normal and she would also need help to express them. This would not be possible if she felt that she would be labelled as 'mad' or complicit, said Carpenter.

Elisabeth Fritzl faced other issues not usually seen in victims of sexual abuse. She was the mother of six children – children about whom she was likely to have ambivalent feelings. They were all active, daily reminders of her unwanted incestuous relationship with her father. All of them, to a greater or lesser extent, had also been abused. As a parent, she was likely to feel guilt that she did not protect them – even though she had done everything in her power to save them from harm.

As a parent of more than one child, you always wants to be even-handed in dealing with your children. In Elisabeth's case, this would have been particularly difficult. After all, she knew the children who shared her imprisonment far better than those who had been taken from her soon after birth. Also, it would be hard not to favour those who were, like her, the victim of Fritzl's sadistic decision to imprison them in a cellar over the children who lived a comparatively easy life above ground in the fresh air. The children would, of course, be similarly conflicted and would also need extensive support to help them understand and cope with those complex feelings.

Elisabeth Fritzl's reintroduction to Austrian society is likely to be long and traumatic; it may even be as traumatic as her first few months in captivity. To start with, she needs to be shielded from the eyes of the world as she is helped to reconcile the very complicated and conflicting emotions that she is probably now experiencing. However, there is the shining example of Natascha Kampusch to follow – Natascha has been strong enough to turn her suffering to her advantage. She has not wallowed in victimhood, but rather used her ordeal as a springboard to build a new life and career and she has offered Elisabeth Fritzl her help.

Of course, if one can compare such things, Elisabeth's suffering has been far more profound and long-lasting than that of Natascha, but she has survived it, when many weaker souls would not have done so. One can only hope that she has enough self-possession to use that ability to flourish in the outside world.

For now, though, she is having to cope with the abrupt transition from a world where she would have felt very alone to one where she is constantly surrounded by other people. She has moved from a world where the only other adult she knew was the man who monstrously abused her to a world where she is attended by people who want to care for her.

And she will have appreciated very quickly that her feelings are far from unique – many others who have suffered abuse and ill-treatment have similarly relied on professionals to ease them through the pain of their past and the discomfort of the transition period. But many have come through with their lives – and their futures – intact. One can only hope that Elisabeth will also begin to feel that relief and release from her past, and look optimistically towards her future as soon as possible.

The question remains – what was the role of Rosemarie Fritzl in this horror story? It seems certain that she had no direct knowledge of the imprisonment and abuse of her daughter in the cellar. However, there were signs that could have alerted her, questions she should have asked and clues that, had she followed them up, would have unmasked the secrets of the House of Horrors.

Her passivity demonstrates the peculiar nature of marital dependency and the lengths to which some women will go to preserve the façade of normality and respectability. Misplaced loyalty, fear or self-deception allow all kinds of women – from battered wives to the partners of paedophiles – to suspend disbelief under the most extraordinary of circumstances. Like Rosemarie Fritzl, they learn not to question for fear of receiving an answer they do not want to hear, or for fear of the repercussions. To some wives, a husband can simply do no wrong, whether he is a philanderer, a violent drunk, a junkie, a thief, a spy – or a murderer, even when evidence mounts up to the contrary. Rosemarie Fritzl playing 'the perfect grandmother' simply demonstrated an extreme form of what therapists call 'cognitive dissonance'.

Incredible though it may seem, psychologists agree it was

possible that she refused to question her husband about his strange absences. She did, after all, tolerate his sex holidays in Thailand and his visits to brothels and swingers' clubs. Abused and tyrannised herself, she may have reached a point where the only response to each implausible story was denial.

'It is perfectly feasible that she did not know,' said Dr William Conn, an expert in child abuse and neglect. 'Living with a tyrant who exercises immense control eventually prevents the dependent partner from being able to process the information or challenge anything. Challenge ceases to be an option.'

Dr Conn believed that exercising this control would have been a turn-on for Fritzl. 'The element of power over other people would have been part of Josef Fritzl's sexual arousal,' he said. 'He seems to have orchestrated a system where he was unchallenged. This was not just a secret world; he appears to have been arrogant enough to believe he could police everybody inside it.'

Curiosity, in those circumstances, would have been unwise. After her other children had flown the coop – and no longer wanted as a sexual partner – Rosemarie Fritzl would have found her life empty. The three babies that turned up on her doorstep gave the middle-aged woman a renewed sense of purpose. To question their appearance might have risked losing them.

'Maybe it was to her advantage – and she knew it – not to ask questions,' said Michael Berry of Manchester Metropolitan University's department of psychology. 'He is in control; he tells her what he wants her to know. She knows her place and keeps her mouth shut. They live almost separate existences. That is not uncommon – but here it is taken to the extreme. The fact that he travelled to Thailand on his own for weeks at a time, without her making a fuss, is interesting in itself. I am amazed at how utterly confident he appears to have been in his own ability to run a double life without detection.'

Fritzl's ability to dominate his partner so utterly, and thereby avoid detection over the truth of his secret activities, is by no means uncommon. 'I am familiar with cases where a woman has not known she has been living with a paedophile for 20 years and with women who do not know they are married to a spy,' said Berry. 'The wife has often ignored the signs that others would see.'

These women are in a state of denial and refuse to ask questions because they do not want to hear the answers. The case of Rosemarie Fritzl merely takes this to the extreme. 'The difference here is that the crimes were committed under their own roof,' said Berry. 'If his wife has been in denial, the revelations will have been a major shock for her. She will not want to believe it. It will challenge all her values, beliefs and expectations, but there will come a time when all the pennies start to drop.'

However, most parallels from the psychology of abuse break down in the face of the terrible atrocities perpetrated in the cramped prison beneath the Fritzls' ordinary-looking house. In its locale, there are echoes of the case of Fred West, whose wife Rose became his accomplice in the torture, rape and murder of ten women in Gloucester, including their own daughter Heather, burying them under the house and in the garden. In that case, too, the neighbours suspected nothing.

'Nobody in their right mind would be capable of envisaging such a scenario,' says Berry. 'The secret of Fritzl's success is surely that no one could even imagine this.'

The Wests pursued their murderous careers for 20 years without anybody noticing. Harold Shipman, the Manchester GP who murdered his elderly patients, continued undetected for 21 years.

'The tough question is: how could this have happened for so long?' said Professor Andrew Silke, a psychologist specialising in criminal behaviour. 'It is harder to believe there was no indication of evil goings-on than that there was some, but that it was ignored.'

Austria itself is now in the midst of a period of soul-searching. First, it was the Natascha Kampusch case, now Elisabeth Fritzl – two abductions, two secret cellars. And there has been one admission of failure on behalf of the authorities – and it concerns the statute of limitations. Fritzl's conviction for rape was erased from the record books after ten years. Had it remained, perhaps more questions would have been asked. Following the Fritzl case, the Austrian parliament has begun to consider changing the legislation, although some people believe this will not help Austria to become a more open society.

'We're a country that is very particular about data protection,' said Professor Friedrich of Vienna University. 'We tend to look the other way when a child gets a smack in the face, rather than be brave and intervene, and say what are you thinking? What are you doing? We respect privacy so much that we don't pick up the phone and call the police to send someone over. Everyone is left to mind their own business. We have a saying in Austria: "Don't get involved."'

Nobody did. As a consequence, Elisabeth Fritzl underwent an unspeakable ordeal for 24 years. She has been robbed of the best years of her life and the three children she brought up in the dungeon may never recover.

As the Austrian writer Thomas Glavinic puts it, 'Austrians hardly ever notice anything that might cause them discomfort.' He also asks, 'How many more of the 700 people officially missing in this country are sitting in some underground prison as we speak?' And how many more will join them now that the genie is out of the bottle?

But in the Fritzl case, there is, at least, hope. On 9 June 2008, Kerstin was finally roused from her coma. The doctors made sure that her mother Elisabeth and her brothers Stefan and Felix were on hand when she regained consciousness. Apart from her brutal captor, they were the only people she had ever known. As soon as it was clear she was awake, she was moved to a special medical ward at Amstetten Regional Clinic to be reunited with her mother and brothers in a special room designed to look like the cellar she has known all her life. She would now have to begin the long-term physical and psychological therapy her fellow captives started a month before. The prognosis is good. Her mother has already made a remarkable recovery and, against doctors' advice, she insisted on speaking to the police.

'She's determined to ensure her father, who may claim he is too ill to go on trial, doesn't escape justice,' a spokesman said.

Elisabeth was determined to testify via video link at her father's hearing in July; her children will testify later. They are expected to give their evidence in pre-recorded sessions. The family's testimony is necessary for prosecutors to complete their case against Fritzl, who faces a string of charges including manslaughter, incest, rape and incarceration. The hearings are expected to be closed to the public.

Fritzl himself, apparently, has had a change of heart. The prosecutor in charge of the case, Christiane Burkheiser, who had questioned him twice, said that he was now being 'co-operative'. It has yet to be determined whether he is fit to stand trial.

EPILOGUE

It is, of course, impossible for a writer to know the age of their readers, but if you are over 42, think of all the things you did between the ages of 18 and 42. If you are under 18, think of all the things you intend to do over the next 24 years. Think of all the holidays, all the countries you have visited or want to visit, all the trips you have been on, all the meals you have enjoyed in restaurants, all the nights out you have had, all the films, plays and exhibitions you have seen, all the sporting events you have attended, all the lovers you have had, all the walks you have been on, all the parties you have been to, all the family events you have enjoyed, all the jobs you have had, all the work you have done. Think of how full those years have been or will be, and all the emotions you'll have experienced in that time – joy, sorrow, excitement, love, despair, pride, sympathy, fulfilment ... Now imagine all that has been taken away from you.

Put in place of it hours, days, weeks, months, years of complete inactivity, endless spans of time when all you can do is sit or lie down, barely able to breathe. And remember what the head of the Fritzl investigation Franz Polzer said: 'I believe that, in those 24 years, life must had felt as if it lasted ten times as long as the real time.' Imagine sitting or lying down doing nothing, not just for 24 years, but for 240 years. The depths of boredom you would experience would be unfathomable. Remember, throughout those 24 or 240 years, there would be no end in sight. Your suspension between life and death may go on for ever.

Imagine, too, the dim light and the low ceilings, the feeling of the weight of the bunker-like building pressing down on you. You would feel as if you had been consigned, alive, to your grave. The only hint that time is passing would be the distressing decay of your own body. It would be as if you were locked, fully conscious, inside your own corpse as it rots. This is truly a living death.

How many times would you have thought about killing yourself? How many times might you have clutched at some faint hope of rescue, only to abandon it in the face of the pitiless reality of your situation? How many times would you dream of liberation, or being in the great, big world outside, only to wake to find yourself in the unchanging world of your dungeon? How often would you absentmindedly think about whether it is spring, summer, autumn or winter outside, day or night, raining, snowing or sunny ... or how things outside might have changed while, for you, everything stayed the same? And how many times would you have thought of family and friends, knowing they were blithely unaware that you were close by?

Now imagine that vast expanse of empty time being punctuated only by more suffering. Your only human contact is with the person you hate most in the world, who is coming only to beat, rape and humiliate you. You crave human contact but, at the same time, dread it. Remember, he is not just going to abuse you physically, he will torment you constantly with the hopelessness of your situation. He is going to remind you on every possible occasion that your friends and relatives – everyone you care about – and the authorities who are supposed to protect you, have given up on you. They are not looking for you; they don't care. You are, in their eyes, as good as dead. Even the master of the genre, Edgar Allan Poe, did not manage to conjure up this horror. You exist solely in a dimly lit, living nightmare.

Then there is the whole business of childbirth. The baby growing in your belly is the product of incest. Will it be hideously deformed or retarded? Will you survive the birth if there are complications? How will you cope with the baby if something goes wrong? In this situation, you are young and utterly alone. There's no one you can call on for help if anything happens – even though your own mother is but a matter of metres away, no one can hear your screams. There is no loved one, or even a sympathetic stranger, to hold your hand. You even have to cut and tie off the umbilical cord yourself.

Think of the pain of giving up your children, even though you know they will be better off than those who remain with you. Think of living with your little ones, seeing them so full of curiosity and life, and watching that life being slowly snuffed out of them day by day by the endless monotony to which they have been confined. Think how selfishly you love having your children around you, just for the company of another human being, although you would give everything, including your own life, to free them.

Your monstrous father – a man so utterly in control and so utterly evil – is robbing them of their lives as well as you of yours. But you once had a life; you knew what it was like to be outside. You have felt the rain on your face, the wind in your hair. Your children have never known that and may never know it. As far as you know, they have been condemned to the House of Horrors for ever. On top of every other atrocity your father has subjected you and your children to, he may well allow you all to die of starvation and neglect down there. There's no reason to believe that he will ever let you go free. You have been locked away for eternity without hope.

Now what should be done about a man like Josef Fritzl, who inflicted such a living hell on his own flesh and blood? And his lawyer Rudolf Mayer is right: Fritzl is a man, not a monster. Being a man makes his crimes all the more abhorrent. Fritzl did not have to behave in the way that he did towards his daughter and their children because he had to, because it was his nature; he *chose* to behave in that way, which makes his actions worse.

At the time of writing, doctors have roused Kerstin from her coma and it looks as though she may live. This means that Fritzl will not face a murder charge in her case, at least, though he may be charged with murder over the death of baby Michael. But, in some ways, it is immaterial. No punishment could be devised that would possibly fit the enormity of what he has done. He is already 73 and he is going to die in prison or a mental hospital, possibly even before his case comes to trial. But even if he was released from prison tomorrow, where could he go and what would he do? Everywhere in the world, he would be shunned and vilified. Someone would surely take the law into their own hands. If he was beaten or tortured, would the authorities intervene? Who would protect him? The likelihood is that he would be killed within ten minutes of being set free.

But never mind about him; he is beneath contempt and deserves no concern at all. It is Elisabeth and her children who have earned the respect and admiration of the professionals who are treating them as well as the media and wider public. They are the ones who deserve to feel the love, sympathy and admiration of the whole world. Elisabeth has been through an ordeal that I am sure most people could not have survived without going mad or simply giving up the will to live. She endured the 24 years of privation and horror with enough strength and practical sense to seize the opportunity to escape when it came. A shining example of courage, an inspiration, she has shown what heights the human spirit can soar to, just as her father has demonstrated to what depths it can sink.

In the writing of this book, I spent five weeks sitting in my basement flat. Elisabeth Fritzl spent 1,235 weeks in her cellar – 247 times as long. My own weeks have hardly been an ordeal, but sitting in one place for five weeks has left me stir-crazy. I keep jumping up from my desk and pacing about. It is time to go out into the sun. After being acquainted with the ordeal of Elisabeth Fritzl and her children over these weeks, I am grateful that I can do so.

POSTSCRIPT

Since I completed the manuscript for *House of Horrors* there have been some significant developments. Firstly, after nearly eight weeks, Kerstin has been fully awoken from her coma. Her mother and brothers – the only other people she had seen in her life, apart from the monster who sired her – were present throughout the whole process It was thought that awaking to be greeted by others might have proved too traumatic.

She was also aided into consciousness by the playing of her Robbie Williams' CDs. 'She still had the breathing tubes inside her but she was sitting up in bed waving her arms and dancing in bed,' said Dr Reiter. 'She wants very much to go to a Robbie Williams concert.'

Doctors have said that she is expected to make a full recovery.

'For all of us, Kerstin's surprising recovery is a great relief,' said Berthold Kepplinger, who will oversee her psychological adjustment. 'We are going to give her a special diet with extra vitamins and an exercise regime to help her.'

In due course she is to be questioned about whether Fritzl also committed incest with her.

In June, her grandmother, Rosemarie, returned to the family house at 40 Ybbstrasse to pick up clothes and toys for her six-year-old grandson Felix. She also visited the dungeon, Austrian authorities said. According to reports, Mrs Fritzl told friends that she does not want to live in the 'tainted' house again. It is thought that the house will be knocked down.

Since emerging from the cellar the children have been gradually weaned off television, their only contact with the outside world while they were in the cellar, but the ban was relaxed during Euro 2008 so that they could enjoy the football.

Elisabeth was eager to testify against her father via video link at hearings set to begin in early July. She feared her father might die before he stood trial. However, doctors determined that she was not well enough to do so yet. The preliminary hearings have been postponed.

Nevertheless, though initially it was thought that the case might take two years to prepare, it is now said that the trial may take place before the end of the year. Court spokesman Franz Cutka said that the case will now begin this autumn or winter as preparations are running 'at full speed'.

It seems that a woman judge will officiate at the trial. Forty-eight-year-old Andrea Humer, Austria's most senior female judge, has been scheduled to preside over the Fritzl case. One of her first tasks will be to oversee Elisabeth's deposition. Prosecutors also need to interview Elisabeth's children and her mother Rosemarie.

Meanwhile, a disturbing number of similar cases have now

been reported. It appears that women have been imprisoned and sexually abused in makeshift dungeons in France, Belgium, Hungary and Italy. The latest case comes from Skopin, in Russia, where factory worker Viktor Mokhov held two local girls for three years in a five-metre-square bunker under his garage equipped with an electric oven and a bucket as a toilet. At the press of a button Mokhov was able to cut off the ventilation if his victims refused to fulfil his sexual fantasies.

Mokhov admitted to being a copycat. He said he got the idea after watching a documentary about the criminal Aleksandr Komin, who, ten years ago, built a vault where he forcibly kept two slaves. He tattooed the word 'SLAVE' on their foreheads and made them stitch robes for his makeshift enterprise. When Mokhov saw Komin describing how he built the cell on television, he said to himself, 'I can do better than that!'

One can only pray that there is not a wannabe Josef Fritzl out there.